There We Are Human Again

Nothing exists but you and I
And if we two be not
Then god is no more god
And down must fall the sky

Angelus Silesius (1624–1677)

There We Are Human Again

A Diplomat's Journey to Anarchism

by Carne Ross

In memory of the anarchist poets, my allies and guides,
John Burnside and Benjamin Zephaniah.
Rest in Power

PERSPECTIVA

First published by Perspectiva Press, 2026
An imprint of Perspectiva (trading name of Perspectives on Systems, Souls and Society,
a UK-registered charity no. 1170492)
London
www.systems-souls-society.com

For distributor details and how to order please email greetings@perspectiva.co.uk

Text copyright: Carne Ross, 2026

ISBN: 978 1 914568 10 7

A CIP catalogue record for this book is available from the British Library.

Design: Lapiz Digital Services

Illustrations and cover design by Christopher Burrows

UK: Printed and bound by CPI Group (UK) Ltd, Croydon, CR0 4YY
Printed in the US by S&S

The manufacturer's authorised representative in the EU for product safety is:
eucomply OÜ – Pärnu mnt 139b-14, 11317 Tallinn, Estonia,
hello@ eucompliancepartner.com,
www.eucompliancepartner.com

Contents

Preface: Two Forms of Anarchy

I WAS born into chaos; I live in chaos.'

These were the words of a young Californian woman spoken to me as I finished this book.

I tend to reject binaries, the posing of two opposites to frame a choice. The binary always seems simplistic and reductive, when reality is always so much more complicated. But, paradoxically, it is a binary that stands before us now, in a clarity that we could not have foreseen a few years ago.

Anarchy is routinely presented as chaos and violence. Indeed, 'disorder' is the common dictionary definition of anarchy. But there is a very different definition to be found lower on the dictionary's list, a very different kind of anarchy. This might be called a 'gentle' anarchy, found in the absence of top-down authority and the joyous assertion of our own autonomy, negotiated freely and directly with those around us. An anarchy of love, mutual aid and cooperation, not competition or conflict. An anarchy that allows us to be our most human.

These two forms of anarchy are now emerging from the future's haze; indeed, one is already upon us.

The first definition of anarchy can be witnessed in the mounting chaos of today's world. Accelerating climate catastrophe of floods and fires, and failed government attempts at remedy. In the winter of '23/'24, Arctic temperatures were a breathtaking 20°C above the seasonal average.* A president in Washington who threatens to invade a supposed ally's territory and who endorses genocidal ethnic cleansing in Gaza. War in Ukraine, Sudan and across the Middle East. War crimes conducted in Ukraine and Palestine, with total impunity. Headlines announcing the collapse of the 'rules-based order'. Seemingly 'random' terrorist attacks of cars ploughing into crowds in Germany or France, while young children stab each other to death in small towns in England. An endless 'cost of living' crisis which is, in fact, a misnaming of endemic inequality.

A deep sense pervades that the teachers have abandoned the playground; things are out of control. And 'we' have no power to put things right. There is allegedly no alternative to the liberal democratic model. Some 'switch off' from the news, some stop reading social media, let it all wash over them, another 'bingeworthy' series on Netflix (I watch them too). Sheep with glazed eyes placid as they await their demise.

In response, the new authoritarians offer the illusion of control, but it is not ours, it is theirs. They promise those who feel ignored and left out that at last it's their turn. This is the world of Putin, Trump and Xi. A world of a state that represses dissent and offers satisfaction to its angry constituency through unashamed nationalism and the alleged promise of material wealth (often in an undefined future). This is a world of interior and exterior violence. The interior becomes a place of hate and assertion of difference: Them and Us: a narrative that can then justify, externally, genocide against the Hutus in Rwanda and Muslims in Bosnia or the cruel expulsion of millions of those seeking safety and a better life ('illegal immigrants').

---

* Source: "Temperatures at north pole 20C above average and beyond ice melting point": https://www.theguardian.com/environment/2025/feb/04/temperatures-at-north-pole-20c-above-average-and-beyond-ice-melting-point

This 'order' separates the child from their parents in concentration camps in the US, beats dissidents to death in Siberian jails and manufactures threats from alien hordes crossing our borders or invented images of strange countries we have never bothered to understand. Those who resist are abused, ridiculed and persecuted. Even to the dominant who perpetrate that repression, there is a secret knowledge that order built on violence cannot last, that its nemesis must at last find expression somewhere, somehow. The prison guard is no more free mentally than the prisoner. This is control and domination, not harmony and fulfilment, perpetrated through violence, both actual and threatened, everywhere, all the time.

This appalling state of affairs has been brought about by the slow collapse of the 20th century ideal of representative 'liberal' democracy, of the few elected to govern the many, and a form of capitalism that is supposed to bring wealth to everyone, but hasn't. That is supposed, through government modulation, to protect the planet, but hasn't. These are the elements of the mental orthodoxy. More and more people have become disaffected with this model; they rightly feel disenfranchised, cheated in a system that celebrates only a narrow success for a minority, and denied agency over their own lives, a fundamental necessity of human wellbeing.

Economically, that model has worked only for the few, not for the many, as wealth inequalities have deepened and wages, for most, have flatlined, an injustice unacknowledged by politicians of the so-called 'centre' (Democrats, the Labour Party). The authoritarians have turned this disillusionment to their advantage with their loud complaints about 'the system' and their bogus offer of remedy, their claim that only they can speak for the ordinary man. Lack of freedom and autonomy has eroded peoples' sense of individuality and expression, a deficit manipulated into hatred of the 'Other', the immigrant, the asylum seeker — that we should define ourselves not by what we are free to do but by what we oppose, that 'they' are somehow to blame for what we lack. Meanwhile, the climate crisis threatens us with impending catastrophe and fuels our existential dread. Some offer no solution to this fear except all-too-tempting denial, but that too seems to work.

It is a depressing picture of enfeebled democracy vanquished by arbitrary dictatorship, where unrestrained (indeed amplified) aggression and hostility reign over human compassion, where fearmongering and violence are the language of the state and indeed of society itself. Here, the only security the state provides is that of the prison and ubiquitous surveillance perpetrated by unaccountable private companies in cahoots with equally unaccountable authorities. It is a pseudo-order of domination and control; there is no internal cohesion to society; indeed, the authoritarian can only succeed by creating division. Any fragile stability rests on violence and coercion.

Faced with this threat, 'liberal democracy' has proven incapable of reforming itself. That is because it is not what it claims to be, a vehicle and enabler for human freedom. Instead, it is the enforcer of a system that, in a thousand subterranean ways, denies us true freedom by forcing us into the reductive boxes of modern capitalism, the tedium and frustration of the workplace, the constant burden of debt and fear of poverty, offering as compensation the paltry dream of fulfilment through consumption and thereby a dream forever denied. A myth of liberty belied by our permanent lack of control over our own affairs. We know it because we feel it, even when told that this is the best we can hope for, that there is no alternative. It is made possible by a political system that is by its very structure corruptible. When the few govern the many, it is always the most privileged who exercise power and influence, thus denying true representation of the whole. Those who call instead for mass democracy are peremptorily dismissed.

The new authoritarians pretend a supposedly 'anti-state' ideology that in fact is enforced through the power of the state. They are already far advanced in theirs campaign to seize the 'narrative' and, with it, power. They are multiplying and combining their forces. Witness the growing collaboration between the Orbáns and the Putins, the Farages, Musks and Trumps. Political forces are now joining with those of capital, the bankers, hedge-funders and tech titans: a blatant and utterly shameless manifestation of the self-interested partnership of capital and the state. As their arguments are more loudly heard, these begin to comprise the 'discourse'; opponents find themselves on the back foot, unable to advance a positive alternative — because they simply don't know what it is.

But there is a different form of anarchy. An alternative that might, just might, resolve the disorder we now confront, that counters the modern-day Mussolinis and the failing model of contemporary, supposedly 'democratic' politics, 'the system' in which so many have lost faith. It is the other definition of anarchy.

Where humans negotiate in equality over the things they care about, they are likely to agree, and division to diminish. When people have agency over their own affairs, they feel fulfilled and empowered to determine their own fates, not to be carried along and encased by an immutable, impenetrable 'system'. In social relations of equality and respect, the most important elements of what it is to be human find expression (and these things may have no names, though 'love' is one). In self-government lies the possibility of societal cohesion, where humanity exists in peace because it is a stability woven from the ground up, directly debated and collectively decided, not imposed from above. And that circumstance is the most propitious for the flourishing of love.

The chaotic form of anarchy is already gathering force. The gentle kind must be constructed brick by brick in individual acts of courage and self-determination, then bolstered, cheered on and built upon by the solidarity of others. It may be driven purely by a beautiful imaginary, a vision of utopia, or inspired by the example of others, including those who have lived long ago — or those who are practicing these ideas right now across the world. Its origin may be found in a poem or song. It is a vision of the possibility of what it is to be truly human. For this is a struggle common to us all, the struggle to live as fully and meaningfully as we can. It is an anarchy of different elements: democracy, agency, negotiation, equality and respect, which together create the possibility of something much greater: a whole that is greater, much greater, than its parts.

Instead, the planet burns. We flounder in a ghastly quicksand of inaction and conformity, drowning yet passive, anaesthetised by commodities and pale, and soporific culture, convinced of our own impotence. The deep, deep sleep that presages disaster.

One form of anarchy is the deepening instability and conflict, an invitation to the neo-fascist who offers order only by fostering violence between us and within us. Its eventual demise is woven into its being, but only after many have suffered and died. The other form offers more enduring stability, cohesion and joy. But one form of anarchy is no more inevitable than the other. There is no dialectic of history at work where antithesis follows thesis in an eternal pendulum swing of events, indifferent to human action. There is no end to this battle, no ultimate destination; there is only what is happening *now*. And it is we who create that present, either through our acquiescence to the horror or through the withdrawal of our consent to today's dispensation and determined construction of another reality.

The necessary revolution can only be created between us. But it already lies within us.

Introduction: Two Lives

Y APARTMENT lay on the south side of Union Square in Lower Manhattan. To some, 14th Street was the boundary between downtown and the rest of the island. After the attacks of 9/11, it formed a real barrier, marked by police tape and barricades, south of which ordinary traffic was not permitted. Only fire engines, police cars and the awful refuse trucks laden with rubble from the smoking ruins were allowed to cross the line. South lay a kind of quiet, dark wasteland, populated only by the wandering, traumatised and silent, phantoms.

My apartment was a 'penthouse', although in reality it was three floors below the top of the building (it was so named doubtless to extract more rent from the tenant). Two bedrooms, two bathrooms, one living room, around a thousand square feet, it was by Manhattan standards fabulous and spacious for the needs of a bachelor in his late thirties. Its wall-spanning windows looked downtown, the view encompassing the East River and Hudson to the west. In between, a glorious New York cacophony of buildings, skyscrapers and apartment blocks, the roofs studded with the city's iconic barrel-like water reservoirs, with the twin towers at the centre, shooting upwards from the tip of the island.

I would often stand at that window, contemplating the vista. What was I thinking? I remember mostly only the bad bits, the loneliness and the depression, the Post-it notes I left around the flat, telling myself to keep going, the sofa where I spent long weekends reading, listening to music, alone. But when I began living there, at the start of my tour, I remember whooping with joy in the shower one morning. I was delighted with my work, a member of the UK delegation to the United Nations. I was delighted with myself. This was a pinnacle of personal accomplishment: a diplomat in the cockpit of international affairs, of war and peace, at the UN Security Council. I was, at last, a member of the elite who ran the world, the fulfilment of a long-held ambition, fulfilment of a long-held parental dream.

By day, I would stride the UN's corridors, waving my all-access pass at the security guards, walking fast to indicate my busyness. Usually, I was on my way to or from the Security Council's 'informal' chamber where the Council's true business, its arguments, its conflicts, took place, outside the public gaze of the more well-known 'formal' chamber with its big U-shaped table, unintelligible tapestries and high curtains covering all light from outside. My 'area' was the Middle East, that festering bed of contested borders, religious and ethnic strife, dictatorship, conflict and repression, a place almost designed to reassure the Western mind of its superiority and escape from atavism. Moreover, though almost completely ignorant of a more controversial history, I was likewise regarding of my country's 'historic role' in the region. We knew the region, we pretended, even though I knew almost nothing, barely having visited and speaking none of Hebrew, Arabic or Farsi, let alone Kurmanji, the language of the Kurds. Indeed, I didn't know that Kurmanji existed, no more than I knew about the Peel Commission, the Exodus, the Nakba, the bombing of Iraqi villages by British aircraft, the concentration camps.

By then, after nearly ten years in the diplomatic service, 'I' had become 'we'. When words left my mouth, we were speaking for Britain.

We were representatives of the state and all that it stood for — in our version, democracy, human rights and the rule of law. My own self had been thoroughly subsumed. I no longer thought as an individual with my own judgement and conscience. My thinking was thoroughly framed and constrained by the strictures of the state, a narrowed range of choices premised, above all, on the utterly invented notion of British 'interests', a construct of the idea that states have agency and identity, and are not merely the fictive creations of men (usually men) with certain needs to satisfy, above all the need for meaning, power and the hunger to dominate.

I knew those needs. For if I wasn't a diplomat, what was I? As a professional diplomat, I had purpose. I had status. I had people who nodded reverentially when I mentioned my profession, as I was always careful to do. I was not much more — or less — than a diplomat. I was living the life dreamt of by my parents.

The signs were there all along, though I could not see them. Many weeknights I would meet up with my American 'opposite number', John, who also 'dealt with' the Middle East on the Security Council. My purpose was to go drinking, with company. I guess his was the same. So we drank. Mostly on the Lower East Side, in the dive bars of Stanton and Ludlow Streets. Since we drank for several hours, we drank a lot, but mostly nothing stronger than draught beer, Sierra Nevada or Brooklyn Lager, sometimes finished off with shots of Jack Daniels. Many were the mornings when I attended work heavily hungover. If my bosses noticed, they never told me.

At weekends, I would try to find a party to go to, but often failed. I would then spend most if not all of the weekend alone. On Saturday mornings, I ritually visited a diner on Broadway for bacon and eggs with the *New York Times* or *New Yorker*. In the afternoon, I would run to one of the piers on the West Side, jog to the end, and stare out for a few minutes over the Hudson River before running back.

For a while I had a girlfriend, but my heart wasn't really in it. I dated her because I was scared of being alone. It wasn't fair to her, but I didn't know that at the time. We watched *Seinfeld* in her studio apartment near the UN (she was another diplomat). Eventually, I realised that a certain blackness had descended upon me. There were days when I could barely drag myself to work. I felt a profound existential dread. I began to see a psychotherapist. On Friday, at lunchtime, I would walk from the mission on 49th Street and 2nd Avenue up to 59th Street, cross Central Park to the Upper West Side, where I would see 'Josh', a prototypical New York Jewish shrink whom I came to like very much. But he couldn't do much to 'fix' me. My depressions became a regular occurrence, a freezing of my brain into a leaden mass barely capable of thought.

But in the upcycles, my doubts were few (these were to come later). I was convinced I was where I wanted to be, little realising that the act of having to convince myself was itself a signal that not all was well. My country was largely right about the world. The values we told ourselves we stood for, democracy, human rights, law and all the rest, were the right ones. It was the late nineties and early aughts. The Soviet empire had been vanquished. History was at its teleological end, as Francis Fukuyama had so rashly claimed. The Western model was supreme. And I was one of its foot soldiers, preaching to the rest of the world, benighted in autocracy and pre-modernity (indeed, my previous boss, whom I had considered brilliant, divided the world into pre-modern, modern and post-modern — guess which one we were?). At the Security Council, we cleaned up the rest of the world's mess, wilfully oblivious to our own role in creating it in the first place.

Though I questioned myself, I never questioned the system I represented. It was comfortable to live in moral and political superiority. We were sustained by the myth of Western progress. That things would always get better for us and future generations. That wealth would trickle down from the rich to the poor. That parliaments and congresses truly represented what people want. That there was justice. If you worked hard, you could succeed. It of course helped that I was one of those who benefited most from that system. A white privately educated male, moderately good-looking, healthy, mentally competent (at least most of the time), the world was designed for —

and indeed by — people like me. I never wondered about the innate solipsism of my view of life — that what worked for me must work for everyone else. I never asked or listened to those for whom it might not be working so well.

I was an *apparatchik*, no less than a bureaucrat of a totalitarian state. I could debate policy inside my ministry but never question its basic premises. I was obliged to represent what my government thought about the world, and never deviate from that line, on pain of dismissal. I could have moral qualms (and indeed I would), but these were always to be kept private. I thought I was independent of mind, cognisant, a moral agent, but in fact I was none of these things. I was that most pathetic of specimen, an unfree person, but of his own choice. I had chosen the trammels of the state. Indeed, I prided myself upon them. My life had all the appearances of success in our status-conscious age, a job with kudos and reputation, overseas postings, my own flat, an embossed business card, a hefty expenses allowance. Other diplomats sought me out, because Britain matters at the UN, as a privileged veto-wielding 'permanent' member of the Security Council. But as I was to later find, they did not seek me out because of who I was, the real me (if that person even existed then); they wanted me because of *what* I was, a First Secretary covering the Middle East for the UK Mission.

People like me governed the world. We made decisions in the form of legally obligatory resolutions stating the way that things should be and the means, often violent, to get there. The press who questioned us, only a little, were kept outside our chambers, forced to trot after us as we strode down the carpeted corridors of that beautiful UN building. We met in private rooms to plot and decide the fates of others, sometimes in the many millions. I was transported to secret 'bilaterals' with our main ally, the US, to confer, take instructions and, sometimes but rarely, seek to influence. I had a neat little diplomatic passport bearing Her Majesty's command that I was to be well-treated. On my wall in my taxpayer-paid apartment was her commission, calling me her 'trusty and well-beloved' servant and representative. I wore well-made dark suits and polished black shoes. My shirts were always a crisp white. My ties were sensible and often blue, with barely the faintest of patterns.

It was a life of power and status, of regard and comfort. My career lay before me, with its culmination in ambassadorships, my own embassies and, maybe, a knighthood. I was doing well. I was well thought of in the 'service'. I ensured that my name appeared in telegrams issued from the mission. I was expected to reach the summit of my profession.

****

It's now twenty years later. I am making toasted sandwiches for my twin children to take to school. I put the bread in the toaster two slices at a time. When all eight slices are ready, two slices with honey and two with mashed avocado (my daughter's favourite). I rinse the sandwich boxes after they have been in the dishwasher overnight. I cut up some cheese for my daughter. I slice an apple into sixteen small pieces so my son with his new braces can eat it without the bits getting stuck in his teeth. I pour fresh water into their water bottles, which I then slide into the side pockets of their backpacks, into which I also place their 'cold bags' which contain the sandwiches, apples and cheese (plus a 'fruit roll', a package of dried fruit, for a snack).

I've also made their toast for breakfast. My son also gets a chocolate brownie (it upsets my daughter's stomach). After they've eaten their food, I make them a 'cocktail', a mixture of about twelve different supplements — vitamins, minerals, tinctures. I have to be very careful to get the measures right, for each child has slightly different amounts. A long list of instructions is blu-tacked to the cupboard to remind me. Once all the additives are mixed in, I pour in a generous sluice of apple juice to sweeten the mixture. All the while, I am drinking copious amounts of instant coffee and listening to the news on the radio. Slowly I am waking up.

Sometimes, I help them knot their ties. When they've eaten their breakfasts and drunk their 'cocktails', I hustle them into their coats, load up their backpacks, ensure that they have their epi-pens (both have potentially dangerous allergies). Usually, by this point, we're running late, so K. and I have to nag them to get their things ready and into the car. Then I drive them to school. It's a fifteen-minute drive, and there is no available public transport for the route (we live in North Wales). After I've dropped them off, I return home, make yet more coffee, perhaps read the newspapers on my phone for a while, then prepare for work.

I do many things today, various consultancies. I'm no longer a diplomat. Once I wrote speeches for the foreign secretary for a living; today I write wedding speeches for a bit of extra cash. But sometimes I'm working again on something diplomatic, like a UN summit. No longer am I an insider on the privileged track, with power and influence. I am an outsider. I send submissive emails to low-ranking diplomats, importuning them to talk to me. My emails to their ambassadors often go unanswered or are passed to junior staff without the courtesy of a direct reply. Some of these ambassadors I once knew when I was a British diplomat and they were of more junior rank than today; some of them would seek me out as someone who mattered. Today they ignore me.

My onetime contemporaries in the Foreign Office are now ambassadors and permanent secretaries. Some have been knighted. Sometimes I feel bitter about this and resent them. But this feeling passes quickly. For I am free, and they are not.

My life today is altogether humbler. I am not listed in any directories. I do not write UN resolutions or negotiate international law. I no longer have the fate of nations in my hands. I have no power. All I have is my voice. But it is my own, and no one else's. I say what I think, and this requires me actually *to* think, something I did all too rarely when enacting the instructions of my government. So I have become aware of the true complexity of the world. No longer do I think of the world as a chessboard neatly delineated into our side and theirs, us and the Other, nation states in their formula machinations, predictable … at least, depictable. Instead, I see it more as a Jackson Pollock painting, a chaotic swirl of different connections and flows, some natural, some human, some intellectual, some material, entirely unpredictable but with deeper patterns and rhythms that can be depicted and analysed, though they are never comprehensive and all-explaining. This is a much richer, more absorbing canvas, if also a more frightening one.

I have no 'security' in my work. No longer paid a steadily rising government salary with the comfort of an index-linked pension at retirement, I worry about making ends meet. I have a mortgage until I'm seventy. I juggle several 'projects' at the same time. I must neglect my true love, writing (with this exception). I constantly 'network', firing off myriad emails to connections old and new, trying to find ways to sound authentic but professional, polite but also 'real', trying to remain true to myself and my beliefs without succumbing to the deadened, soul-destroying language of the discourse of modern work, "I just wanted to reach out to connect with you…"

I have few friends. But they are friends because they like me and I like them, not because of what I am, because I am a nobody. I had a brief moment in the public spotlight, but that is now forgotten. When I meet someone new, I have to spell out my name and tell people how to pronounce it. I can expect no public recognition and no honour (I would reject it in any case: the government has no right to decide who is worthy). Once I held court in government press conferences of scores of journalists. Today, I write to those who remember me with requests that they not forget the cause of Rojava in North East Syria or the people of Western Sahara, little known places and peoples whose moral needs and cases are as strong as any but who lie outside that self-referential body of information known as mainstream news.

But today I feel no shame at what I do. I have chosen my own path; I am the captain of my own ship. When I'm making the twins' sandwiches, I feel purpose; I feel needed. In fact without my wife, my children (the twins) and the daily rhythm of my chores (for there is school pickup, tea and supper to follow, fruit salads, special drinks and vegetables), I would feel wholly lost. I do not expect to reach some pinnacle of career and success. Indeed, I may already have passed it if it existed at all. Instead, I look ahead and behind to see a rockier and more uneven road, of moments of triumph and deep disappointment, of victory and defeat. Not of ease, but of struggle. But it is my road; I chose it. Its failures belong to me, but so do its glories.

Once, I had a set of certain beliefs, of order in the world and my place in it. That democratic governments ruled in the interests of all. That markets made everyone better off. That the system was ultimately fair or at least correctable through courts, elections and a free press (Popper's triumvirate). That 'nature' was eternal.

I no longer believe this.

Some time ago now, I was awake with my baby daughter in the middle of the night. Slumped on the sofa, I was blearily watching pay-per-view TV and saw an advert for a series of recorded lectures called the Great Courses on complexity theory. I decided to buy the set of DVDs, and I learned about complexity from a balding Minnesota professor.

Complex systems comprise perhaps billions of actors in constant dynamic motion, acting, reacting and reacting once more. It is impossible to know the state of the system at any one moment. Most remarkably, a complex system can demonstrate 'emergent' properties which are not manifest from its components alone — where the sum is greater than its parts or shows different characteristics, like wetness arising from the aggregation of otherwise nonwet water molecules. Those emergent properties can suddenly change across the system, a 'phase shift' triggered by a 'tipping point'.

For such a phase shift to happen, the system has to be at 'criticality', a state when the system's many parts are in some way primed for change. No one can predict that moment; it may become evident only long after the event. A moment when everything changed.

I realised with a jolt that of course humanity — and Earth — was a complex system. It is one of the ways, though not the only way, to understand what's going on in the world.

I believe that our political and economic system — indeed, how we think about life — may be approaching that state of criticality, if it is not already there, the state necessary for the system to 'tip'. Events are unstable. Existing structures seem weak and under threat. Global institutions — the international rule of law, for instance — are ever less effective. The presumption of liberal democracy's triumph over autocracy seems stupidly naïve. Wars have become interconnected across continents — Syria's war is affected by Russia's overstretch in Ukraine; the invasion of Iraq in turn helped form the chaos and rise of ISIS in Syria, and is still used by Russia to justify its invasion of Ukraine. A hundred million refugees are on the move, a number that will inevitably rise as a warming climate threatens the survival of billions. Nuclear powers are increasing their arsenals while agreements to limit their number and spread are breaking down. On the battlefield, drones are usurping heavy armour, and guerrillas triumph over armies. AI threatens mass dislocation of workers and the very nature of work and, perhaps most perniciously, is already manipulating the form and content of information and thus perceptions of truth itself. The climate is heating, triggering floods, droughts and hurricanes. And in this incipient chaos, disillusionment with the system of government, the state and allegedly free markets is rising. Across the globe, incumbent governments are overthrown, replaced by those promising dramatic change — any change! I could go on. Things seem very much 'out of control'.

We are therefore at a moment of great jeopardy. We may see the rise of the authoritarians promising to control these turbid forces and stand up for the 'little man' ignored in the current system. So far, this seems to be exactly what we're witnessing — nothing less than the rise of a new fascism.

But this may instead be the moment of great possibility, of the advent of a new kind of system, where the people are genuinely in charge of their own fates — the planet preserved — and at last learn what it is to be fully human.

There is no inevitability about what will happen, except that the system and circumstances we experience today will certainly change. Humans make their own history, in a million different ways.

This time, it's up to us.

1
Truth and Testimony

THE UN headquarters in Kosovo is a grim tower block in the centre of Pristina, Kosovo's capital, ringed by high fences and guards. It was once the secret police headquarters, when Kosovo was part of communist Yugoslavia and later dominated by Serbia while Yugoslavia collapsed in the 1990s. Some local Kosovars were given to saying that nothing had changed. One oppressive overlord, Serbia, had been replaced by another, the UN.

My office was a small room on the seventh floor. Dulled paint, a cheap desk, an office chair and a computer with a big, old-fashioned monitor. Notebooks and stacks of files lay around. A small window looked out onto a fire escape. The sky is grey. It is April 2004. That day I am sat at the computer, pondering a decision that would change my life. On the screen is a draft email to a Whitehall official, submitting a seven-page testimony about my earlier work as a diplomat at the United Nations in New York. I had negotiated the terms with that official, a former colleague from the Foreign Office. My testimony was to be kept secret, to protect me from the inevitable reaction should it ever become public with my name attached to it.

As the evidence of the government's dishonesty grew after the invasion of 2003, the Blair administration agreed in 2004 to organise an official inquiry not into the war itself but rather into the use of intelligence in the run-up to the war. This limited mandate was given not to an independent judge or person of broad experience, perhaps from civil society or the private sector, but to a former senior official of the government, Sir Robin Butler. To gather the necessary data for his investigations, he sent an invitation to all the officials who had worked on Iraq and its infamous Weapons of Mass Destruction. I was one of them. My response was a seven-page document which detailed my knowledge that the government had exaggerated the evidence that Iraq's WMD posed a threat, had ignored available alternatives to war (which I had advised upon) and had breached the terms of the UN resolutions, which it itself had voted for and often drafted (sometimes by me) — in other words, international law.

My finger hovers over the return button on the clunky, grimy keyboard. But my hesitation doesn't last long. I know I have no real choice. There is truth and untruth. And once you know the one from the other, there is only one to follow, lest you destroy a piece of your soul. Everyone I knew and respected, including the one closest to me, my wife, would want me to press that key. Every part of me that I valued, the same.

If I didn't send the testimony, I knew what awaited me. A coveted job back at the Foreign Office in London. It would be my first job as a senior diplomat, a head of department, ironically the reconstruction department, responsible for building from the ruins of the countries we had invaded.

If I pressed the button, the unknown. A life without structure or security. An abandonment of the career that I had once loved.

I pressed the button. The email flew to its destination.

Immediately after that message, there was another I had to send, as necessary as the first. It was addressed to the foreign secretary, my ultimate boss: my letter of resignation. My testimony meant that it was impossible for me to continue as a British diplomat, a member of the diplomatic service. I knew that I could never again sit with my colleagues, let alone a minister or the prime minister, knowing what they had done. I could never trust them again; I could never respect them again. It was very personal; perhaps I might have wept, but I remember feeling stern and sure. I was turning my back on my clan, my tribe, my friends and close collaborators. Men and women of 'the office' with whom I had shared drama and sometimes tears. My ambassador whom I had once admired, whose words calmed us at the UK mission on that devastating day, 9/11, who once attended a play I wrote off-off-Broadway (i.e. a very small theatre). Mine was not disloyalty but a declaration of separation, a declaration that they were wrong and I was right. I said that in doing what they did, they had created a war. They had known what I knew but did nothing; in fact, they went along with it: some of them enabled it. It was a short letter — I told my minister to please read my testimony as an explanation. It took a couple of minutes to prepare that email, but it too was fired off into the electronic ether. Two quick emails; the end of my career; the casting out and turning point of my life.

I sat up straight, stared at the screen for the last time and left the office. The emails meant that my job for the UN was finished (I was there on secondment from the British government). I crossed the grey-tiled corridor to the clanking communist-era lifts, descended slowly to the ground floor, handed in my pass and walked out onto the streets of Pristina. I would never return.

****

Many years earlier…

We were driving home from the countryside. It was dark. My parents were in the front and my brother, sister and I in the back. For some reason we were talking about our ambitions. I was twelve years old.

"I want to be a diplomat", I declared.

My father turned in his seat.

"You have to be very clever to be a diplomat, Carne".

Thus was an ambition sealed. About ten years later, I received a letter from the Foreign and Commonwealth Office telling me that I had been accepted to join the fast stream of Her Majesty's Diplomatic Service.

I would like to pretend that I became a diplomat because I was fascinated by the world and its machinations. This was true. I wanted to be a player on the global chessboard, not an observer. But, looking back, it's all but certain that it was my father's doubts that drove me. My sister and twin brother were more academically accomplished. My twin brother was put in the year above me at school: there is no more direct a comparison than with your twin. I was the one of whom little was expected. At sports day, with my short pudgy body, I was excluded from athletics but put on the tug-of-war team with the other misfit boys.

Several of my family members had tried and failed to join the Foreign Office. My much revered grandfather, who had worked at the secret code-breaking centre Bletchley Park during the war, had been in the Foreign Office. So joining the Foreign Office was thus an emphatic way of turning my family's expectations of me against them. *That* showed them. And I'm afraid that to this day I am still given to mentioning, not so subtly, that only twenty fast streamers were selected from five thousand applicants that year, or that the contemporaries I had joined with are now ambassadors and senior mandarins. I would have been one of them, I want to imply. Sir Bufton Tufton.

I joined the Foreign Office in 1989, the year the Berlin Wall fell. The sought-after postings for the young diplomats of my cohort were to Eastern Europe to spread the 'know-how' of democracy and free markets.* I was sent to Germany, then struggling with its own extraordinary transformation from two countries into one. When I

____

* Their job was to disburse money from something literally called the 'Know-how Fund'.

returned to London in the mid-1990s, I ran the "Arab-Israel" desk in Near Eastern Department during the happier days of the peace process. I visited Israel and the Occupied Territories; I accompanied Yasser Arafat around London.

Thanks to a speech I had written on that tormented issue, I was appointed speechwriter to the foreign secretary. My first boss was a Conservative. His successor was 'New' Labour. In those days, British civil servants, even the speechwriters, were expected to serve ministers of any party, regardless of their personal sympathies. The new foreign minister, Robin Cook, fired me, however, despite my private warmth towards his party: he simply didn't like my speeches.

In fact, no one is ever really "fired" in government, but my dismissal was nevertheless something of a humiliation. But my seniors were kind, and as a consolation, they sent me to the sought-after posting of the British mission to the United Nations in New York. I did not realise it at the time, but this place was to prove my nemesis.

I was thrilled to move to New York. The UN, a cockpit of negotiations of war and peace, was a hub of political and diplomatic drama; the city itself seemed to me to epitomise excitement. I had a job on diplomacy's frontline. I was head of the Middle East section of the Mission. I attended the UN Security Council as part of Britain's delegation. I negotiated resolutions on things like Morocco's illegal occupation of the Western Sahara, the Lockerbie case and, of course, Palestine.

But by far the largest part of my time was spent on Iraq, where I was responsible for the numerous and lengthy resolutions which required the Saddam Hussein regime to disarm itself of so-called weapons of mass destruction.

I was a tough and aggressive negotiator. I spent a year fighting line by line over a resolution that reframed the sanctions on Iraq and established a new weapons inspections body. One night, I invented the name for that body by assembling various letters standing for things like Inspections and Verification into a pronounceable acronym

"UNMOVIC" (this is my tiny footnote in history).[†] Resolution 1284 was at that time the longest resolution in the Security Council's history. It was also among the most unintelligible.

But I believed that "we" — my government — as we called ourselves, were doing the right thing. Saddam was a threat to the world. Sanctions were necessary to contain him and force him to comply. If others disagreed, we deployed sophisticated and oft-repeated arguments to dismiss them. We worked hard.

The diplomacy was ferocious, demanding and confrontational. It was also utterly absorbing and, in its own slightly sick way, fun.

****

The day after the 9/11 attacks, I was deputed by the ambassador to negotiate for the UK the resolution condemning the attacks. It was a simple negotiation — of a French draft — that unusually lasted less than an hour. I discussed words of the text with the US delegation who, as usual, sat beside the UK. Their eyes glassy with shock, they could barely take anything in. The mood in the informal chamber was subdued. A couple of hours later, the resolution was adopted in the formal chamber. For the only time in the Council's history, the diplomats stood in silence at the adoption.

A couple of months later, I delivered the letter to the UN, in which Britain (like America) justified its invasion of Afghanistan as self-defence. Like many of my colleagues, I was eager to go to war. A few weeks after the Taliban fell, I spent a memorable six weeks in the Kabul embassy, touring the country with British army bodyguards, flying low level through the Hindu Kush in a special forces Hercules to

---

[†] The acronym UNMOVIC stands for the United Nations Monitoring, Verification and Inspection Commission. This commission was established by the United Nations Security Council in December 1999 as a successor to the United Nations Special Commission (UNSCOM). UNMOVIC's primary mandate was to ensure Iraq's disarmament of weapons of mass destruction (WMD) and to monitor its compliance with United Nations resolutions.

parley with warlords in mountain hide-outs. I still believed the official line while I was there.

As the embassy's political officer, I wrote telegrams confirming that indeed "the Afghans" wanted democracy and peace, choosing to ignore those who didn't. I omitted the fact that my every meeting with Afghans was with those already allied to us and that in every encounter I was accompanied by several heavily armed men.

I chose not to mention the intelligence officers in the embassy who told me of the suitcases of cash they were delivering to politicians to win their support, or the simple but never-uttered reality that we had over-run no more than half of the country at most. In fact, not even that, as the allied 'presence' in much of the country amounted to small squads of special forces posted to the major towns to act as liaison with the local warlords who actually ran things.

A closed circle of diplomats, intelligence and military, with scant contact with actual Afghans, we repeated the same beliefs over and over to each other. No one, including me, risked testing our wisdom against reality.

I returned to New York exhausted. After fourteen years of diplomacy, I was dimly aware that something was wrong with the system that I had for so long promoted and defended.

I needed to stop and think. So I took a year off. I had fallen in love, very suddenly, with a New Yorker. I swapped my government-rented penthouse on Union Square for a one-room, six-story walk-up in the East Village. I became a fellow at the New School University. I got hold of a library card for New York University. I spent my days in the Bobst Library, a red stone cube on the corner of Washington Square.

I was looking for *something* to help guide me out of the mire of disillusionment I had fallen into. I just didn't know what.

As I pondered all this, another drama was playing out only thirty or so blocks north, at the United Nations.

I was well aware of it, even if I was holed up in the sleepy quietude of the Bobst Library. I kept in touch with my colleagues at the missions of various members of the Security Council. I was friends with senior officials of the UN weapons inspection body, which I had named and helped design.

My studies took me into new realms, beyond the tight boundaries of the theories of economics and democracy that I had learned as a student and civil servant. I began to realise that there was something profoundly wrong with those theories. But it was the actions of my own government — my own colleagues — that convinced me that *government itself* was not to be trusted. And there were things I had done too, things I would rather I had not done, that played their part in this disillusionment.

The story of the lies about Iraq's WMD (Weapons of Mass Destruction) is still serially misunderstood. I had worked for four and a half years on the issue. Each day, I had received a thick folder of intelligence reports, their origins — human or signals intelligence — denoted by different colours and strange acronyms ('Top Secret Umbra'). I spoke regularly to the weapons inspectors who were highly expert in the various and considerable complexities of chemical and biological weapons, and the ballistic missiles which were also considered part of Iraq's WMD.

I was one of a small group of British officials consulted in the preparation of Joint Intelligence Committee analyses on WMD which were used to brief ministers and the prime minister.

I knew the designations of Iraq's "special weapons" regiments; I knew the chemical make-up of the residues of the highly toxic VX nerve gas after a missile warhead had been left in the desert for years. I knew about extended-range Scud missiles and exactly how many had been launched and destroyed during the (first) Gulf War.

During my posting, I attended every US-UK bilateral meeting on Iraq at the State Department or Foreign Office, sometimes flying to London overnight to return the next day after hours of talks (cosseted in taxpayer-funded business class).

It is often not appreciated that on any particular piece of foreign policy, even one as important as Iraq was to the UK, there is usually only a small group of officials who work on the matter. I was one of them, and indeed, after four and a half years in New York, I had spent longer working on the topic than any other British official, barring a few of the weapons experts.

One of these weapons experts was a scientist called David Kelly, whose speciality was biological weapons or BW.

At the British mission, I regularly organised briefings by Britain's top weapons experts for the other Security Council missions to tell them what we knew about Iraq's WMD. Foremost among the experts was David. He was able to synthesise the complex and technical data on Iraq's WMD into a coherent picture: what we knew and what we didn't know. There was much more to say about what we didn't know than what we did.

Before the 1991 Gulf War, Iraq had possessed very large quantities of what might be called "basic" WMD, including relatively crude chemical weapons and medium range ballistic missiles, none of which had been used to deliver CW or BW. We had little to no hard intelligence, like satellite photos or communications intercepts, indicating that there were still significant stocks of these weapons.

There were various "humint" (human intelligence) reports from defectors or, very rarely, agents inside Iraq, but we tended to think that such data were unreliable, because the source had an inherent interest in exaggerating it, particularly if a defector.

By the turn of the century, when I was at the UN Security Council, our main argument for maintaining the comprehensive economic sanctions on Iraq was that it had failed to account for getting rid of its stocks. In other words, a kind of accounting issue, albeit of a rather grave kind. We called it the "material balance" — the difference between what we *knew* Iraq had once possessed and what Iraq could *prove* had been destroyed. In other words, not actual weapons but a statistical discrepancy. This discrepancy could have meant hidden weapons, but we had zero actual hard evidence of such.

It is now well-known how this negative knowledge — what we didn't know — was turned into "positive" allegations: that there were real weapons, and lots of them, that posed a threat.

I took part in that process, albeit reluctantly, as drafts of the government's propaganda passed across my desk, each draft with ever more confident and strident claims of imminent danger. Somewhere in the Foreign Office archives there is a letter from me to the non-proliferation department querying the evidence for these loud new assertions, which were dramatically at odds with the account we had been giving at the UN for many years.

By the time Britain and the US presented these claims to the UN Security Council in a failed attempt to win legal authority for the coming war, I had left the mission. I watched from my library perch, incredulous. I literally could not believe what my government was doing.

A few months later, after the invasion, I invited David Kelly to the New School to give a talk about weapons inspections, which he did with his typical meticulousness and humility. Afterwards, at lunch in a diner on Sixth Avenue, we talked about the government's WMD claims, including the infamous 'Number Ten dossier'. Neither of us knew of any new intelligence that would justify the overheated assertions made by the UK and US.

It was the last time I was to see him alive.

Soon afterwards, David was exposed by the Ministry of Defence, where he worked, as the source of the allegation, reported by the BBC, that the dossier had been "sexed-up." He was attacked and publicly humiliated by the government he had loyally served for decades. Anonymous spin doctors, doubtless at the behest of Prime Minister Tony Blair and his press chief Alistair Campbell, insulted Kelly and claimed that he was only a junior figure who could not have known the "full picture."

But that was a lie. In fact, David was Britain's foremost WMD expert, upon whom we relied considerably. He was told he would never work again in his professional field (there are no private employers of biological weapons scientists). I wrote to David to offer my solidarity.

A few days later he was found dead in an Oxfordshire wood near his home, his wrists slit and painkillers in his system. I do not think that

David Kelly was murdered, although I don't rule out the possibility. To me they are both morally equivalent: outright murder or humiliating a man so that he is driven to take his own life.

I attended the ugly circus of his funeral, where fevered gangs of press gathered at the gates of the country church where he was buried. Some of the small group of officials who had worked on Iraq's weapons travelled together to the ghastly event. On the train to the ceremony, I asked aloud: Did any of us think that the government was telling the truth?

There was silence.

David's death shook me to the core. Somehow the death of a man hit home much harder than the knowledge of an epic lie. He was a decent man, a loyal servant, a man defined by his hard-earned but lightly worn expertise. Bearded, bespectacled, of medium height and build, he was the sort of man one can rely on, the rational, reasonable substance of a system. That system hounded this kind man to his death. It destroyed its own. If it could kill David, none of us was safe. No truth was sacrosanct or inviolable. Any lie could be told. My faith was broken, forever.

****

Waging war is the gravest and most solemn activity any government can undertake. It is at the heart of the Hobbesian 'contract' between the people and the state: citizens give up certain freedoms in return for security.

My government had lied to provoke a war. As I was later to testify to two successive official inquiries, the government had ignored available alternatives to war. These crimes were not the actions of a dictatorship or Putin-like despot: they had been committed by a nice, liberal democratic government staffed by people just like me, the large majority of whom had done absolutely nothing to stop it.

And to this day, not one of them, from the prime minister downwards, has been held accountable for it.

During my library idyll, I had read Karl Popper's brilliant argument for democracy, *The Open Society and Its Enemies*. Popper argues that government is kept on the straight and narrow by a free press, independent courts and, ultimately, the electorate itself: the 'Open Society'. In the case of the Iraq invasion, every one of these mechanisms failed abjectly. The courts did nothing. The press utterly failed to scrutinise the government's claims, even though they contradicted what the government itself had earlier stated.

After I resigned from the government over these lies, there was a general election in the United Kingdom which Tony Blair won. Popper had been proved wrong. Today, Blair is regularly given a platform on the BBC to be interviewed by sycophantic journalists. His spin doctor Alistair Campbell hosts a successful podcast and presented Channel Four's general election coverage. There has been no popular or cultural accountability either. Both have been — warmly — welcomed back into the 'mainstream'.

Look grave, pretend competence, keep lying long enough ... and the people, at least enough of them, will accept it. If caught, keep lying. After not too long, they will stop complaining.

****

It is hard after such an experience to keep one's faith in so-called democracy or in the integrity and honesty of government. I nonetheless wavered for months. I had been promoted to the senior ranks of the Foreign Office, but I chose not to return to London and instead took a secondment to the UN mission in Kosovo.

From there, I testified in secret to the first official inquiry into the use of intelligence before the Iraq war. I sent my secret testimony to the foreign secretary along with my letter of resignation. He never replied.

The Foreign Office did, however, get in touch with me a few weeks later. One letter invited me to visit my personnel officer who offered me psychiatric counselling, presumably to save the government fresh embarrassment if I chose, like David, to commit suicide. Another letter, from a different department, threatened me with prosecution under the Official Secrets Act if I spoke publicly about my work.

It was only thanks to the patient support and counsel of my wife that I survived this period. I had lost the profession I thought I would pursue for life, a job I had once loved. My disillusionment was complete. I knew, however, that I did not want to become the bitter man propped up on the end of the bar, endlessly rehearsing the lies and injustice of a disappearing past. In a few years, no one would care. I needed a life. I needed beliefs. I was political to my fingertips.

And so the reconstruction began.

2
Reality Is Relationships

I N OUR garage sits a bag of my fishing gear: a fly box, reel, net, waders and, of course, a fishing rod. I haven't used this gear since I retrieved it from my sister's house a few years ago. Now I ask myself why.

When I was a boy, I loved fishing. Indeed, in my memories of childhood, the episodes of fishing stand out with astonishing clarity. I spent most the time at a pond in the grounds of a large house in west Somerset, in Exmoor National Park. It was a beautiful, serene and silent place. I remember the exact spot where I would make my base to prepare the line and tie on the fly, the arc across the pond where I would cast my fly, most often what's called a nymph, a tiny hook wound around with cotton, fur and an exquisitely tiny spiral of golden tin foil. I remember the precise details of my fishing rod, its scratches and runnels, the green jacket I wore. I tied my rod to the frame of a small, one-gear bicycle we called 'the little red bike'. I would ride it back to my family as the night drew in, speeding down a tiny country lane, the bike rattling, the road a dark tunnel with thick trees and bushes on either side, forming a canopy above.

I ask myself why I remember this so clearly. Much of the rest of my childhood is cast over with fog. I remember hardly any of it. Memories of my school days are compressed into a few short moments — a fight with Barry Porter under a conker tree (I won, albeit tearfully). Running in my RAF cadet uniform to meet my gorgeous girlfriend at the main gates of the school. Curled up on the floor outside the science lab where various classmates took their turns kicking me until my twin brother arrived to push them away. My glee in repeatedly firing a rifle (shooting blanks) at attacking schoolboy soldiers during a woodland exercise. In his extraordinary memoir, *Memories, Dreams, Reflections*, written when he was eighty-three, Carl Jung writes that he only remembers moments of emotional or spiritual salience from his childhood. So it seems with me (it also seems that my memories of sex and violence predominate).

I have realised that those fishing moments were when I could be truly myself. Somehow, at home, I felt invisible. Instead, I burrowed my mind into a kind of mental anaesthesia. When I think of that boy fishing, I feel sad. He was a lonely boy but also a boy who separated himself from reality, who only allowed himself to exist when alone with his fishing rod during long summer evenings at that pond or, sometimes, when playing with my twin brother, my greatest friend.

That act of separation served me well. It protected me from emotional hurt at being ignored. It protected me when my twin was put in the year above me at school because he was clever and I, clearly, was not, a very public humiliation. But that separation, in saving me from pain, also saved me from experiencing anything, including joy. Only after leaving school, when I went to Zimbabwe to work as a teacher, did I begin to emerge from my burrow, enraptured by the blue, blue skies and the infectious energy and laughter of the pupils at my school, many of whom, ex-guerillas from the war against white-minority rule, older than me.

But as I encountered the travails and difficulties of adulthood, I retreated once more. I now ask myself whether I became a diplomat at least in part because the profession offered a pre-formed identity, into which I could enclose myself and, zipping myself up, be insulated from the vicissitudes of confronting actual adult human existence. It provided immediate social status, a uniform (dark suits, leather-soled shoes) and even a language, the formulae of diplomatic speech, where wars, deaths and conflict are reduced to terminologies and euphemisms, evenly spoken. I should have read the signs of dissonance between a fully formed, rigid and all-embracing professional identity and the other pulsing, vulnerable, raw human unacknowledged within, with emotional and spiritual hungers unsatisfied. In three years at the embassy in Bonn, my stand-out Jungian memory is the moment when I first took a drink alone at home in my dismal flat in Bad Godesberg, a suburb of the small town of Bonn, possibly the most boring town in Germany if not in Europe. Thirty-five years later, I can still see clearly the bottle of Absolut vodka, the glass in my hand, the despair I was feeling. After I moved to a flat in the town of Bonn itself, I remember weekends spent watching the drunks and junkies outside the railway station, envying them and their company as they yelled and consorted with one another. Some nights, I would drive fast up the autobahn to Cologne to visit dance clubs, only to stand alone, pressed against the walls, afraid to approach anyone. But I also remember my good friend Andress, a Singaporean diplomat, with whom I hosted fancy dress parties and travelled to Moscow and New York and an exquisite dinner party where a Danish diplomat cooked fresh lobster. Amid this luxury, it wasn't all loneliness and self-hatred.

As I grew older, however, the separation between the self and my reality only grew. By the time I was posted to New York, I had a stellar career and a pathway to ambassadorships opening ahead of me. But I was a quaking, unexplored bloody mess within. The mountain climb back to reality only began when I left the mission in 2002 for a sabbatical year. My life started to have contrast, expansion. I had fallen in love with a woman who was — is — a soul of great courage, moral rigour and intelligence; she challenged me in every way possible.

But my habits of denial and retreat were hard to shake. The complexities, difficulties and roller-coaster existence of marriage, family life and fatherhood drove me back into my hole. I lived a separate life in my head from what was actually going on. I hurt those around me with my foggy detachment. I denied myself the richness of being alive, its pain and transcendence. My favourite quotation is from Camus:

'There is no sun without shadow, and one must know the night.'

But I didn't live the maxim. To avoid the pain of life, I avoided actually being alive. It took me decades to see what I was and the habits I used to separate myself and the harm that I had caused, above all, to those closest to me. Only now am I slowly learning to be with the world, unprotected, uninsulated. And it is wonderful and painful. I weep and I laugh, both more easily. I dream vividly when for years I didn't dream at all. Each morning, I wake up with a new song in my head. I would like to say it's cool indie music. But actually it's Mariah Carey or Wham.

Once I had to force myself into patience when my children touched me (my separation techniques were physical as well as emotional). Now I relish their touch. The other evening, I sat with a twin on either side of me, going through their English homework. My son rested his head on my shoulder; my daughter put her legs across my lap. *Aha*, I thought, *this is what happiness looks like*. I see you now.

And this, I realise, is why the rubber of my green waders is slowly cracking and perishing in our garage, unused along with the rest of my fishing gear. When I fished as a boy, I was alone in order to feel real, to be present to myself, to be a person, a human, a humanity that was too often un-noticed in my family home. But this cannot last. Retreating into a burrow doesn't work as a method for life. In fact, it is profoundly destructive to the one thing that can sustain your humanity, affirm you as a person, rich, emotional and aware: the relationship to other people.

I don't need to go fishing anymore. In fact, I don't want to go fishing. Because going fishing means being away from my family. I am only truly alive when I am with them. They make me. And it is not only my children and my wife. I now seek this connection with everyone I meet. I try for intimacy with my friends and new acquaintances: each creates not only a new experience but also a new existence. Instead of casting artificial flies with my fishing rod, I now throw the bait of my own confessions before others in the hope of achieving real connection (much as I am now throwing this bait before you, the reader). It has taken far too long, and some of the damage cannot be undone, but I am learning how to live.

****

For several months after I left the mission, I sat in the Bobst Library on the southeast corner of Washington Square Park in downtown Manhattan. I tended to take the same desk on a mezzanine floor overlooking Bleecker Street to the rear of the library, a big red modernist block. Usually I was surrounded by NYU students, coughing and sighing over their laptops. It was a wonderful, quiet place to work. I would wander the shelves, sometimes taking books almost at random. I was exploring and wanted to go down the paths untaken.

I had taken a sabbatical from the Foreign Office, an incredible privilege, doubtless rare in the private sector, whereby my job would be guaranteed for my return — as long as my activities during the time off were deemed by officialdom as 'legitimate'. I had told the Foreign Office that I intended to study the empirical basis of policymaking. Little did they know, little did I know, that this would form my first steps towards anarchy.

I had begun to wonder why governments and policymakers took the decisions they did. Perhaps I was motivated by the loose connection between facts and reality in British policy on Iraq. I had been struck by how we made decisions based almost entirely on abstractions for which we then gathered the evidence to justify — the opposite of the scientific method. But my doubts went broader than British foreign policy. I was concerned with the whole system: capitalism, neoliberalism, representative democracy, whatever you want to call it, where I looked at the outputs and found them wanting. This was the era of Clinton and Blair, later Bush, Brown and Obama, where 'our' way of doing things was supposed to be superior — so superior, in fact, that it could be imposed on other countries including, when necessary, by military force.

But why was it so superior when the deficits were so glaring? Why were economic policy makers so willing to accept the obvious negative consequences of their policies — punitive inequality and carbon emissions, starving children in uptown housing projects and global warming? Were these decision-makers also basing themselves on tempting abstractions with little relation to reality? Why was democracy in trouble with widespread disillusionment and apathy? Were people somehow unconvinced by the reality when the theory was so convincing? Since those days in the early 2000's when I was in that library, these concerns have only become more widespread as the evidence of the inadequacy of traditional theory becomes more urgent.

So I took books off the shelves and pondered. I read and read. Marcuse, Smith, Marx; Hayek and Friedman but also Camus, Orwell and Kafka. Critiques of democracy and neo-classical economics, as well as the textbooks that students learned from at college: the elements of the dominant paradigm. What were the theories that formed our understanding of the world and drove the policies that arbitrated that world? And why were they so wanting? And then, in turn, what might replace them?

I began to formulate a crude hypothesis. I made notes for a book. My thesis was simple: human needs and wants should be at the centre of any political and economic philosophy. Everything should flow from this.

****

The human mind craves patterns with which to understand the world. It craves order. This sounds reasonable, but it may in fact be mistaken. For while the world obeys certain rules, ordered it is not. It is something else.

I have long sought out organising systems to interpret the world's machinations, both human and otherwise. I love graphs and schematics, drawing lines, boxes and arrows to depict systems and relationships. I think it was this hunger that led me to economics and politics, which I studied at university. I wanted to understand how the world worked.

But *how* and *why* are two different questions. One is about the workings of a system, the other is about its reasons. And it is a mistake to confuse the two. I fear that that is a trap I have often fallen into. You think you understand how a system works and that this knowledge amounts to an understanding of fundamental causes. But that's wrong. While the practice of a system may reveal itself, the reason and meaning of that system are elusive. In fact, they may remain forever mysterious, and perhaps they should always be so.

Orthodox economic and political theory claim to answer these questions. They claim both to explain how the system should work and — they go further — to explain what it is *for*. This is why I studied them. I wanted theories and a systematic understanding to explain the world. My studies offered a well-honed and thoroughly researched answer. Neo-classical economics proposed a neat and logical system where supply matched demand through price, where markets came to equilibrium and, above all, where humans were able to satisfy themselves through consumption.

During my sabbatical, I read the current textbooks that are used to teach economics. There I found the same mythologies. Resources are allocated most efficiently in a free market; growth is thereby maximised to the ultimate benefit of all. Everyone gets richer, even the poorest — and even if some get more than others (indeed this is one necessary cost of the process). Anything outside these neatly drawn models were mere "externalities" and could be safely ignored. The textbooks are easy to understand; the intersecting lines and parabolas of their graphs offer a pleasing and convincing aesthetic.

Underpinning it all is a theory of how individuals choose to live, what drives them, and here we encounter the 'why'. The answer offered — nay, assumed — by conventional economists, and propounded in the textbooks, is that people wish to maximise 'utility' — that this is what humans want. 'Utility' is an invented concept, created in order to fit the theory. It is the idea that people want more in order to be satisfied — in the jargon, they want to 'maximise' utility. And what is the thing they want?

I suspect that no one, not even orthodox economists, would describe their needs, wants, desires, ambitions and longings in this way. The things that drive them. If we could put words to them at all, we would never use the language of maximizing utility. It would sound absurd. Yet this is the founding premise of neo-classical economics, the idea that dominates our world to this day.

This fundamental failing is compounded by a further gross distortion. For the purposes of the theory, anything people want must satisfy one condition — it can be measured. For if it can't be measured, it doesn't count, and indeed you literally cannot count it. Thus, everything we might want is reduced to things — goods, services, things you can buy, the material. All these things can be consumed; thus, the pursuit of utility is in fact another way of describing consumption. Thus, all of life is reduced to accountancy. This fundamental deficiency — the tyranny of measurability — has had countless ramifications for our society and planet; indeed, it has shaped them both — in some ways for the better, but in others catastrophically for the worse. Life expectancies have dramatically improved (for the richest more than the poor), and people's material circumstances globally have never been better. But the price has been great. A psychological crisis of ennui and destruction visited upon the planet upon which all life depends.

Meanwhile, the discourse of politics, albeit with less pseudo-scientific precision, offered an equally convincing and parallel philosophy. Democracy produced order through the imposition of laws to which the people consent. Its antithesis was totalitarianism where order was simply imposed without consent.

Centuries of democratic practice had evolved highly sophisticated institutions, where complex policies could be successfully arbitrated between different interest groups. The two philosophies — of democracy and markets — reinforced one another. Democracy could only flourish when markets were free, while any "market failures" could be successfully corrected by government. If government diverged from the collective interest, then the people would see to it that it would be thrown out by democratic elections.

As the foreign secretary's speechwriter, I had written nice, clear speeches celebrating and propounding these ideas. I had honestly believed that since my government was democratic and staffed by mostly decent people like me, it must be right.

But the evidence told a different story.

Only in the solitude of the library, away from the echo chamber of my government ministry, could I confront it. Mounting inequality, accelerating atmospheric warming and what already appeared to be a state of perpetual global war.

Just a few miles from where I sat reading in downtown Manhattan, in the northern reaches of New York City, children were going hungry. These were the indices of a failing system.

Meanwhile, other signals, without statistics, told of a society ill at ease: the suppressed but ever-present violence in public spaces; the constant desire for escape, whether alcoholic, narcotic or merely distracting; individuals stuck in tedious, mind-numbing work which, to their enduring humiliation, they must pretend to love.

I read and read. Following one particular byway, I came across an extraordinary book by Ludwig Wittgenstein, his *Tractatus Logico-Philosophicus*. I read a lot *about* this book, because on its own it was more or less impossible to understand. What it said, I realised one afternoon, changed the way I thought forever. I vividly remember the burst of light.

In the *Tractatus*, Wittgenstein attempts to find a perfect symbolic language to represent reality. The book mostly comprises austere statements of logic which, building upon one another, make his case. What he demonstrates is a kind of paradox, but also an essential truth.

He finds that there is no symbolic system and no language that can fully represent reality. Even logic itself can only be *shown* by symbols, never proven. He concludes with a series of short, devastating statements which, in a way, explode everything he has just attempted to prove.

These statements are not written in logical symbols. They are just ordinary sentences, almost poetic.

We feel that even if all possible scientific questions are answered, the problems of life have still not been touched at all. Of course there is then no question left, and just this is the answer.

There is indeed the inexpressible. This shows itself; it is the mystical. The right method of philosophy would be this. To say nothing except what can be said.

At first, this revelation might strike you as esoteric. But to me, trapped in conventional theories of economics and politics, it came as a shattering epiphany. For what Wittgenstein was saying was that *everything that really mattered could not be described*. Indeed, he said it couldn't be spoken of in the quotation most commonly taken from his book*. It couldn't be measured. It couldn't be put into symbols or equations or graphs. It wasn't rational because it couldn't be proven.

But it was the most important stuff of life.

What is this metaphysical stuff? Wittgenstein talks of God, death and the mystical. But this indescribable, ineffable realm also

____

* 'Whereof one cannot speak, thereof one must be silent'.

comprises things like solidarity, hate, compassion, grief, meaning and, of course, love.

Words can suggest and hint at these things, but they can never fully capture them. These things are wholly ignored in logical, "rational" theories such as neo-classical economics. But they are what matter most. They save us from the empty materialism and rationalism of modern life. As Marcelo Gleiser puts it, 'This unknowability may well be what will rescue what is left of our humanity from the unstoppable mechanization and objectification of modern existence'.[1] This realm may be far greater than what can be captured with rationalist terms. As Rilke put it, 'Things are not as graspable and sayable as on the whole we are led to believe; most events are unsayable, occur in a space that no word has ever penetrated'. Another book I read exploded the myth of rationality, a cardinal assumption of neo-classical economics: that people are able to make the best choices for themselves. It was a remarkable book by two Israeli-American academics, Daniel Kahneman and Amos Tversky (the former has since become famous). In it they demonstrate a basic finding — that people's choices depend on how the question is framed. Frame a question differently, even if the options are exactly the same, people make a different choice. Again, this should be obvious, but rationality remains a core assumption of neo-classical economics to this day. We are emphatically not rational; we are creatures of emotion and context. We do not crunch the numbers like sentient computers. We are swayed by myriad forces, some of which we may not even understand.

Most people don't need psychologists or fancy philosophy to tell them this. They already know it. While we need food, houses and stuff to be comfortable, these things are not ultimately the things that matter most.

I need patterns and shapes to explain an otherwise incomprehensible world. I need theories to interpret its otherwise unintelligible machinations. But if my theories *fail* to account for what was most important, then they must be wrong.

****

It felt as if I had been locked inside a neat and tidy little box where everything internally seemed ordered and made sense: at least in terms of the box. But outside was the world in all its complicated, ineffable glory: fantastic, beautiful, incomprehensible, mysterious.

With a few dry but devastating phrases, Wittgenstein had smashed the box apart forever. But not only were the theories I had hitherto relied upon inadequate, their imposition upon the world through our dominant economic and political systems was causing indescribable trouble.[†] Orthodox theories were being forced upon the world, and yet, humans weren't really like that. Humans are not rational actors; they are not mere maximisers of utility. Measurable economic growth is not the thing that everyone aspires to above all else.

It's hard for me to convey the importance of this moment. I looked at the world with fresh eyes, liberated from the false constructs that had for so long confused me.

At last, I was able to see the limits of theory, indeed the terrible dangers of theory — particularly theory that bases itself only on the material. As Wittgenstein implored, I was invited to see the world as it really was, not as a rigid and imprisoning construction of ideology and fake science.

Of course — how could I have missed this! — what mattered to people should be what mattered in economics and, indeed, politics. Unfortunately, that which most matters to people is *not* what most economics and indeed contemporary politics, even allegedly democratic politics, is about.

The economy and government have diverged from what humans really want and need. They have been perverted by false theory. And specifically, corrupted by those who benefit from this perversion, who

---

[†] I was nervous about this 'political' interpretation of the *Tractatus*, so I checked with Ray Monk, a philosopher biographer of Wittgenstein. He concurred with this potential interpretation.

enforce these ideas through power, policy and their dominance over the narrative of what society, indeed life, is 'about' and what matters.

Questions, however, remained. What system would be better? How should you design a society which is governed not by theory — or by the powerful — but by people's authentic wishes?

For evidence of the truth of Wittgenstein's logic of illogic, you need not look far. Unless you're a hedge fund trader, most of the people you know are not primarily motivated by money and material acquisition. There are far more teachers and nurses than there are currency speculators. God knows, we all want a nice house and not to have to worry about money, but only a minority would argue that these are the *most* important things, goals to which all else should be subordinated.

How are we to explore what really matters to people? I find it hard to explain to myself the deeper forces that drive me, that strange amalgam of childhood inheritance, adult experience, unspoken motives and vaguely understood emotion. I have attempted to write novels and screenplays that explain it. I have always come up short. The closest I have come to a representation is the intersection of a line and the curve, that infinitesimal dot where the circle meets the plane, where the rational meets the irrational. But this symbolism too, I know to be simplistic and inadequate.

As for other people's motivations, dreams, drives and ambitions, I can only guess: a sharp contrast to the presumptions of orthodox economists and theorists of 'representative' democracy. Indeed, this has come to form the core of my political credo. It's hard — very hard — to know what others want or need. If we don't know, we have no alternative but to ask them. We must respect their own voices. Indeed, it follows that our voices, mine as well as others', are the only source of political legitimacy, the only thing that should have weight. This, I came to realise, has profound implications for the kind of system we might seek.

I can, however, speculate on the motives of others. I can seek out evidence of what they say and do. I have often sought the testimony of those at the extremes of life, for perhaps this is the most revealing, when people are liberated from the suffocations of normality and routine.

There are few greater extremes of life than those who are confronting death. The regrets of the dying are never that they should have made more money. They are of neglect of family or friends or of joy itself. Many regret living for work alone, when it is the things beyond work that give the most satisfaction.

Jake Seliger, a man dying of cancer:

What really matters, sustainably, over time? Other people and your relationships with other people. That's it. That's the non-secret secret. As the end approaches, you're not going to care about your achievements or brilliance or power or lack thereof; you're going to care about the people around you and how you affected them, and how they affected you. That's what will matter.[2]

Another datum of the point of living can be heard in the words of those confronting death by execution: the condemned. Here's one person facing their death at the hands of the state, Dawn:

The day I got my execution date, I learned something that's never left me. You have to be right here, in this moment. Like a child. They're not thinking about tomorrow or last week. They're just here. Now.

Seeing a smile on someone's face, the light in their eyes, is enough. That's perfect contentment. That's joy. It's taken me a lifetime to learn that life's deepest meaning isn't found in accomplishments, but in relationships.

All there ever is, is this moment.

You, me, all of us, right here, right now, this minute, that's love. And that…

That's a whole lifetime.[3]

This is the immeasurable, the metaphysical, the transcendent. It is certainly beyond numbers and cannot be bought. The power of relationships and love, in this — our only — moment, is arguably beyond all words. It is certainly something that makes us happy[‡]. Few of us would question that these ineffable things are what life is, or should be, about. But this stuff doesn't fit neatly into scientific quantification. It is the realm of the irrational, the kingdom of art, poetry, music, mysticism and even religion.

Later in life, I was to discover other philosophers who echoed Wittgenstein's revelatory conclusions. Carl Jung also believed in the human need for the infinite, the limitless:

> The more a man lays stress on false possessions, and the less sensitivity he has for what is essential, the less satisfying is his life. He feels limited because he has limited aims, and the result is envy and jealousy. If we understand and feel that here in this life we already have a link with the infinite, desires and attitudes change. In the final analysis, we count for something only because of the essential we embody, and if we do not embody that life is wasted. In our relationships to other men, too, the crucial question is whether an element of boundlessness is expressed in the relationship.[4]

Here we again encounter the infinite, the limitless, that mysterious something at the heart of all humanity, that thing beyond words. The conventional theorists of capitalism don't deny that we need the arts, religion and the ineffable and to satisfy the need for self-expression. But they claim that these needs can only be addressed once material needs have been satisfied. If you like, we can only experience god once our bellies are full and our houses warm. Abraham Maslow's famous hierarchy of human needs has played an influential part in

---

[‡] A 75-year, $20m Harvard study found that the strongest indicator of happiness over a person's lifetime is the depth and meaningfulness of relationships.

this assumption, namely that humans' first needs are food and shelter, and only once their material needs are taken care of do they become concerned with "higher" needs — love, self-expression, fulfilment, the spirit. This thinking is implicit in the logic of capitalism, as another of its rarely questioned assumptions. Attend to the material first, then only later can we take care of the rest.

I came across other theories that counter the neo-classical mythologies. Manfred Max-Neef argues that human needs are not insatiable but are in fact limited. It is more than possible to fully satisfy human needs. In other words, there can be limits to consumption, to materialism itself. These needs cannot, moreover, be simplistically divided into material and immaterial needs. We have perhaps nine basic needs, including subsistence, security, affection, meaning and freedom. He also suggests transcendence as a human need, though he is not convinced that it is universal (I believe it is). A crude materialist measure like Gross Domestic Product (the measurable sum of what an economy produces) cannot be adequate to capture this diversity and subtlety of what matters to us.

The 'human givens' hypothesis, originated by Joe Griffin and Ivan Tyrell, makes a similar claim: humans are born with certain innate needs, emotional as well as physical, for security, love, connection to community, autonomy: agency. These matter as much to our mental health as any other need. Part of me resists the parcelling up and listing of something as subtle and complex as human needs, but it's surely the case that this approach, or Max-Neef's, lies closer to the truth than the simpler Maslowian hierarchy.

And indeed the data suggest that wealth and happiness are only weakly correlated, only up to a point. In fact, inequality is a more important determinant of happiness: the greater the inequality, the less happy the society.[5] A recent book about how to be happy, based on the findings of an 84-year Harvard study, also emphasises the importance of relationships, as well as the freedom and capacity to make important life decisions: relationships and freedom. Good relationships also make you less likely to contract heart disease or arthritis: the more socially connected you are, the more likely you are to live longer and live well. These factors are important across countries, cultures and social classes. One of the authors boiled down the definition of a good life: "Being engaged in activities I care about with people I care about." Robert Waldinger declares that he has had a happy life apart from the times characterised by disconnection from other people.[6]

I am unconvinced that 'happiness' should be the goal. Whenever I ask myself whether I am happy, I start to feel depressed. And, indeed, psychological studies suggest that seeking happiness is a false god and that we can only achieve it in the seeking, in the 'flow' states of absorption and activity, that only there will we find fulfilment. And I would suggest that even this happy state of affairs is all but fleeting.

But my failure to attain happiness does not rob me of purpose, motivation or meaning. I tend to bleakness. I prefer the painting of Caravaggio and Rothko, one a literal representation of human torment (in one painting, the severed head of John the Baptist has Caravaggio's own face), the other an attempt, perhaps forever futile, to capture in dark colours alone that thing that animates us, possesses us, the ineffable. I prefer cold mountains over beaches, rainswept moorland over manicured flowerbeds — "there is no sun without shadow and one must know the night", as Camus put it in his existentialist masterpiece, *The Myth of Sisyphus*.

I have spent periods of my life fascinated by the Holocaust. I have visited the death camps of Auschwitz, Dachau, Buchenwald and the modest building in Wannsee near Berlin, where the final solution was plotted by Nazi officials. I wrote a presentation about the Holocaust when I was a diplomat in Germany. One reason I was intrigued is that this horror had happened in (then) one of the most advanced and 'civilised' countries in the world, the birthplace of Schiller, Beethoven and Goethe. It is as plausible a destination for humanity as the idiotic triumphalism of those who believe democracy and capitalism are the ends of history.

But another reason for the fascination is the human experience of those caught up in the Holocaust, at least those who survived. Members of my family, some of whom had comprised the Polish government when the Nazis invaded, had been exterminated in Auschwitz, so there is something of a personal connection, too. Primo Levi's *If This Is a Man* had a profound effect on me as a young man. When I was posted to Germany, I read the chilling memoir of Rudolf Höss, the commandant of Auschwitz, a boring, quotidian man who talked of family outings, gardens and bureaucracy while overseeing mass murder. And finally, and most devastatingly, Christopher Browning's extraordinary book, *Ordinary Men* about one battalion of shopkeepers, teachers and postmen who killed tens of thousands of Jews behind the advancing German army on the Eastern Front, who day after day obeyed orders to march old people, women, children and men into forests, force them to dig ditches, then line them up and shoot them one by one at close range, calmly adjusting the aim of their rifles to ensure that they were not spattered with brains and blood (a side-effect, by the way, that encouraged Himmler to build the gas chambers; thereby avoiding this sanguinary awkwardness for the perpetrators while ensuring the industrial efficiency necessary for killing millions of people).

What of the human experience amidst this horror? Can a point of life be located in this darkest of places? The idea of happiness, utility maximisation and all the rest becomes grotesque, absurd. Yet there was meaning and purpose to be found, as Viktor Frankl testified:

> Everything can be taken from a man but one thing: the last of
> the human freedoms—to choose one's attitude in any given set
> of circumstances, to choose one's own way.

> Those who have a 'why' to live, can bear with almost any 'how'.

The fallacy of contemporary orthodoxy is also to locate meaning and purpose in the individual, that it is the individual who seeks to maximise their satisfaction. But this seems wrong. Any one of us knows that it is our relationship to others that matters as much as anything. It is certainly true for me. I only feel that I matter when I am making those sandwiches for my children or talking with my wife, experiencing both the banality of the everyday but the depths of the sublime. And vain as I am, I feel that I matter when I'm opining on the radio or writing this book, but only because I think that other people are listening. Alone, I would be pointless.

I would go further to argue that there is one immaterial need that stands out above all others. That is our need for other people. Solitary confinement is a form of torture because it denies all human relationships. In this way, it denies what it is to be human. Two unexpected thinkers have helped me give shape to this realisation, one an alleged terrorist, the other a quantum physicist.

****

Abdullah Öcalan is today imprisoned on an island off the coast of Turkey, designated a terrorist both by his government and by the rest of the world (whether he is or not is another argument). He is the leader of the Kurdish liberation movement, the Kurdistan Workers Party, the PKK. He is the author of the ideas that today hold sway in Rojava, in northeast Syria, a place I have visited. Öcalan posits that the fundamental problem of Western culture is the subject/object distinction. What he is criticising is the notion that we are separated from others, whether people or nature. A neat way of understanding this distinction is grammatical: subject/object.

Instead, Öcalan believes in a more connected reality, that there should be no distinction between subject and object, that they only exist in relation to one another, a subject/subject relationship, if you like — or rather, just a relationship.

Curiously, this echoes discoveries in physics about the most fundamental relationship between particles at the quantum level.

Here we turn to the second thinker, the physicist Carlo Rovelli, who argues that the *relationship* itself is the fundamental (or, if you like, the 'ontological primitive'). Thanks to the reality that a particle's quantities (its velocity, its position in space) are only established when the particle is observed, it follows that the particle only actually exists in relationship to another entity.

> We have discovered that, at the core of the physical reality, it's not particles, it's relational connections.

Rovelli says:

> Each object is defined by the way it interacts with something else. So when it's not interacting, *it's just not existing* [my italics]. An object is the ensemble of the ways in which it affects other objects around itself — an object exists reflected in everything else.[7]

In other words, reality is composed of relationships.

Is this an echo — perhaps even a fundamental — of the very nature of being human? That we only truly exist in terms of other people and, indeed, of the natural world around us. To exist alone in a black void, disconnected from everything, is truly a nightmare, one that is unsustainable for any individual. This is not a kumbaya statement that 'we are all connected' but an observation, founded on our deepest intuitions of what it is to be human, that our reality, our very existence, is dependent on other people. If we take this on board, we begin to see other people as functions of our very selves. We only truly exist in their eyes, and vice versa. In the African concept of *Ubuntu*, a human being cannot be complete without the affirmation of other human beings. The Akan of Ghana would say: 'onipa na oma onipa ye onipa': it is a human being who makes another person a human being.[8]

Nick Montgomery and Carla Bergman see our very freedom within our relationships with others:

> If relationships are what compose the world—and what shape
> our desires, values, and capacities—then freedom is the capacity
> to participate more actively in this process of composition.[9]

For Ivan Illich, 'friendship will be the soil from which a new politics will emerge…'[10] Society is a network of relationships, not an aggregate of discrete individuals (indeed, the notion of the individual is a 'bourgeois fetish').

The anonymous French revolutionary collective, the Invisible Committee, noted that freedom and relationships have the same linguistic roots: "freedom isn't the act of shedding our attachments, but the practical capacity to work on them, to move around in their space, to form or dissolve them."[11] Originally, freedom meant simply having friends. Marx also defines freedom in terms of a successful relationship to others:

> Only in community [with others does each] individual [have]
> the means of cultivating his gifts in all directions; only in the
> community, therefore, is personal freedom possible.

At the moment, we live in a society oriented towards growth and consumption as its highest priorities: the primary of the individual's aspirations. These are the wrong priorities, as evidence, theory and philosophy, as well as our own personal experience, all suggest. The problem is exacerbated by the dominance of those who choose wealth over other priorities. The hedge fund manager has more economic and political power than the nurse: their choices are more influential in shaping our lives, our culture and the policies of our governments. It was hedge fund traders, not nurses, who drank champagne with the Chancellor the evening after he cut taxes on the wealthiest. The wealthy enjoy more political access and sway. Witness the donors' clubs, who are granted direct access to government ministers (of both major parties, notably). British political giving is increasingly dominated by the rich.[12] But their choices also shape a culture by promoting obsession with materialism and luxury. The rest are caged by their power, their influence and their cultural choices. The most materialist kind of people create a culture that dominates the rest.

That culture is sickeningly familiar; it is constantly in our faces: the 'influencers' basking in swimming pools in Dubai; the Mercedes racing along a deserted road, steered by a bestubbled man, a beautiful woman by his side. The very idea of luxury requires the projection of exclusivity. If we could all have it, it wouldn't be worth having. I too am susceptible to the insatiable craving such messages are designed to provoke.

Instead, I think that humans desire a society not only where they are comfortable but also — and perhaps above all (though here, as everywhere, we should avoid making hierarchies) — where the ineffable qualities of meaning, community and solidarity are maximised. A different order or indeed no order at all.

But I can only claim to know this. I don't know for sure. I cannot claim to know what other people want or need any more than a neo-classical utility-maximising economist can, or the prime minister. I'm not even sure I know what I myself want, let alone other people.

So how can we tell? Well, obviously, people need to be free to choose their own path. They need to be free to declare their own wishes and requirements and, perhaps above all, to negotiate their own relationships, their own place in society. Only then can we know. And only then if we listen and pay attention to what they say, which is not always easy when one disagrees.

But what if people's declared wishes do not truly reflect their deeper and authentic desires? Wants are often created by culture: by advertising, by invidious comparison with others, by our craving for self-expression in a society that smothers it in conformity and compliance. To be a follower of fashion is, of course, in a way to be unfree.

The challenge then is to create the conditions where people can be free to choose and make such declarations, to have their own voice, ideally in circumstances of genuine freedom, cut loose from the pernicious influences of those who manufacture our wants in search of profit and the narcissistic impulses of those whose only route to meaning is through ostentation and their desperation for attention — itself a symptom of a poisoned society, a place where some commit murder in order to win fame. Perhaps some would truly want this kind of society; I shudder if so. But even then, they should be free to choose it.

Without agency, no one can express what they need, even if sometimes that expression is the result of sometimes silent manipulation, escape from which is the ultimate precondition of freedom. There are thus two levels of true freedom — the first, to decide for ourselves; the second, for the *circumstances* to enable free, unfettered choice. We shall come to the second condition in a later chapter.

My political journey has taken me to this point and to this conviction — that the primary requirement is that everyone should have a say in matters that concern them. I have helped refugees form the first-ever delegations to take part in international negotiations about refugees so that they, at last, have a say in their own fates. I have joined struggles for self-determination in the Western Sahara, Kosovo, Somaliland and Catalonia. But these were would-be states that wanted their own freedom, away from the controlling domination of other states. Self-determination has another, more microcosmic meaning. That we ourselves should be free.

That freedom of course is not absolute. It has to be negotiated with others. I am not a die-hard libertarian like the anarchist Max Stirner, who believed that we should be free to do whatever we want. It follows from my conviction that it is other people who make us matter, that we are concerned with other people. They matter to us too. My freedom cannot be obtained at the expense of theirs (it wouldn't last in any case because they would resist, ultimately with violence). My behaviour has consequences for them. Therefore, we have to deal with things together. So-called 'representative' democracy is supposed to take care of this, as we elect political parties to aggregate and then negotiate our views. But this doesn't seem to be working. We don't feel represented.

We feel we are denied agency. Most people feel, as surveys suggest, that politicians do not listen to them and do not represent them. Of course, politicians cannot represent the richness and diversity of our wishes, only aggregations of the generalised desires of many. But perhaps we don't in fact want to be represented at all: we want at last to speak for ourselves.

So what might be an alternative that gives us this agency back, gives us control and choice over our own lives, a space for us to negotiate together while accounting for the needs of the whole? I have been in search of this alternate dispensation, not knowing what I would find.

3
A Radical, New Dispensation

*'Go to work, send your kids to school, follow fashion, act normal, walk on the pavement, watch TV, save for your old age, obey the law, repeat after me: I am free'.**

COME from privilege. I was brought up in a large house in a relatively wealthy suburb of London. I was sent to private school (I hated it). In class terms, we were firmly Upper Middle Class.

My grandfather was obsessed with class. A professor of linguistics, he became fascinated by the language of class. What were the linguistic distinctions between the classes? He came up with a taxonomy of class language, which he called 'U' and 'non-U': upper class or non-upper class — a pretty revealing binary. He regarded himself as upper class. He had been raised on a country estate with servants. He defined 'U' (upper class) speech as how he spoke.

Alan's class taxonomy became famous in the 1950s when it was picked up by Nancy Mitford. Together, they authored a book called

---

* This quote may have originated as street art; its author is unknown.

Noblesse Oblige, which was well-known to a certain — now rather aged — segment of the population. For a while U and non-U became a thing. U was loo. Non-U, toilet. U was napkin, and non-U serviette, and so on and so forth. In the aspirational status-conscious days of that decade, U and non-U became so popular that my grandfather wrote and sold several books on the subject. Despite his professorial status, there was little rigour to his analysis. His language distinctions were based solely on his own experience and prejudices. Today his books read as manuals for blatant snobbery. To older people, I used to show off *Noblesse Oblige*. Today, I'm rather ashamed of this part of Alan's work. Instead, I talk about the secret, more worthy work he did as a codebreaker at Bletchley Park during the Second World War.

We inherited these prejudices. My father would become angry if we called the bag in which you keep your toiletries a 'wash bag' (non-U) instead of 'sponge bag' (U). Likewise, our pronunciation, which was that particular brand of 'well-spoken' English that, while neither 'posh' nor aristocratic, denoted a certain class status. To this day, I can garner an awful lot of information about an English person's background by listening to how they speak. I've noticed that I am careful about my own diction. When I testified in person to the 'Chilcot' Iraq Inquiry, my speech was at its most polished. I can do 'U' pretty well, and obviously, I thought it added to my authority. When I'm speaking to a group of anarchists or inner-city school children, however, it is my South London roots that my speech evokes, with its glottal consonants and elongated vowel sounds.

Doubtless, my speech was pretty arch when I was interviewed for the Foreign Office. You won't hear many working-class accents among its senior ranks. In fact, you will hear none. Membership of Her Majesty's diplomatic corps affirmed if not elevated my class status. If I had stayed in 'the Office', as we called it, perhaps by now I would have a knighthood, like several of my contemporaries have. But all that is behind me now, along with — alas — my index-linked pension.

Instead, I have a more average but still privileged class and economic status. After I left the Foreign Office, I founded and ran a non-profit, or non-governmental organisation as it's known in Britain. Today, I work as a consultant, earning significantly more than the average wage.

Nevertheless, my choices are constrained as they are for everyone save the ultra-rich. Throughout my life, I have worried about money. Thanks to a mortgage and other pressures, I will be in one kind of debt or another until I'm seventy. My family has chronic health needs; we have had to reach deep into our own pockets to fund various treatments. We have had to sell houses to pay off medical debt. For myself, I have long been diagnosed with a long-term condition for which the care under the National Health Service is abysmal, requiring me to fork out of pocket for private care. I am lucky that I can.

A few years ago we moved to Wales to better attend to family's needs, including education. North Wales, like so much of the country, suffers an acute shortage of affordable housing. There are virtually no long-term rentals available. Whenever we saw a listing for an available rental, we would call the estate agent only to find that no fewer than forty families were somehow ahead of us in the queue. Even if we got close to the front of the line, we were then humiliatingly obliged to reveal — with written proof — every detail of our personal finances — our income, savings and debts — in order to convince the landlord of our credit worthiness. Instead, we lived in a succession of Airbnb rentals at vast expense, for these were rented by the night rather than the month. We moved twelve times in one year.

I tell this story not out of self-pity. On the contrary, I tell it because we are well-off by national standards. I have preserved a small pension pot that the Foreign Office granted me when I resigned. My income puts me in the top 20% of earners. The relative wealth of my and my wife's families provides a foundation of financial security: we will never starve or be homeless. For people like us, life should be easy. Yet every step of my life since my resignation has been shadowed by worries about debt and financial insecurity.

And yet I am lucky. For most people, it's so much worse. I do a job which I can manage by sitting at a computer and talking over video calls. I don't have to heft bricks or forty-pound crates of cheese (a truly backbreaking job I once did as a student). I am white and do not have to deal with the baked-in injustices and persistent obstacles for people of colour in a system built by people like me, or the micro-aggressions and prejudice they regularly experience. I am male and have never faced the systematic expressions of sexism and male power experienced by women. For centuries, the system has been set up to preserve the privileges of people of my race and gender. This is my point. The system was designed *for* people like me.

I am so much better off than someone struggling on a low income or living off benefits. I do not suffer the pain, humiliations and frustrations of not being able to afford the basic necessities of life, whether food or heating. I do not experience the chaos of a life of poverty, juggling debts and bills. Mine is by comparison a very small burden. Yet I do not feel free.

Thanks to the overspecialisation of the economy, I'm not really qualified to do anything else except jobs like my current one. Especially when I'm filling in tax declarations or wondering how to pay my council tax, I do not feel free. Rather the opposite. I feel as if I'm working *towards* something, rather than doing the thing I love. One day, I think, I will be able to spend my time as I wish. But that day never seems to come.

After the 9/11 attacks, the *New York Times* ran thousands of mini-obituaries of victims from the World Trade Center. It was striking and tragic how many of them were working in the Twin Towers, frequently in some boring back-office job in order to do something else, such as pay for a master's degree or open a restaurant. And yet their dreams ended when the hijacked planes smashed into their buildings. There was to be no future. And this is a cardinal lesson. Life shouldn't be about the future. It should be good enough here and now.

In a society driven by material consumption, there is an endless race for more money. If we have more money, we believe, we will at last be free. Unfortunately, except for a tiny minority, that day never comes. Unless you are at the very top of the pyramid, where there's precious little room, you will always be subject to the force of money and the power of those who have more. As they say in America, almost every one of us is working for the Man in some way or other.

Meanwhile, in other ways, my choices are constrained. I have never voted for a political party that became the government. I have written to MPs about various issues but only ever received perfunctory form replies (the first I wrote was about the regulation of air rifles). I have never talked in person to an MP about my concerns. I could hate all politicians, but I don't blame them, and I abhor the abuse and threats they now routinely suffer. They are largely powerless functionaries of the system too. Most can't do much either unless they happen to be one of the tiny few who serve in the cabinet where they might have some sway over the only person whose decisions actually matter, the prime minister.

Like millions of others, my family has enduring and profound needs in terms of healthcare and education. I have absolutely no power over how those needs are met, whether by the health service or by the local council. In different places, including in London and New York City, we have had to threaten the council with court action in order for the statutory obligations to our family to be met. We have been forced into years-long legal actions. Those legal obligations, in turn, are in the hands of various national-level secretaries of state, whose names I don't know and to whom I have precisely nil access and nil influence.

The needs of my family could not be more central to my concerns. Yet even here the paltry tools that I enjoy are not available to most. My wife and I are determined advocates for our family's needs. On occasion, we have had the resources to buy legal advice on how to take on the authorities in both the US, where we once lived, and the UK. I am well aware that because of these advantages, we ultimately — and unfairly — get a better deal than those without them. The truly worst off have no tools at all. They are entirely subject to the force of legislation they had no part in writing and to the arbitrary whims of officials' interpreting those rules, over whom they have no sway whatsoever. We have dealt with many kind and thoughtful local officials in both the US and the UK, but we have also witnessed the worst kind of petty power-wielding by nameless bureaucrats who can change our life circumstances profoundly with the tap of a computer keyboard in an office whose location I will never know. They have the power literally to ruin us.

The richest can buy their way around these obstacles. For everyone else, they are a fact of life. We have become so used to this awesome lack of agency over the things that matter to us that it is just accepted. We may fight it as individuals, but without collective power, it is a losing game.

Government reaches into every part of our lives. This is supposed to be part of a so-called 'contract' whereby we give up our freedom in exchange for the public goods that the government provides us, above all, security (for without authority, we would end up killing one another, as the 'theory' of democracy would have it). But I never signed up for that contract. I was never asked if I wanted this so-called bargain. Your freedoms are taken away at birth when your parents are legally obliged — under threat of penalty — to register your existence with the authorities. Government authority has suffused our lives and culture to such an extent that it is almost never questioned.

Through taxes, government controls our money. Government decides how to manage our health and when we should be treated. It even controls what we put into our own bodies — arguably the last realm of our sovereignty — by banning certain drugs and making us be vaccinated (here, of course, there is an obligation on us to protect others, though I suggest that this obligation be voluntary — chosen through our sense of social responsibility, not coerced by law).[†] Through a humongous body of law, of which most we are wholly unaware, government arbitrates and dictates our social relations. We are obliged to tell government where we live and with whom we live. Government decides whom we're allowed to marry (only recently

---

[†] And it is notable that anti-government resistance was triggered by the COVID vaccine, where our own bodies at put at stake (though I am not an 'anti-vaxxer' and accept the case for general vaccination).

were people of the same sex 'granted' that right) and what kind of sex we're permitted to practice (watch out, you sado-masochists out there! Remember 'Operation Spanner'[‡]). Through its massively intrusive mesh of social policies, it decides who gets priority in education, care and welfare and who doesn't — and somehow it's always the most vulnerable who end up worst off. It tells us where we can live and in what kind of buildings we must live.

There is legislation and rules for almost every aspect of our lives. Even if I want to get away from it all and go fishing, there are rules about when and where I can go and what fish I'm allowed to catch. I have to buy a licence to fish in the local river. We are free in almost no aspect of our existence.

Jean-Pierre Proudhon put it rather vigorously:

To be GOVERNED is to be watched, inspected, spied upon, directed, law-driven, numbered, regulated, enrolled, indoctrinated, preached at, controlled, checked, estimated, valued, censured, commanded, by creatures who have neither the right nor the wisdom nor the virtue to do so. To be GOVERNED is to be at every operation, at every transaction noted, registered, counted, taxed, stamped, measured, numbered, assessed, licensed, authorised, admonished, prevented, forbidden, reformed, corrected, punished. It is, under pretext of public utility, and in the name of the general interest, to be placed under contribution, drilled, fleeced, exploited, monopolised, extorted from, squeezed, hoaxed, robbed; then, at the slightest resistance, the first word of complaint, to be repressed, fined, vilified, harassed, hunted down, abused, clubbed, disarmed, bound, choked, imprisoned, judged, condemned, shot, deported, sacrificed, sold, betrayed; and to crown all, mocked, ridiculed, derided, outraged, dishonoured. That is government; that is its justice; that is its morality.

[‡] In which 16 men were prosecuted for consensual acts of sadomasochistic sex.

This list may sound extreme, but except for the bits about being choked or shot, it is all more or less still true (and there are those that still suffer the choking or the shooting, particularly people of colour).

Above all, we are powerless in the things that most matter to us. The state has absolute power over us. It alone decides when to use violence and wage war. It alone can imprison us and punish us. Meanwhile, the power we have over the state is slightly greater than zero, but only slightly — a paltry vote every five years. By contrast, the power the government has over us is absolute in almost every aspect of our lives. It's an absurd and grotesque imbalance. This is what we call 'democracy'.

This lack of agency is a pernicious force. It surely lies behind the rise of the Right in the US, Europe, Latin America and Asia. Fascists and the Far Right appeal to the 'little man' who feels ignored and overlooked. That man is right to feel angry: he *is* ignored and overlooked. But the Far Right have the solution wrong. Their strongmen, their would-be dictators, their Bolsonaros, Orbáns and Trumps, offer to speak for the ignored and marginalised, but this is a lie. They are deniers of true agency. They don't want true democracy. They want the opposite.

Agency is at the heart of our well-being. We cannot enjoy a life of freedom and flourishing without it. As long as authority imposes upon us, we are denied the ability to live as we wish or to negotiate our needs directly with other people. There is only one solution: give agency back. What this means is not less democracy, as the fascists threaten, but *more*.

This is not complicated to understand, much as the opponents of truly participatory democracy would have you believe. It simply means that people should be part of the decisions about them: *nothing about us, without us*.

My lack of agency over my family's circumstances distresses me and constrains us. For others, that lack of agency is literally deadly.

In 2024, the public inquiry into the Grenfell Tower disaster released its long-awaited 1700-page report. Grenfell Tower was the

London block of flats where 72 people lost their lives in a terrible fire in 2017.

The report pointed the finger of blame at multiple actors: the architects who designed the refurbishment of the building; the building companies who used the flammable cladding that caused the fire and covered up the fire risks; the tenants' association that didn't listen to the vocal safety concerns of the tenants; the local Council that failed to conduct adequate safety checks (and didn't listen to the tenants either); all the way up to central government whose Conservative party minister, in a 'free market' frenzy to cut regulation, abolished the fire safety laws that governed public buildings. The report described the failures as 'systematic'.

Various individuals were named as culpable and wilfully negligent: a few may be prosecuted, though it appears that thanks to government austerity, the overburdened criminal justice system won't be able to bring the cases to court until more than ten years after the fire, though the police investigation has so far cost £100m. The report has been in the headlines for a couple of days. The prime minister gave a short apology in parliament the day after the report. MPs could be seen leaving the chamber as he spoke, many had already left.

I'm sure some are glad that the culprits have been named and that some of them at least may — eventually — face justice. The guilty companies will probably face fines; the guilty individuals will probably not be sent to prison. I hope the victims' families get lots of compensation, but it will be paid by the taxpayer not by those responsible for their relatives' deaths, and nothing can truly compensate them for their loss. Perhaps the public is reassured that the catastrophe has at last been properly investigated and blame duly assigned.

But the report, while liberally using the term 'systemic', doesn't actually talk about the system that produced the eventual outcome of the fatal fire. That system — its ideology, its structures, its rules — is the very one that governs all our lives. What is that system?

Starting with the private companies: Why did the architects and building companies neglect and ignore the risks of the inflammable cladding that would turn the building into a deadly inferno? In private emails, company employees and directors were pretty clear: safer cladding would cost too much. What about the — *known* — dangers of the unsafe cladding? They should be covered up. Safety concerns were raised with one senior company manager. He replied that the critics could "go fuck themselves".

So what was the motive for choosing the lethal cladding? The profit motive. It was cheaper. As *The Guardian* put it:

> The picture that emerges [from the report] is of companies with a drive for profit and commercial success at the expense of anything that gets in their way.[13]

In capitalism, everything else — even lives — is subordinated to the profit motive. The government minister in charge of housing was driven by the same factor — to maximise growth, cut regulation, even if that regulation's purpose is to save lives. Capitalism is, literally, deadly.

And what of government? Government is supposed to correct the market and protect the public. Instead it did the opposite. It sought to enable profit maximisation at the cost of people's lives. Arconic, the multibillion pound American company that made the deadly cladding, was, according to the inquiry report, "determined to exploit what it saw as weak regulatory regimes ... including the UK". Notably, the minister directly responsible for that regulatory regime was scornful of the inquiry, complaining that attendance wasted his time. He obviously did not feel responsible: he said so.

Needless to say, the minister, as all those who made the rules governing public buildings, such as blocks of flats, had zero contact with the tenants of Grenfell House. He would not even have been aware of their existence. But in our system he is supposed to be responsible for their safety. Instead, he chose the ideology of the free market as his guiding credo. (It is thought that the minister concerned, now an unelected Lord in the chamber which scrutinises government legislation, is unlikely to be prosecuted). And it wasn't just one minister. His decisions took place during years of the Cameron government's deregulatory 'bonfire of red tape'.

> The report is clear that this goes back decades ... It's not just the Conservative government that [the inquiry chair is] pointing the finger at. But it is clear that in the [Prime Minister] Cameron years, this drive to cut red tape dominated decision making, and that the policy dominated the thinking in [the] department.[14] It's sometimes opaque how supposedly 'representative' democracy enables the exploitation and destruction wrought by capitalism. In a searing, tragic moment, Grenfell precisely, inescapably demonstrates this mechanism at work. The result: the supposedly 'democratic' system of government and capitalism conspired to kill people. They were a lethal combination.

And what of the people most affected, including those who died? Tenants voiced their concerns about the building's safety. Ed Daffarn sent a message directly to this effect eight months before the fire. He was ignored by the tenants' association, by the local Council, and of course his concerns never made it to the inboxes of central government officials, let alone ministers.

The inquiry report threw the local community a bone: "those who emerge from the events with the greatest credit, and whose contributions only emphasised the inadequacies of the official response, are the members of the local community".

But the inquiry itself hardly put them first either. In a process that lasted more than seven years, the 'Grenfell families' were not allowed to interrogate the witnesses themselves. This was the preserve of highly paid lawyers (the inquiry is estimated to have cost £200m). The fathers, mothers and children of those killed were granted precisely four days out of seven years and over three hundred hearings of the inquiry to put their concerns and questions directly.

Such is the quality of accountability in our current system, as well I know from my own experience at the 'Chilcot' inquiry into the Iraq War to which I testified, which likewise took many years at vast expense to produce an enormous but mealy-mouthed report, resulting in precisely nil prosecutions for the lies and war crimes of the Blair government, whose former members, like Alastair Campbell, enjoy lucrative careers and their index-linked government pension. Victims had even less of a look-in with the 'Iraq Inquiry': no Iraqis were invited to testify; none is named in the several hundred page report. 500,000 died in the illegal war. It was all about 'us' and never about 'them'.

Like Grenfell, Chilcot's report was in the headlines for no more than a day; the prime minister gravely told parliament that its recommendations would be implemented. A few months later, I checked with a friend in the Cabinet Office (the central part of central government). Of course, she told me, the report had been entirely forgotten. Not even an all-staff memo (perhaps telling civil servants not to tell lies or break international law) had resulted from its publication.

It was the political and economic system — capitalism + 'democracy' — that killed the people of Grenfell. They died horribly from inhalation of smoke and toxic gases, and in terror, some also died trying to escape. Grenfell might be an extreme case. But the truth is often revealed in extremes.

Others have gone further. Gillian Slovo, who wrote a play based on the testimonies of the victims, has said that the system worked exactly *as it was supposed to*. She quotes Karim Musilhy, who lost his uncle in the fire:

The system isn't broken. The system was built specifically this way to keep us where we are and them where they are.[15]

'Us' are the tenants; 'them' the government. One of the reasons the tenants were ignored is that many were first-generation immigrants, some asylum seekers, mostly non-white. A more politically marginalised community is hard to imagine. If instead the inhabitants of Grenfell had been white middle-class lawyers and TV producers, would the Council have ignored them?

And there were marginalised among the already marginalised. About 40% of the building's vulnerable and disabled residents, for whom escape plans were never prepared, died. In his lengthy statement introducing the report, the inquiry's head, Sir Martin Moore-Bick, never mentions the words 'race' or 'disability' (though he does mention 'vulnerable people').[16] Neither word appears in the 52-page executive summary. These persistent and structural marginalisations are, as ever, relegated.[§] By ignoring them, Moore-Bick has in fact reinforced this exclusion. His statement is a recitation of institutional failings by the companies and authorities concerned. He never mentions structure or system. Black, brown and disabled people died in grossly disproportionate numbers on that terrible night. This fact receives from the inquiry no special attention. So we can add the systemic exclusion and marginalisation of non-white races and the disabled to the list of root causes. The inquiry report doesn't say this any more than it cites the ultimate and deadly effects of our system of government and economy.

The inquiry report did not touch on the deeper systemic reason for the tragedy; the media reporting barely touched on it because the deeper system of our society is never really questioned. This can be summed up in a simple question:

Would the residents of Grenfell have died if they had been in charge of the building?

Probably not. We cannot know for sure. But we can confidently assume that the residents would have taken their safety and the risks of building work, and the use of cladding, *very* seriously. They surely would have checked the flammability of the cladding before permitting its use. The Council was supposed to do this, but did not. If all residents governed their own buildings, there would presumably be

---

[§] Likewise, Chilcot invited no Iraqi witnesses to testify to his inquiry into the 'Iraq War'. No individual Iraqi is named in his report.

networks of shared information about dangers. Centralised authority failed in that basic responsibility. We can speculate why, but surely one factor is that they — the decision-makers — were not themselves living in the building. They had less at stake. Their own bodies were not at risk.

But it's easy to imagine a system where a group elected by all the tenants takes the decisions, informed by independent disinterested experts (who would of course cost much less than all the government officials currently charged with the building's safety) and mutually supported by a network of likewise self-governing buildings. Not really so implausible. I lived in a self-governing building like this in New York City. It's called a cooperative.

Will this happen? The report didn't recommend it (instead it recommended safety reviews and more regulators). Neither did the prime minister mention it in parliament. In fact, as far as I can see, no one has suggested it, so trammelled are we by the mental boundaries that define what's possible.

The covert purpose of public inquiries is to reassure the public that lessons have been learned and that catastrophes like Grenfell — or the Iraq War — will not be repeated. It's a process of re-anaesthetising the public into its mistaken belief that the 'system' works for them; after all, we can tell ourselves, the system is capable of correcting itself.

Truth is often revealed in extremes. Grenfell is an extreme case but revelatory of something that is usually invisible in plain sight. It shows that the hierarchical and un-transparent system of government and administration of our daily lives serves not to protect us, and particularly not those at the bottom of the pile, but that its transcending purpose is to *protect itself.* The witnesses to the inquiry were fully prepared and lawyered up; their stories were often convincing: 'they did their best'. Memories were found wanting. Responsibility was shunted around, never taken. No one asked whether the system itself, rather than its functionaries, was to blame.

What Grenfell demonstrates is surely an obvious truism. People know — and attend to — their own circumstances best. It is incredible that this truth is totally ignored in our current political dispensation. Instead, the opposite assumption informs the design and practice of the system: that people *cannot* be trusted to run their own affairs. Instead, authorities, sometimes occasionally elected, sometimes not, are entrusted with those affairs.

When I tweeted the idea that the residents should run their own building, someone responded with the usual criticism of self-government: that the tenants neither had the desire nor competence to manage their own building.

I used to think like this. As a British diplomat, I was encouraged to think that only we, the anointed officials, were capable of considering all the complexities of the world and British foreign policy — to take care of the needs of the British people in the world at large. We explained things to our ministers who, in turn, would explain them to parliament (in truth, this barely happened). This arrogance and unaccountability led me to do terrible things (we shall come to that). But my beliefs were implicit and baked in throughout the system of government: ordinary people are not capable of running their own affairs. Like so many assumptions that inform and sustain the system, this is never stated. It is just taken as understood. Therefore, the reasons government makes this assumption are never questioned either. We don't really know. Members of parliament would never be crass enough to admit this, but sometimes in private others confess their prejudice: ordinary people are too ignorant, feckless and irresponsible. Simply not capable.

But citizens' assemblies are already showing that this prejudice is unfounded. Time and again, they have been shown capable of debating and arbitrating complex decisions. The trouble is that the very system helps perpetuate the negative myth: When responsibility is removed, people behave irresponsibly because their actions do not matter. When given responsibility, the opposite is true. Moreover, responsible citizens are free of ideology, untethered from party politics, free to decide simply what is best. There is space for uncertainty, reflection and wisdom.

****

No decision about us, without us. If there is any political principle that I stand by, it is this one. It is a right I have fought for around the world, from the Pacific islands to Kosovo, Syria and the Western Sahara. In places like Britain, what it means is putting decision-making power back in the people's hands. Simply put, all people should have the right to take part in decision-making about them. But how do we put this into practice while ensuring stability, security and the effective management of our common affairs, from running schools, hospitals and roads to defending ourselves against Putin or the Islamic State?

Some anarchists argue that stability will naturally result when individuals are free to negotiate with one another directly without the interference and inevitable coercion of authority and institutions. While sympathetic in theory, I am not so sure about the practice. Society and the modern economy are complicated, with highly specialised functions from the fire brigade to administering the internet or air traffic control. It seems to me that some kinds of institutions are necessary to organise affairs. But how do we build institutions that guarantee a voice for those most affected, that remain accountable and uncorrupted?

The origins of true participatory democracy lie long in the past, where citizens in ancient Greece took turns to make decisions about their 'polity' (though notably not if you were a woman or an enslaved person). In fifth-century Athens, as many as six thousand people of a city of thirty thousand would attend mass meetings to make decisions. A 'Council' of five hundred citizens, selected at random, would decide regular day-to-day affairs. Sometimes juries would be elected to tackle particularly difficult decisions, but their choices were always ratified by the whole. Slavery and patriarchy show that the Athenians did not fully understand democracy or mass participation, but the philosophy of citizen government is nonetheless clear.

When Athens was at the peak of its success, Pericles declared:

> Our constitution is called a democracy because power is in the
> hands not of a minority but of the whole people. When it is a
> question of settling private disputes, everyone is equal before
> the law; when it is a question of putting one person before
> another in positions of public responsibility, what counts is not
> membership of a particular class, but the actual ability which
> the man possesses. No one, so long as he has it in him to be
> of service to the state, is kept in political obscurity because
> of poverty. And just as our political life is free and open, so
> is our day-to-day life in relations with each other ... I declare
> that in my opinion each single one of our citizens, in all the
> manifold aspects of life, is able to show himself the rightful lord
> and owner of his own person, and to do this, moreover, with
> exceptional grace and exceptional vitality.[17]

The intimate connection between the political freedom of self-government and personal agency in life is striking.

Today, as then, participatory democracy means that decisions about matters that affect us should be taken *by* us. This might start at the local level — the town or the village, the 'commune' — with decisions about things that matter in those places. The New York political theorist Murray Bookchin thought through how genuinely participatory democracy might work. There are a couple of obvious principles that must be followed: participation by all affected; transparency to ensure accountability and honest administration.

A few years ago, I began to hear about a place where Bookchin's ideas were being implemented in reality. It is a surprising location: a corner of north east Syria called Rojava by Kurds. I was in the throes of making a documentary film about my journey from government to anarchism, so it seemed important that we went and filmed this living experiment in the ideas we were examining.

I was nervous about this journey. The Foreign Office was advising against all travel to Syria because of the civil war. There was a 'hot' war between the forces of the Syrian Kurds, the Syrian Democratic Forces (SDF), and ISIS: the SDF held a chunk of northeast Syria; ISIS held a chunk, including its 'capital', Raqqa. A war-correspondent friend of mine recommended I take D. as a security adviser. He was hard and experienced, a hostage negotiator and a former intelligence officer in the British army (I didn't ask too much about his time in Northern Ireland). I bought a flak jacket and helmet. I took a course in warzone safety, learning, among other things, that when you hear an artillery shell coming in, you should lie down with your feet pointing to the impact, though how you were supposed to know where the impact would be, I never learned. I felt a bit less nervous.

I travelled to Rojava from northern Iraq, my first visit to that country despite my many years of work about it (another sign of my dubious status as the Iraq 'expert', as we were known, at the UN Security Council). Accompanied by D. and Javier, our cameraman (the director had decided not to risk a visit), we crossed the Tigris to enter Syria. I felt rather excited as, rucksack on my back, our small boat puttered across the river. There is only one entry point into Rojava because Turkey lies to the north and not only has closed the border but also is deeply hostile to the administration in Rojava, claiming that it is nothing but a wing of the PKK, the Kurdish Workers Party, the Kurdish liberation movement that has long fought the Turkish state's systematic repression. Turkey is essentially at war with Rojava, a war that has only intensified since I went there. To the west of Rojava, the SDF's advance against ISIS along Syria's northern border has been halted by Turkey's declaration of a so-called "safe zone" between the front line and the Kurdish-controlled canton of Afrin in the northwest.[1] It is rarely reported because of the West's perverted relationship with Turkey's authoritarian government, but Turkey occupies a substantial chunk of northern Syria. Rojava

---

[1] Since early 2026, invaded and occupied by Turkey.

was a revelation. Unlike most foreign visitors and journalists, who are understandably mostly interested in the war with ISIS, I wanted to see what the people were fighting *for* — their politics, their democracy, how women led this unique project of self-government. Those journalists who do get there naturally gravitate to the front lines like the devastated city of Kobani; similarly, images of the photogenic young women who make up the female Kurdish militia, the YPJ, are more eye-catching than the village hall meetings that comprise the reality of an innovative grassroots democracy. But it is in those dusty assemblies across Rojava that a democratic revolution is taking place.

The extraordinary reason for the strange emergence of communal self-government in Rojava became clear during my visit. Abdullah Öcalan, leader of the PKK party, is seen by Kurds in Syria, as well as those in Turkey (where the party is banned), as the leader of Kurdish liberation. This despite — or in defiance of — the fact that, since 1999, he has been held in a Turkish prison on an island in the Sea of Marmara.

Öcalan was once a devotee of Marxism-Leninism but came to believe that, like capitalism, communism perforce relies upon coercion (in capitalism's case, coercion is necessary inter alia to enforce the exploitative contract between capital and labour). By chance, one book that was passed to him in jail was the masterwork of Murray Bookchin, *The Ecology of Freedom*. Like Öcalan, Bookchin rejected communism when he became disillusioned with Stalinism's authoritarian bent. A passionate believer in equality and freedom, he spent years teaching and arguing about anarchist philosophy in the bars and radical political groups of New York's Lower East Side. Bookchin believed that true democracy could only prosper when decision-making belonged to the local community and was not monopolised by distant and unaccountable elites.

Outside the radical and bohemian circles of 1970s New York, Bookchin's ideas have remained obscure, despite their pertinence today. Bookchin married what we now call environmentalism with anarchism. He believed that anarchism's fundamental precept, the rejection of power of one over another, should apply to mankind's relationship with the natural world. Entrapped in concrete cities, people were alienated from themselves and nature. The disasters of pollution and pillaged resources would persist as long as the false hierarchy of mankind over nature endured.

Bookchin ultimately eschewed the term "anarchist", which he saw was tainted by those who vaunted mere selfish individualism, "lifestyle anarchism".[**] Some kind of organised administration was, he believed, necessary to make collective decisions, as long as it included everyone: government can only be for the people when it is truly by the people. Bookchin called it "communalism".

On his prison island, Öcalan saw that Bookchin's concept of government without the state was ideal for the Kurds — a people who had been denied their own state. In pamphlets and books, he interpreted Bookchin's communalism for the Kurdish context and termed it "democratic confederalism".[††] If you want a society freed of coercion, you must abolish the ultimate practitioner of coercion, including violence: the state itself. In 2004, Öcalan wrote to Bookchin and invited him to Kurdistan, but Bookchin was by then too unwell to undertake such a journey. He died two years later.

Öcalan's new ideas were distributed across the PKK and, through them, to the Syrian Kurdish PYD. His influence in propagating a system of democracy without hierarchy presents one of the ironies of the situation in Rojava: a system that emphatically rejects all authority was inspired by a singular leader who has in the past used harsh methods to enforce organisational discipline. I was perturbed to see that every soldier I met carried a patch depicting Öcalan on their arm. On a hillside in Rojava, I spotted a massive outline, delineated by rocks, of his visage. For many Kurds, Rojava is deeply connected to their struggle for liberation in Turkey and elsewhere (Kurds are spread

---

[**] I also reject the 'anarchism' of the libertarians who see the individual's needs as primary and paramount. Anarchism is a broad church: I am at the communitarian end of the spectrum, where it is the community and relationships that are paramount, but where these relationships can flourish because everyone is free to express their needs on equal terms.

[††] *Democratic Confederalism*, Abdullah Öcalan, the Anarchist Library, 2011.

across southeast Turkey, northern Iran and Iraq, as well as eastern Syria; they should have been given their own state when the Ottoman empire collapsed after the first world war).

Moreover, perhaps as a demonstration of the persistence of cultural patriarchy and the masculine model of singular leadership, even here, I was only later to discover that women cadres in the PKK played a central role in developing and propagating these ideas across the movement. I would later write about Rojava as the 'most feminist revolution in the world', an understanding shared with me by Bookchin's daughter, my friend Debbie Bookchin, whom I got to know back in New York when we started a Rojava solidarity movement, and Dilar Dirik, another activist and writer, whose book about women in the Kurdish struggle is fascinating and instructive on this remarkable story of self-generated and self-educated social revolution.[18] I was struck by the echoes of another under-reported story, the central role of women in the Paris Commune of 1871, a story best told by Carolyn Eichner, whose book, *Surmounting the Barricades, Women in the Paris Commune*, pays particular attention to the leadership and innovation demonstrated by feminists in that brave attempt at people-led revolution.[19] Women spoke out forcefully in political clubs, often chiding male Communards for political timidity. "Men," charged one, "are like monarchs softened by possessing too much authority ... it is time for woman to replace man in directing public affairs." In many ways, they were the engine of the revolution, much as they have been also in Rojava.

What is happening in Rojava is remarkably — and, sadly, uniquely — perhaps the most explicitly feminist revolution the world has witnessed, at least in recent history. Previously, Rojava was home to traditional patriarchal peasant norms, including child marriage and keeping women at home. These traditions have been overturned: child marriage, for instance, is now illegal. There are parallel women's organisations in every field, ranging from the separate women's militia, the YPJ, to parallel women's communes and cooperatives. Self-defence is a principle of the Rojava revolution, which is why women are so active in the armed struggle — but the concept extends towards the right of self-defence against all anti-woman practices and ideas, including those of traditional society, not just the extreme violence of ISIS/Daesh.

During my visit to the autonomous region, I was taken to see the frontline in the war against ISIS. It consisted of a huge earthen berm that spanned the horizon. The observation point we visited was 'manned' by a unit of women soldiers, many young, from the YPJ, the female militia of Rojava, which fights alongside the YPG, the male units. I interviewed one young woman, who gave her name as Viyan, who was clad in camouflage with a Kalashnikov slung over her shoulder. She told me how the ISIS fighters that dug in only a few hundred yards opposite their position were afraid of attacking them because they didn't want the shame of being killed by women. I asked her why she was fighting. She replied:

> For over five thousand years, women have been oppressed here. People here think women can do nothing. We reject the idea that women cannot defend their own land. Because of the history of power in our society, it's assumed that women cannot protect themselves and women can't carry a weapon. The YPJ and YPG reject that idea. Our aim is to protect our homeland, our culture and language. Because it is our own homeland, we have to live free on it. First you have to free women. Without having free women, you don't have a free society.[20]

Viyan was later killed, fighting ISIS. In addition to ensuring complete equal rights for women, the feminist politics of Rojava aims to break down domination and hierarchy in every aspect of life, recasting social relations between all people regardless of age, ethnicity or gender, with the aim of achieving an ecologically and socially harmonious society. In terms of historical comparison, this project resembles most closely the short period of anarchism witnessed by George Orwell in Republican Spain during the Spanish civil war in the late 1930s. But the representatives of Rojava also reject the label of anarchism, preferring Bookchin's 'communalism' or Öcalan's 'democratic confederalism'.

In this radical new dispensation, authority is vested primarily in the communal level — the village. At one assembly I attended, villagers gathered in a spartan town hall to debate their affairs. An old man began by retailing all the decisions of the previous meeting. The audience grew restive with boredom until a very young female co-chair gently stopped him. Then others took turns to voice their concerns. These were the stuff of day-to-day village life: anxiety about deliveries of medical supplies; celebration following the announcement of the opening of a small new factory for laundry powder. But the rocketing prices of bread and other basics were lamented at length. The prosaic found its voice, too: someone complained about children riding their bikes too fast around the village.

Not all decisions can be made at the most local level. Those that need broader discussion go to district or cantonal assemblies (Rojava, with a population of an estimated three million, comprises three cantons). Here, as in the villages, care is taken to give non-Arab minorities and women prominence. Every assembly I encountered was co-chaired by a woman. In one town, a very young Kurdish woman enthused to me that never before had people like her — "the youth" — been included in the actual government. At meetings across the region, I was struck by the sense of a population trying to get used to methods of self-government that were entirely unfamiliar after generations of dictatorship.

I was repeatedly told that special efforts were made to include the Arab, Assyrian and Turkmen minorities. Some Arabs confirmed this to me directly, with something resembling bewilderment. In Jazira canton, the two co-chairs of the district's "institutions of self-government", as this collective system is awkwardly named, consisted of an aged Arab sheikh and another young Kurdish woman. Accustomed to the traditional hierarchies of the Middle East at such gatherings, I unthinkingly addressed the senior-looking man. Without speaking, he turned to the young woman to speak for the group. She then spoke Arabic for the benefit of non-Kurdish participants.

For the people of Rojava, these radical ideas on self-government offer a democratic model for all of Syria. One man, steeped in the philosophies of Bookchin, Kropotkin and, of course, Öcalan, argued to me that the traditional centralised state of the Middle East resembled the "ziggurat", the massive, stepped structure that housed the authorities and dominated the cities of Mesopotamia. He claimed that this model had been a catastrophe for Syria and Iraq in recent generations, an argument hard to dispute. It was self-evident, he contended, that a decentralised and inclusive structure of democracy had a better chance of producing stability — woven from the bottom up rather than imposed from the top down.

One problem, however, is that outside states continue to prefer other states that resemble themselves: the model of top-down government with its illusory offer of control is deeply ingrained. Decentralisation, particularly in the fullest sense advocated by Bookchin, threatens those who are used to authority — and particularly those who wield it. The diplomatic advisory group I founded was to help representatives of the autonomous administration address diplomats of the UN Security Council, and to this day I continue to advise the Rojava self-government myself on their diplomatic strategy. But even those states who are collaborating in military operations against ISIS with the SDF do not grant a formal political relationship with Rojava for fear of the hostile Turkish reaction. I am of course reminded of states' interactions with would-be states, such as Somaliland, Kosovo and South Sudan, before independence. But Rojava is different from these places seeking recognition as sovereign. Rojava doesn't want to be a state, despite Turkey's claims to the contrary. Indeed, Öcalan saw it as a dispensation for a people without a state, the Kurds.

One irony of Rojava's democratic experiment is it was only made possible by the rupture of war and the effective collapse of state authority. What is happening in the west is less dramatic, but is a crisis nonetheless. The model of supposedly "representative" but hierarchical democracy as manifested in western capitals is seen as less and less representative by the people it is supposed to answer to, as survey after survey — and the numbers who no longer bother to vote — amply demonstrate. The fissure between the power of the wealthy and connected and everyone else is painfully evident. The desire to take power back is growing.

Rojava may seem exotic and its democratic experiment radical, but that word radical means a return to the root, and that is exactly what is happening in this remote corner of Syria: rule by the people; democracy returning to its roots.

After my visit, Rojava was included in the documentary film, *Accidental Anarchist.* I wrote about it in the *New York Times* and *Financial Times*. But, at best, this exemplar of alternatives to Western democracy was treated as a kind of Middle Eastern curiosity. When I was in Rojava, I was often asked why other countries didn't want to emulate their political project. I struggled for an answer. Rojava is of course remote and dangerous to visit and in a complicated political situation. The West sucks up to Turkey and ignores the plight of the Kurds in Turkey and Syria, because Turkey stops refugees from crossing the Mediterranean to Europe (an ugly bargain that is admitted publicly only by Turkey). On the hard Left, Rojava is sometimes characterised as a CIA-backed construct, pointing to the American military presence and backing for the SDF against ISIS. For both right and left, Rojava's geopolitical position doesn't fit into their simplistic narratives of anti-Islamism or Western imperialism. The fact that the adaptation of Bookchin's ideas for a region of Syria was led by a jailed man designated a terrorist — in another oversimplification of a complex situation — surely also inhibits his ideas' being taken seriously.

But I believe that the reason Rojava's example is ignored is deeper. Its model poses a direct threat to the Western model of top-down 'representative' democracy. People in the West clearly find it difficult even to imagine life without a state. It's interesting too that the Rojava system and its philosophy comprise an explicit rejection of patriarchy and traditional male domination in society. Perhaps this too is threatening to Western biases.

I think that there's classic Orientalist racism at play, too. Westerners are steeped in the mythology that their system is superior to all others. They find it unsettling that a plausible and perhaps better model may have been innovated and introduced by those from the Middle East, who are explicitly rejecting their colonial heritage of top-down authority, fixed borders and the state itself. It's not possible, goes the presumption, that our own system might be inferior to a model that comes from the 'primitive' Other.

There are other concerns about the relevance of the Rojava model that carry more weight. Until there is peace, it will be difficult for outsiders to assess its practice in detail: Does it live up to these claims? (Everywhere has its shadow, after all). One structural question about its relevance for us is that Rojava must be simpler to govern than other more technologically 'advanced' and complicated economies. How can anarchist self-government administer things at scale?

Rojava demonstrates Bookchin's concept of democratic confederation, where decisions that need a larger scale — a new road, a hospital — can be taken by a sort of commune of communes — a democratic aggregation of local decision-makers. This is not like the ill-named 'representative' democracy of today's model whereby the people elect a few to take decisions for them. Instead, in this system, representatives are appointed at the communal level. They can only 'represent' decisions made at the communal level. When needed, decisions can be aggregated to a bigger scale (let's avoid the up-down nomenclature of hierarchy). Decision-making needs to be at a small-enough scale for participants to know its context and, most importantly, each other. But in this way, collective decision-making, which works best when in smaller groups, can be *applied* at large scale.

Bookchin distinguished his philosophy from that of pure anarchists who are hostile to all institutions. His 'communalism' instead assumes that some form of governing institution is necessary to take and administer decisions in a complicated society. But crucially this is government by *consent* — of everyone — not by coercion, consent that must be continually reaffirmed, not given once every five years. Representatives to the bigger scale assemblies must be recallable if they do not represent decisions taken by their local assemblies. Their appointments should also be temporary in order to avoid the creation of a self-interested political caste.

The Zapatistas in Chiapas, Mexico, have since 1994 instituted a similar system of self-government without the state. As Anna Rebrii has reported, a key principle underlying the Zapatista project, which ensures that autonomous institutions serve the people, is *mandar obedeciendo*, which means to lead by obeying. It implies that political leaders do not make decisions on behalf of their community as its representatives but rather act as the community's delegates, implementing decisions made in local assemblies — a traditional decision-making mechanism. These exist on a village level and, in contrast to traditional assemblies of Mexico, include women, whose empowerment has been at the centre of the Zapatista revolution. Assemblies elect delegates to a municipal council — the next level in the Zapatista administrative structure. Next, on the regional level, several autonomous municipalities are represented through delegates in *Juntas of Buen Gobierno* (JBG), or Councils of Good Government — called so in contrast to the "bad" Mexican government. JBG members serve for three years on a rotating basis in shifts as short as a few weeks. Such frequent rotation is intended to prevent the emergence of clientelist networks.[21]

****

The idea of more 'participatory' decision-making is beginning to filter into the ossified and troubled democracies of the West, and even into more authoritarian states such as China. So-called citizens' assemblies are lauded by the likes of mainstream commentators, such as Martin Wolf and Rory Stewart, for their potential contribution to restoring democracy. The OECD talks of a 'deliberative wave'. The inevitable raft of philanthropically funded NGOs is creating a 'field' and, with it, defining the limits of what's possible.

But these mainstream commentators and NGOs are not calling for true bottom-up democracy and self-government. Instead, they propose assemblies whose members are randomly chosen by a method called 'sortition' to represent the population as a whole, a bit like a jury chosen to attend a court case. This group then takes time to deliberate an issue. And there is plenty to celebrate in this model. Recent examples show that inclusive, deliberative citizens' assemblies are in fact *better* than top-down legislatures at considering decisions about complicated and tendentious issues such as climate.

It's hard to imagine, for instance, a more difficult and controversial issue than euthanasia and assisted dying. Yet this is the topic taken up by a citizens' assembly in France. Demonstrating that such groupings are fully capable of deliberating complex policy, the assembly produced sixty-seven recommendations which were then approved by the legislature and implemented by the government.

This result was made possible by the lengthy deliberation of several months that the assembly's participants undertook to understand the subject, as well as the testimony they received from all those affected — the terminally ill, their families, doctors, experts in ethics. Refuting the common claim that 'ordinary citizens' are not capable of making such complicated and tendentious decisions, one observer commented that "the diligence and intelligence of the participants are the first qualities that strike any witness."[22]

Such a reflective, deliberated process contrasts with the supposedly superior British system (the 'mother of all parliaments') where unprepared ministers, who are often in office for months rather than years and, inexpert in the issues of their ministry, take decisions in a hurry, with short-term political advantage inevitably at the forefront of their considerations, without the deliberation that momentous decisions require and without consultation of those most affected. In Britain, there was no public consultation on a proposed law to permit assisted dying; instead, the vote was left to the 'consciences' of individual members of parliament, many of whom did not bother to seek the views of those who had voted for them. Some did, but even then, could they capture or arbitrate the deep-seated differences over this tendentious issue? Where is the debate, the deep reflection, the exploration of compromise, all of which characterised the deliberative process?

But while sortition-chosen assemblies can inform policy decisions by government, they are ultimately only *consultative*. They do not include the whole population. They do not take binding decisions. Governments, as the British government has shown with its own climate assembly, are free to ignore their recommendations. Worse, governments may simply dismiss citizens' assemblies as lacking the alleged legitimacy supposedly granted by elections — after all who elects citizens' assemblies, why is sortition more legitimate, who gets to be in charge of the process? Most cynically, governments may see such assemblies as mere legitimising devices for subsequent decisions by the centre. They will eviscerate their meaning.

And when the decision-making power of a collective forum declines, unsurprisingly so does enthusiasm and participation. Brazil has led the way in introducing mass democracy for decision-making, most notably in Porto Alegre, a city which witnessed extraordinary social progress (and the end of political corruption) as a result of mass debates about budget priorities.‡‡ But with the departure of the Workers' Party governing party, the mass democracy was downgraded: public assemblies became more consultative than decision-making; as a result, unsurprisingly, participation declined.[23] What we really need is decision-*making*, not consultation, by the people themselves. True agency. This is not a jury of citizens, however much better that may be than decisions by a politicised elite, any more than it is a Facebook page or online forum. I worry that when NGOs receive funds from foundations created from the profits of hedge funds or when the OECD anoints an innovation, those NGOs and

---

‡‡ The Porto Alegre experience is discussed in *The Leaderless Revolution*.

that innovation are not really challenging the status quo. They are instead reaffirming it.

These randomly chosen assemblies are not what is going on in Rojava. It is a much more thorough-going political and social revolution, where not only top-down political institutions are replaced with self-government but also social relations — an end to men's domination over women — and indeed the relationship with the environment. For, in Rojava, there is also a 'green revolution'. It is a much deeper revolution than just renovating decision-making.

Only Bookchin's communalism or the self-government advocated by other anarchists offers true independence and autonomy — government that is *by* the people and indeed *of* the people, thus making it genuinely *for* the people. It isn't just incremental improvement to our current hierarchical system, a gradual re-democratisation. It is something else entirely. For only then can you achieve the fundamental benefit of a system where we negotiate our affairs directly with one another as equals with no politicians or others to speak for us (the type who grabs the mic first to tell us what to think), where we gather to tell each other our truths, maybe through tears, and at last be heard.

There is a deep and persuasive power when people finally have the chance to express their own needs. How does it feel to see someone break down in tears over their unlivable housing or skipping meals to make ends meet? For all but the hardest hearts, we experience empathy — fellow feeling. We might not agree on how to fix their problem, but we can appreciate their human need. This organic humanity and connection transcend the petty argument and transactional bargaining of what we traditionally regard as 'politics'.

I am autistic. I find it difficult to be with other people. Their mere presence, the energy they emit, can be overwhelming. But I nevertheless retain the capacity to be greatly moved by authentic expression, the honest, heartfelt declaration of our needs or desires. This is precisely the opposite of what we hear from politicians, who are required, I suspect to their great frustration, to dissimulate, dodge the question and offer platitudes in place of stark honesty. This is perhaps why we find reality shows and social media influencers appealing: they offer at least the *possibility* of authenticity, even if we are often disappointed. We crave authenticity, an acknowledgement of our true humanity.

Perhaps the reimagining of democracy might start where our concerns are most at stake. I would attend a local gathering because I care about what goes on at my children's school or the hospital where they or I may be treated. These are what matter to me. And, though I cannot be sure, I believe that others would show up to such meetings, belying the oft-made criticism that people would not turn up to local assemblies. When there is something at stake, people want to have a say.

This was the problem at participatory assemblies I attended in New York City. The mayor had given a small proportion of the city budget — around $2m each — to local councillors to divvy up, in a half-hearted attempt to foster 'citizens' democracy'. In that corrupt city, most councillors didn't bother consulting their constituents but gave the money to their cronies and donors. But some councillors with greater integrity instead arranged local participatory processes, where they invited their voters to decide how to spend the money. I attended some of these sessions but found that the attendance was low and those who did participate tended to have time to waste or had a particular niche hobby-horse to ride. Their proposals were for things like a cycle path or a war memorial to the civil war dead. In other words, not big enough things for most people who are showing up to a long, boring meeting to care about. I think it would be different for your hospital or school. Start where the people are and with what they care about.

As our local and inclusive assemblies begin to assert their own views and decisions, they will start to come up against the traditional authorities, local councils and the government who already claim to manage affairs, whether taxation or healthcare or education. In Frome, Somerset, this is precisely the problem a group of independent councillors found when they tried to have local, participatory assemblies take decisions. The local authorities — and there are many layers of them — simply claimed that they had the power, not the citizens. The conclusion of one the leaders of the independents, Peter

McFadyen, was that we needed to take over the whole council with those committed to more participatory methods of decision-making. This is what they've done in Bogotá, Colombia, where the mayor introduced participatory budgeting.[24] Activists called it 'occupying politics'. They work with candidates for council seats in cities and provinces who, once elected, then set up participatory assemblies. "Once they're inside" one activist said, "we basically hack the institution". Local forums will gather *legitimacy* — the essential condition of democracy — through attendance and, above all, inclusion. If all the affected people — staff, patients, families — attend a forum on the future of a local hospital, the decisions of that forum carry weight because their meetings carry legitimacy. The local MP will have to pay attention. Delegations can be sent to the capital; press attention can be sought. In the contest of legitimacy, who should make the ultimate decisions? The local forum, where everyone has a voice, or the inherited and moribund structure of the local council, for whom few have voted (turnout at Council elections is routinely less than 35% of eligible voters), or the MP who has barely a say in what the government does (and who is also elected by only a minority of the people).§§ A debate begins. A new realm of public discourse and politics opens up. We seek a *culture* of participation and decision-making, a habit if you like: legitimacy will come through the very practice of this form of democracy.

Perhaps we fear that the encounter with other people may be hostile. And this is what we are encouraged to believe. But the opposite may well be the case. In the 1950s, the American psychologist Gordon Allport found that actual contact between human beings reduced prejudice. He'd noticed data on the rare cases when Black and white servicemen had served together (against the rules) in the US Army in the second world war. When that happened, the number of white servicemen expressing prejudice against Black people was nine times lower than in segregated army companies.[25]

---

§§ The current government was elected by 33% of voters, which equates to around 20% of the adult population.

It also depends on *what* is being decided. When there is something at stake for people to show up for, surprisingly, they tend to agree more. Stanford University's Professor Stanley Fishkin found that when groups were merely debating an issue, and their decisions had no consequence, the group tended towards argument and polarization. But when they were discussing something of common interest where their decision would actually be implemented, the opposite happened: consensus rather than division. People realised that their decisions mattered and that it was better to account for others' views than ignore them.

This finding explains the ugliness that often characterises the 'public forums' created in an attempt to legitimise the current top-down system, where citizens are given an all-too-brief opportunity to make their voices heard, whether on talk shows or through artificially staged debates. In the US, during the presidential campaign, the ultimate in top-down supposedly 'democratic' systems, one event scheduled during the election campaign is a so-called 'town hall' meeting where a few voters are selected to share their views. Inevitably, these artificial occasions are characterised more by angry dissent and argument than by agreement. We are all desperate to make our point, at last to be heard; listening and accommodation only comes in a longer process.

Technology might help, but within limits. In Taiwan, the extraordinary digital minister, Audrey Tang, has worked to ensure that citizens have a voice in the decision-making process, and has pushed for greater transparency and accountability. For instance, Tang introduced a system called Polis that helps find consensus between thousands of people, using their own words, enabled by statistics and machine learning. She sees the introduction of participatory process as a way to encourage trust in government — "To give no trust is to get no trust. When you radically trust citizens, citizens will trust you back."[26] When she left government, the administration's approval ratings had reached highs of more than 70%.[27] I admire Audrey, a brave and pragmatic innovator. Notably, however, she sees government and people as different things: one doing something for or to the other. I see them ultimately as the same: self-government. There is now a diverse array of technologies to enable online democracy.[28] AI may make it easier to devise statements and policies that attract consensus.[29] It is possible to imagine in the future that technology would enable a process of almost continual decision-making, where our preferences would constantly inform policymaking. However, the necessity of interaction cannot be overstated. Without it, as Fishkin found, positions tend to polarise and compromise becomes harder. A constant, interactive process should be one where my concession to you today encourages yours to me tomorrow, informed above all by the acknowledgement that you are a human being with needs equal to my own and worthy of respect. This necessity is surely best met face-to-face, when I can most literally see you and you can see me. That crucial social element is entirely lacking in a representative system, whether that representation is performed by politicians or computers.

We can only see others as they truly are when they are allowed to reveal themselves, through action and expression, in an authentic way. When someone speaks their truth, we can just feel it, as the hairs on the back of our neck stand up. This doesn't happen online. It can only really happen in person, the intangible yet thrilling feeling of connection we all too rarely attain with other human beings.

When we encounter this, we know it. We live for this. It allows us to be our most human.

There is a broader and, indeed, magnificent canvas here. This change is not merely about politics, new institutions and better decision-making. It is in fact about how to live: the very people and their relationships, their bonds. When I started on my journey to what I now realise is anarchism, I thought it was about the mechanics of democracy and economy, a better way of arbitrating our affairs with one another: system design, in essence. I realised that it needed to put 'the human' at its core, but I didn't realise what this truly meant. I used to think that anarchism was 'just' a political philosophy. I was wrong. It is much, much more than that. It is, I have realised, about love.

4
An Ideal City

WE HAVE been told that without laws and authority, people will turn to killing one another, where life would be 'nasty, brutish and short', as Thomas Hobbes claimed. Governments, and those who enjoy authority, often remind us of these allegedly axiomatic 'truths' which are in fact nothing but presumption. 'Post-apocalypse' movies transmit the same message: as government collapses, humanity collapses into feral bands at war with one another: Hobbes's 'war of all against all'. Notably, this is an untested assumption. Indeed when it has been tested, the opposite tendency has predominated; of course sometimes people fight, but far more often they cooperate. It is partly this very presumption that contributes to the problem: if we expect hostility from others, we will be hostile to them. Social science and experience by contrast tell us that we should instead expect them to help.

I lived through Hurricane Sandy in New York City in 2012. It was a disturbing experience. From our flat in a tower block in the Lower East Side we watched the waters rising up our street. Our building lost power and water for several days, requiring us to walk up the seventeen stories to our apartment.

In the city downtown, services were down, the traffic lights didn't work. For days, there was no evidence of activity by the authorities, whether the city or federal government, to look after the most vulnerable or the population at large. We ended up schlepping food and water to the elderly people on our block. It took a week for the Federal emergency agency (FEMA) to show up. Meanwhile, in the financial district downtown (Wall Street), big banks paid to have walls of sandbags erected around them. I was struck by how well constructed they were, their neatness. They appeared the next day after the storm.

Meanwhile, in Brooklyn, a group of friends who'd met through the Occupy Wall Street protests got busy. They took over a church to collect food, bottled water and clothing for local residents trapped in their buildings. They distributed the supplies with trucks lent by local businesses. This effort didn't have a name until someone called it Occupy Sandy. One of the organisers told me that it can take a crisis for people to see that central government isn't looking after them. It's like a series of waves, she said, ever higher and higher. And, of course, there are more hurricanes, floods and fires to come.

In Rebecca Solnit's remarkable book, *A Paradise Built in Hell*, she describes multiple examples of how the collapse of authority, often because of natural disaster, fostered cooperation, not conflict, just as I had witnessed with Hurricane Sandy. After Hurricane Katrina in New Orleans, it was not violence and lawlessness that predominated, much as the television networks preferred to highlight, but rather neighbours helping one another, a phenomenon the media largely ignored. Even the fourteenth-century Black Death, one of the most devastating pandemics of human history, where fully 50% of the population died, did not trigger anarchy.[30] The recent COVID outbreak demonstrated similar truths. Trust within society was measurably increased by the cooperation brought about by the pandemic. People are increasingly relying on mutual aid — "solidarity not charity" — to get through climate-related disasters. Communities of colour and other marginalised groups have long helped one another when government has not delivered assistance. Today, more communities are realising that mutual aid, a core principle of anarchism, is the way to survive increasingly severe weather. A Tufts University study demonstrated that the more connected a society, the more people survive. Perhaps unsurprisingly, when people are more isolated when facing disease or natural catastrophe, they are more likely to die.[31] As one of its authors commented, "Being socially isolated while trying to deal with an extreme weather event can be deadly, particularly for those who are more susceptible to dying from extreme weather." In the same interview, he referred to a study of the 1995 Chicago heatwave that killed 739 people over five days, which found that social isolation contributed to the death toll.[32] What is the nature of human nature? Without the constraints of authority or 'civilisation', would we kill, lie and cheat? Or would we be cooperative, kind and compassionate? Rutger Bregman, in *Humankind: A Hopeful History*, suggests that most of us think of humans as naturally deceitful and cruel. And there's a lot of evidence, whether war, genocide or slavery. But despite this history of human awfulness, Bregman argues that humans are fundamentally good. Contrary to the novel *Lord of the Flies*, wherein marooned schoolboys end up tyrannising and killing one another, Bregman recounts the true story of Tongan schoolboys shipwrecked on a deserted island, who survived for 15 months in 1965, not through brutality, but by working together and forming a functional community. His book challenges common perceptions about human behaviour during wartime, presenting evidence that soldiers often avoid killing and that bombing campaigns can increase community spirit rather than decrease morale. As for the future of civilisations, Bregman debunks the popular narrative of Easter Island's collapse, presenting evidence that contradicts the tale of societal breakdown and cannibalism.

A different way of governing ourselves will work better for a host of reasons: more inclusive and thus fairer decisions, greater consensus and thus greater social harmony, more consideration and deliberation over the longer-term challenges we face. But unavoidable questions remain. Would there be rules? How do you deal with criminality? How do you prevent the domination of the strong over the weak?

The current system fares poorly on these measures. The rich dominate everyone else. They have more economic power; they have more political influence. They can afford better lawyers and thus better evade and subvert justice. Jeffrey Epstein was able to abuse hundreds of young women because he was rich and powerful and was surrounded by rich and powerful people. Indeed, they joined in the abuse. Two decades were to pass between his first arrest and ultimate imprisonment and death. White collar criminals receive lesser sentences than poorer thieves raiding the local supermarket, even if the amount they steal is much greater. Again, my visit to Rojava was instructive, where, alongside self-government, a new form of justice system has also been established.

In Jazira canton, which I visited, one chair of the justice committee (again a young woman) explained that since courts and punishment represented the coercive dominance of the state, such institutions had been replaced by a kind of community justice, where "social peace", not punishment, was the objective.

Intrigued, though a little baffled by these slogans, I asked to see what this meant in practice. The next day, I attended a mass lunch where one family hosted another. There were well over a hundred people present. A member of the first family had killed a man from the second: the lunch marked the families' reconciliation, the culmination of a collective process of compensation, apology and forgiveness, where the perpetrator, briefly imprisoned, publicly acknowledged his crime. In turn, this act of contrition, supported by his family by including the ceremonial meal, was accepted by the victim's relations.

I asked the brother of the murdered man why he didn't want the killer to face further punishment. His eyes moist with grief, he replied, no: "social peace" was more important than punishment. This was a better way, he argued: what good would be served by a long punishment of the perpetrator? I was staggered and moved. I thought of the barbarity of Rikers Island prison, which I would fly over on my way home to the US. No one in that country would claim that a system premised on punishment over reconciliation has achieved "social peace".

In Mexico, the Zapatistas have instituted a community-based system of justice where all parties are encouraged to find consensus rather than focus on punishment. Sentences most of the time involve community service or a fine; jail sentences normally do not exceed several days. As Melissa Forbis explains, community jail is usually just a locked room with a partially open door so that people can stop by to chat and pass food.[33] Since the perpetrator often has to borrow money for a fine from his or her family members, the latter are also involved, and their pressure helps prevent further transgression. In our own system, likewise, evidence shows that prisoners with greater exposure to family and friends during their incarceration are less likely to re-offend. Women-related and domestic issues are addressed by other women.[34] Police are elected and controlled by the local community.

In an adversarial legal system, such as our current courts, the accused is encouraged to minimise their guilt and the victim to maximise the harm they have suffered. Any encounter between them, usually confrontational, takes place across the arid breadth of the courtroom. Reconciliation is not on the agenda. If convicted, the guilty enter a prison where they do not learn the skills of a life on the straight-and-narrow but instead those of a more competent criminality. Today, a full 75% of prisoners re-offend after release. While I do not doubt the skill and goodwill of lawyers and judges of our current system, it is a system that produces inadequate outcomes.

The collective justice I witnessed in Rojava might point to a better method. Where the community sits in judgement, where the accused is encouraged to tell the truth, where reconciliation and 'social peace' is the aim rather than punishment, though necessary confinement to contain the most threatening offenders remains on the table. In Rojava, however, the absence of women at the reconciliation lunch

I attended spoke of a patriarchal culture, when of course equality of voice and decision is necessary. Any new system would take time to find its feet and broad acceptance as an adequate alternative. Safety is a primary concern.

More broadly, a system of local self-governing communities would, as experience suggests, produce a more connected society, where the currently tattered fabric of society is rewoven. That man down the street who you don't like the look of becomes a fellow dad at the local school, with interests identical to your own. Mutual aid, which Occupy Sandy exemplified, ties an otherwise alienated community together. In an in-person forum, we suddenly witness the bared humanity of our neighbour and, accordingly, respect and acknowledge their declaration of need. Of course, we may witness the opposite, but it would arguably be better than what we see on our streets today, of litter, speeding cars, short tempers, latent violence and, at worst, children stabbing each other. The mere existence of Anti-Social Behaviour Orders speaks of a culture where our duties to and respect for one another have evaporated.

****

'Mutual aid' is a core tenet of anarchism. It was popularised by Pyotr Kropotkin in his book of essays, *Mutual Aid: A Factor of Evolution*'. Kropotkin's own journey to anarchism was itself remarkable. Born into an aristocratic family, he served as a page in Czar Alexander II's court. For his military service, he rejected a commission in a well-regarded Moscow regiment, instead choosing to serve in Russia's remote and isolated eastern provinces. He became a naturalist, geographer and scientist mapping uncharted regions. He undertook a journey of thousands of miles across the East during which he examined nature in the raw, as well as the communities scattered in tiny, isolated villages across Siberia.

Kropotkin's expedition through Siberia profoundly altered his political beliefs. Contrary to the prevailing Darwinist notion of competition that he had expected, he observed that both animals and humans exhibited more cooperation than rivalry:

> I failed to find, although I was eagerly looking for it, that bitter struggle for the means of existence, among animals belonging to the same species, which was considered by most Darwinists (though not always by Darwin himself) as the dominant characteristic of the struggle for life, and the main factor of evolution.

Kropotkin came to believe that the true struggle was not conflict within species but rather the collective effort against the brutality of the environment. The battle was not between individuals of the same species; it was rather "the struggle for existence which most species of animals have to carry on against an inclement Nature." He didn't call this instinct for cooperation love. He saw it instead as a direct and natural response to the drive for survival:

> It is not love, and not even sympathy ... which induces a herd of ruminants or of horses to form a ring in order to resist an attack of wolves; not love which induces wolves to form a pack for hunting; not love which induces kittens or lambs to play, or a dozen of species of young birds to spend their days together in the autumn.

He attributed this cooperative behaviour to 'mutual aid', an instinct developed over long periods of evolution. Surveying humans located in remote Siberian villages, he noticed something surprising. The further the villages were from population — and administrative — centres, the more that mutual aid flourished. Freed from authority and bureaucracy, Siberians displayed almost unbounded cooperation with one another.

Pyotr's brother Sasha argued that this apparent mutual aid was merely disguised self-interest. Kropotkin replied:

It is not love of my neighbour, whom I often do not know at all, which induces me to seize a pail of water and rush towards his house when I see it on fire; it is a far wider, even though more vague feeling or instinct of human solidarity and sociability which moves me. So it is also with animals.

Kropotkin concluded that mutual aid is crucial for species' survival and evolution, contrary to Darwin, describing it as a 'biological law'. This realisation transformed his political views. He wrote:

I lost in Siberia whatever faith in state discipline I had cherished before. I was prepared to become an anarchist.

Kropotkin's belief in anarchism flowed from his scientific work on evolution and mutual aid. He concluded from his journey across Siberia that mutual aid was not only common but also "of the greatest importance for the maintenance of life, the preservation of each species, and its further evolution." He had observed that government was not necessary for people to lead lives of happiness and justice, but instead the opposite was the case: such outcomes were more evident when no government was present. He believed that mutual aid has deep biological roots because animals engage in it despite the absence of anything remotely like a government.[35]

Kropotkin's analysis stood in direct contradiction to the emerging paradigm of Darwin's theory of natural selection, of competition between individuals driving species' evolution. Darwin's actual views were more nuanced, especially when it came to human behaviour, but they were twisted and exaggerated in the popular discourse for *political* ends, exploited to justify the nascent system of capitalism. Darwin believed in the importance of moral values and social instincts in human evolution, but these were not the elements extracted and then emphasised by others for their own cynical self-interested purposes.

Social Darwinism was primarily developed by Herbert Spencer, an English philosopher and sociologist, in the 1850s. It was Spencer, not Darwin, who coined the phrase 'survival of the fittest' and applied evolutionary concepts to social and economic spheres. Spencer manipulated the concept of 'survival of the fittest' to justify *laissez-faire* capitalism, oppose aid to the poor and, indeed, support imperialism and racism. This was the cultural narrative that accompanied the Industrial Revolution and the emergence in Britain, then the world, of what we now call neoliberalism, or capitalism.

To me, the opposition of Spencer's view of humanity and Kropotkin's comprises one of the ideological and cultural pivots of human history, a moment when our species could have chosen a different track but was instead pushed down one, not the other, by the self-interest of the few, for Spencer was himself a wealthy capitalist; the newspapers where he propagated his views were owned by a few extremely wealthy men, a foreshadowing of our own age of Murdoch, Bezos and Musk. Spencer's ideas were embraced by the likes of Andrew Carnegie and John D. Rockefeller to justify their accumulation of vast and unprecedented wealth and power.

The story of what humanity was 'about', reaffirmed over and over again today, was established by those with a profound interest in denying the greater, more humane truth observed by Kropotkin and, indeed, historians and sociologists to this day (for example, Graeber and Wengrow's *Dawn of Everything*). The perpetuation of this story (for it is a story) perpetuates capitalism and its necessary enforcer, the state, to this day.

A portrait of Kropotkin hangs on my wall. Persecuted and imprisoned by the Czarist authorities, he sought exile in England and spent many of his latter years in a small house in a suburb of South London, where I am from. Many of his most important works, setting out the philosophy of anarchism, including *The Conquest of Bread* and *Mutual Aid* were written in London; he spoke in a hall just two hundred yards from where I'm sitting now (we've moved back to London). But he didn't love England and returned to the continent before he died. He formed the conviction that revolution was impossible in England. But in any case, Kropotkin never espoused violent overthrow as the answer, instead proposing a more gradualist approach. For this, he was attacked by other anarchists, some who plotted to assassinate him because they believed he was holding up revolution.

But Kropotkin asked the question, still very pertinent today: Why does capitalism persist even when its flaws — growing inequality, social alienation and planetary destruction (and indeed possible species extinction!) are so abundantly manifest?

5
Prefigurative Politics

ONE REASON for the perpetuation of the 'neoliberal' or capitalist system is, of course, that the narrative of competition driving 'progress' is constantly reaffirmed by the system itself and, inescapably, we are part of that system. Unless we go live in a commune in Costa Rica, we have little choice but to collaborate in it and, thus, reaffirm it by our very participation.

Humans are not innately nasty; they are inherently cooperative. But their behaviour is formed by the system. We are products of a system. The system, the combination of capitalism and the state, separates us from each other and deepens division. Capitalism presents other people as competitive; it casts us as individuals rather than community. The very existence of the state manifests the belief that other people are hostile — only the state can protect us from their inherent tendency to chaos and violence. These negative beliefs about human nature are then embodied in the mechanics and very design of the system. We don't see other human beings as truly human. We see them as hostile, at best untrustworthy. The system has made us Hobbes's (and Spencer's) creatures.

So a self-reinforcing cycle is formed. The system is justified by those who believe in the worst of human nature. We are required to collaborate in that system and are thereby forced to behave in ways that justify the system. Only now, as the planet barrels towards ecological collapse, are urgent voices getting louder as they demand change.

I was a product of the system. When I joined the foreign office, I thought I could hold onto my values and beliefs and, if necessary, pursue them and promote them within the system — perhaps I might even *change* the system. What naiveté, what arrogance. Of course, what happened instead is that the system changed me, not the other way around. In very literal terms, the '*I*' of Carne Ross was converted into the '*we*' of the state. Instead of 'I think', I began to say '*we* think', meaning 'we' the state, the British government. My very identity and sense of self became consumed by the state, the system. And this, in microcosm, is what has happened to us all. Like it or not, we have become creatures of the system.

Of course, I didn't think of myself this way. I preferred to think of myself as an independent mind, even an iconoclast, within the system. I was flattered once when during talks at the State Department, the senior American official described our negotiations as a 'trilateral' between the US, UK and Carne Ross. But of course my independence was practiced within very narrow confines of the system I operated within. I never questioned the existence and reason of that system. I was quite happy to accommodate myself to its limits.

How did this happen? Breaking down what happened to *me* might help shed light on what has happened to *us*. And we shall see the empirical evidence and studies that suggest this, too. But one of the oddities of my experience is that the signs that something wasn't right were evident. It wasn't a one-way street of indoctrination. The counter evidence was right in front of me, just as it's in front of us today, but I ignored it.

How did it start?

My parents did not question the system. My father even tried to run for parliament for the vapidly centrist Social Democratic Party, later to become the Liberal Democrats, a party that very much did not question the system but only tinkered with it (and later, proving the point, it would govern in coalition with the Conservatives). He voted for Margaret 'there is no alternative' Thatcher in the turning point in British political history in 1979. The Thatcher who stated that 'there is no such thing as society' but only individuals. Later, he was to vote for Blair in 1998 and then, most surprisingly, in 2005 after his own son had resigned from the government over Blair's lies that provoked the Iraq War. When I bitterly asked him why, he replied that 'they must have known' (i.e. they were telling the truth about the WMD), even though his own son told him — and the world — the very opposite (yes, I remain bitter about this, much as I loved him).

But the actual lives and suppressed emotions of my parents told a somewhat different story of the success of the 'system'. My father wasn't selected to run for parliament and instead remained politically frustrated, his engagement limited to leafletting in the suburb where we lived. He told me once that he hated his job, the point of which was, in his words, 'to make the rich, richer' — he worked in financial marketing. His parents, both intellectuals, had not been well off, so he chose to work in the private sector to provide for his family. For many years, he drove my brother and I to school across South London, then to his office in a dismal tower block in Croydon, one of the less salubrious boroughs of London. He didn't go with a spring in his step, though he did get a company car. He was eventually laid off from that job, and I well remember the inadmissible atmosphere of failure and shame that hung over the house as he assembled CVs and application letters on the dining table. Later he would join the depressing, silent army of commuters taking the train every day to 'The City'. Both he and my mother had tried and failed to get into the foreign office, so that provided an obvious motive for me. Working for capitalism was definitely seen, but never admitted, as second best. My father only really came alive after he retired. He had discovered fox hunting and drove down to Exmoor at the weekends to gallop over the moor barely in control of his horse (he fell badly twice). More appealingly, he worked for charities that supported the elderly and victims of crime, whom he would visit and console. When he talked about this work, as with the hunting, he became animated — at last, alive.

My school taught me obedience and compliance.* As the 'boys' (as we were known) told each other racist jokes in the playground (Nigel Farage was also a pupil), in the classroom we were taught the elements of the system. But interestingly it was rarely explicit; it was just implied, ever-present but submerged. There was no questioning the status quo. In response, a kind of ironic sarcasm reigned among the pupils. During the Falklands War, one of the boys put up a poster of HMS Sheffield the day after it had been sunk by an Argentine missile. But no one questioned the state system which was the ultimate cause of that ludicrous if bloody conflict (described by Jorge Luis Borges as 'two bald men fighting over a comb'). Those who misbehaved badly were sometimes beaten, hard.

Indicating my enthusiasm for control and domination, that was later to manifest professionally, I was elected as 'form captain' when I was twelve. I invented a system whereby if I took a boy's name three times for disruption between classes, when I was in charge of keeping things quiet, they would *automatically* be punished with detention. Even some the teachers felt I was being unnecessarily authoritarian. But it was no coincidence that I innovated my micro-fascism at the very time that my twin brother had been elevated into the year above me, because of his greater intelligence. I bore this humiliation secretly, but it burned. I have no doubt that it drove my punitive desire for control when given the opportunity. Writ large, perhaps most of us suffer the very same syndrome: our systematic humiliation drives our need for domination.

---

* This was my secondary school. My primary school was also disciplinarian in other ways, but it was named after the English revolutionary of the Middle Ages, John Ball. We were never taught his anarchist history, which included the following speech: 'Things cannot go well in England, nor ever shall, till everything be made common, and there are neither villains nor gentlemen, but we shall be all united together, and the lords shall be no greater masters than ourselves. What have we deserved that we should be kept thus enslaved? We are all descended from one father and mother, Adam and Eve. What reasons can they give to show that they are greater lords than we, save by making us toil and labour, so that they can spend?'. Perhaps things would have turned out differently had we been.

All the pupils came from bourgeois families in South London. There were no poor people, or at least no one that admitted being so. The only time the actual structure of society and the economy became explicit was when I was taught economics at 'A'-level, when I was sixteen. Here first appeared the geometric and tidy diagrams signifying the intersection of supply and demand, the 'utility' curve where the individual — the consumer — bought things until satisfied, the theory of 'revealed preferences', which showed what people wanted through evidence of what they had consumed — a kind of quasi-scientific but irredeemably circular affirmation of the system: it *is* that way because people *want* it that way. We weren't of course encouraged to interrogate this corpus of knowledge (which is in fact a political ideology, not the science it claims to be). Instead, it was spoon-fed to us on photocopied sheets that prescribed the exact answers — to the precise word and number — we were to write in the exam. All we had to do was regurgitate them like vomiting seagulls.

As a consequence of this unthinking robot system, I got an 'A' in economics and, believing that I was learning how things 'really worked', went on to study economics and politics at university. Most of the other boys from school became accountants, bankers and businessmen, like their parents. One, who routinely humiliated me in class was fired from his job running a university for corruption. Only a minority chose a more independent route. Jeremy Deller has become a well-known artist whose depictions — re-enactments, video installations, diagrams — question the received narratives and significances of conventional national mythology, for instance, the miners' strike or dance music. He and I used to play battleships in history class, which, needless to say, comprised the classic orthodox British history of kings and queens, followed by the national glories of the world wars. No alternative narratives there. No questioning, either. One segment was about 'The Scramble for Africa', which was framed as a legitimate contest between colonial powers, but never mentioned were the notions of racial superiority that drove imperialism, or the cruelties of empire itself. But we did learn a lot about the military manoeuvres at the battles of Isandlwana and Rourke's Drift, where the British defeated the spear-bearing Zulus with rifles and Maxim guns, a victory later glorified by Sean Connery and Michael Caine in the egregiously racist film *Zulu*. The teacher gave us 'biltong' — dried antelope meat — that he had bought at one of the sites of the battles. It was in classes like these, and the disappointments of my parents, that my ambition to become a diplomat was gestating. But also a worldview was, unconsciously, being formed.

Education clearly has a crucial role in the necessary revolution. One common factor shared by the revolutions in Rojava and Catalonia during the Spanish civil war is that before they took place, 'vanguard' groups educated the broader population, a challenge that continues in Rojava, local officials told me. Both Öcalan and Bookchin saw the role of education as essential. In pre-revolutionary Spain, Bakunin and Fanelli led the efforts to educate workers and citizens through, for instance, unions where leaflets were distributed at union-organised summer camps. In Rojava, women often led discussion groups inside the PKK (contradicting the account of a top-down male-led indoctrination), the movement that then brought forward the PYD, the main engine of the revolution when the opportunity arose in Syria.

But education too often performs the service of the system. It indoctrinates; it controls by dozens of different means, some covert, some overt. The poet John Burnside talks about being expelled from school and his discovery of Ivan Ilich's book *Deschooling Society*. Illich argues that obligatory schooling perpetuates power elites and fails to address the true needs of learners. The book was published in 1971 and was prophetic in highlighting the corporatisation of education and its inequities. Illich proposed 'learning networks' as an alternative to traditional schooling, aiming for more egalitarian and convivial ways of learning and living. Despite being sidelined over the years, Illich's ideas remain relevant in today's hyper-commoditised education system.[36] My 'pol/econ' university course was scarcely more sophisticated than school, merely more elaborated. Politics was discussed as merely *party* politics, the business of parliaments and elections, not the deeper structures of control and obedience. We studied the outcomes of the system — political crises, financial meltdowns — never the nature and structures of the system itself. On one occasion, a lecturer, fairly obviously a drunk, took us in a minibus to Dartmoor where we looked at a few stone circles and were asked to deduce the political system. It was raining and we soon got back in the bus. But it was the only time we were encouraged to consider alternatives, that there might have been something other than the current dispensation. We studied China and the Soviet Union, but of course these were represented as inferior. The deficits of their systems are obvious and manifold, but nevertheless, they were an attempt at something different, however failed they turned out to be. But their purpose in our education was to stand merely as contrast to demonstrate the superiority of our own system — representative democracy plus capitalism.

Many of our tutors were tired cynics, ground down by years of teaching uninterested youths who were only eager to get to their 'careers' and enjoy their bourgeois pleasures. And indeed for me, apart from the minor distractions of student politics, university was largely about my own entertainment, though leavened by student politics — one of my first political acts was to blockade the local Shell station, when the oil company was collaborating with South Africa's apartheid system.

As graduation approached, I began to think about my own 'career' and sent in my application for the foreign office exams. One of my roommates was to become a general in the Royal Marines who led a brigade in Afghanistan. Another became a senior official in the IMF, where he determined the economic policies of eastern European countries, so-called 'structural adjustment' — the rapacious introduction of capitalism at great social expense. Both — we were all friends — loved bad heavy metal music, a booming accompaniment to my idling and minimal studies. We were not only believers in the system. We were to instrumentalise it, indeed, become perpetrators of it. (One would tragically later commit suicide; the other retired to become a yoga instructor.)

Mark Fisher, in his brilliant book *Capitalist Realism*, dissects the cultural and social mechanisms by which we come to think that there is no alternative to the current system and why it seems immutable and eternal. He analyses popular culture to explain how innocent-seeming TV or music perpetuates and reinforces this message. Not only was I subjected to those mechanisms and unaware of what they were doing to me; I also helped create their more explicit expressions. I was a propagandist for the cause.

In 1996, I became the foreign secretary's speechwriter, in those days a Tory. Today, speechwriters are party political appointees. In my day, supposedly politically neutral civil servants were deemed able to do the job, even if there was an unavoidably ideological element to it. Regurgitating my undergraduate (in fact my A-level) economics, I wrote speeches about the value of free trade. I wrote prescriptions for the future of Africa — of course 'representative' democracy and free markets — paying no attention to that continent's pre-colonial systems of government. I wrote about the two-state 'solution' in Palestine, never questioning why 'we' did precisely nothing to deliver it beyond uttering impotent rhetoric, or learning Britain's role in creating the disaster. I penned confident declarations about the 'rules-based' order, a phrase you will hear parroted today by politicians of both major parties (perhaps they recycled my speeches!), reaffirming a world of states, and laws written by countries like mine that we obeyed only when it suited us, implicit confirmation of states' exclusive rights to use violence, a right of course denied to all others — the very definition, according to Max Weber, of what constitutes a state: the monopoly of violence.

My conscience was not troubled by writing these speeches. On the contrary, I felt very special typing the words of the foreign secretary from my high-ceilinged office that overlooked St James's Park. Educated in the ideas that propped up the status quo, suffused with affirming culture, it was easy never to question. My career was boosted by those speeches, which obviously helped too. I was increasingly well thought of and recognised as a 'high flyer' in 'the office'. And as we all know, it doesn't really pay to question the system. I am reminded of this by the trouble I have finding work now that my political beliefs are so public and abundantly present on social media.

Questioning the system is one thing, believing it is another. Capitalism plus 'representative' democracy — the 'neoliberal' system[†] — offers an answer for every concern. Capitalism is supposed to deliver universal benefit, of course to the rich, but also, eventually, to the poor, even though the data are devastatingly clear that this is not happening, that even the wealth of the 'middle class' has flatlined for a generation and the poor have actually become poorer in that period. The state enforces this system, justified, and rarely questioned, in its claim that it alone can give us security and safety from the threat of one another. These arguments form a kind of complete concept, a 'total concept', that is all but impregnable to rational criticism.

As Fisher argues, this concept is reinforced constantly through the mechanisms not only of political discourse but also, subtly or not so subtly, through culture. We all know that advertising is crass and manipulative, but we continue to fall for it (I know I do). We all know that consumerism does not meet our spiritual needs and leaves us feeling hollowed out and hungry, yet we continue to buy stuff that we do not need. Whether a TV series about affable diplomats or spies, culture reaffirms the 'system' in a thousand ways. We might not realise that zombie films help reaffirm the unstated justification for government, that without it we take to killing one another. But such reaffirmations are everywhere. Even the heroic tales of those who stand against the system — the sinister machinations of the CIA, perhaps — serve to lull us into complacency. The system can be beaten; all we need to do is watch.

[†] 'Neoliberalism' is a sometimes confusing term. I like Will Davies's definition: the state-led remaking of society on the model of the market or the 'disenchantment' of politics by economics. Others, including the Oxford English Dictionary — which offers multiple and not wholly consistent definitions — lay less emphasis on the state and instead talk about neoliberalism as the *reduction* of government regulatory control of the free market, i.e. the promotion of individual rights and profit over the public interest (or indeed that rights plus profit is itself the public interest).

According to the Frankfurt School's Theodor Adorno and Max Horkheimer, we have been distracted from overthrowing capitalism by what they called a *Verblendungzussamenhang*, a total system of delusion. Advertising is one of the more overt tools.

> The triumph of advertising in the culture industry is that consumers feel compelled to buy and use its products even though they see through them.[37]

Adorno and Horkheimer wrote this in the 1930s. Nearly a century later, however, that delusion remains. Indeed, the consumerism and materialism that characterise the delusion have only grown more sophisticated. Capitalism is so clever that it develops products to fill the deficits it creates — the hollowness at the heart of the system, the fundamental lack of meaning or purpose. Selling product is now about 'buying meaning', as one branding executive described it to me. A consultancy I know now offers to advise companies on how to achieve "ESG + Purpose". Another even calls itself Purpose.

And to offer satisfaction to our craving for control, many are the products that claim to 'put you in control' or give you freedom (there's even a credit card called the 'Freedom Card', whose real, concealed purpose is the direct opposite of its name), that mere claim only underlining the ironic reality that we are not 'in control', we do not enjoy freedom. But I suspect that we see through these delusions too, while dementedly buying those products in a futile attempt to capture what we feel is missing.

But there is a more pernicious mechanism at work too. While government signals by its existence that we are incompetent and cannot be trusted to manage our own affairs, capitalism controls us and humiliates us by reminding us of our failure.

The night before writing this passage, I met a man who had created a world-famous video game. The event was a fundraiser for a project to promote people's democracy worldwide, a cause obviously close to my heart. He was very nice and friendly, but when I was introduced to him I instantly felt inferior. He had won the game that capitalism has created for us; I have not. I am convinced of the inadequacy and inequity of that system, and its destruction of the planet (and indeed he and I talked about climate change), and I am a trenchant critic of that system, and yet still I felt inferior. I thought of my mortgage and my debts, my insistent anxiety that I have failed properly to provide for my family. He mentioned that being rich made him uncomfortable, though his affect was one of satisfaction. I liked him, and he 'got' what we are trying to do with the democracy project. And yet, unwittingly, he still made me feel like a failure.

I have devoted my life to public service of one kind or other, imperfect though I have been. At times, to fund this work, I have often had to 'pitch' to philanthropists. Some are currency speculators or hedge fund traders who've made billions by betting on exchange or interest rates. A less socially useful activity is hard to imagine, indeed the very opposite — one famous trader I know cost the Bank of England £1bn by betting against the pound. That's one billion taken from the pockets of taxpayers and put into his, and now I have to grovel to him to persuade him to use that ill-gotten money to fund my worthy projects.

I had lunch with him once at his enormous house in Chelsea, one of his many homes around the world. The night before, I was so nervous that I didn't sleep a wink. The power imbalance between us was grotesque. He had the power to make or break my — allegedly socially useful — dreams. Luckily, he chose to make them and decided generously to fund my project (though his generosity was limited, amounting certainly to a good deal less than the interest on the interest on the interest of his enormous wealth). I felt like a ragged commoner petitioning the Emperor, for these of course are the new emperors, whose political and cultural choices are infinitely more important than mine or anyone else's. And, yes, this is biting the hand that has literally fed me and my family. I know other billionaires who have won the lottery of a market-beating internet app, who are funding wars or the illegal colonisation of the West Bank. They have the power of life and death.

That sense of inferiority and failure is a product of the system. Many if not most of us feel that we have failed in some fundamental way. Notably, this is an individual mental feeling — we feel it alone. We do not share our shame. To my friends, I pretend that all is well, and that I don't suffer from this pernicious money and status anxiety, not least because it illustrates the weakness of my character. So the system defeats us one by one, even though we are all in the same boat. As the German-Korean thinker Byung-Chul Han puts it:

> People who fail in the neoliberal achievement-society see themselves as responsible for their lot and feel shame instead of questioning society or the system. Herein lies the particular intelligence defining the neoliberal regime: no resistance to the system can emerge in the first place ... [U]nder the neoliberal regime of auto-exploitation, people are turning their aggression against themselves. This auto-aggressivity means that the exploited are not inclined to revolution so much as depression.[38]

This is how the system maintains its subtle and insidious power. There are far more of us, the failed and humiliated, then there are of them, the Ferrari-drivers and internet influencers, newspaper owners or yacht-racing financiers. But they are the ones who get the attention; they are deemed successful. We remain alone and isolated in our humiliation. I know it, because I feel it, even as I write these words. This is the cultural power that *we* have given *them*. Why?

Other mechanisms that perpetuate the system are more overt and explicit. Thomas Piketty has demonstrated how wealth accumulates faster than wages rise (in his formulation, the growth rate is higher than wage growth). Unless you already have wealth, you are playing a losing game. However hard you work and save, you will *never* catch up. And more and more the wealthy are those who inherit it, not the innovator in her garage or student dorm, who creates a world-beating new product. So the wealthy have not even done anything to merit their power other than be born to the right parents. And, just to remind ourselves of the obvious, money is power. In Bertrand Russell's definition, it is the ability to make other people do things they would not otherwise choose to do, whether washing laundry or varnishing the woodwork on the yacht. In contemporary culture, wealth is presented as innocent, even joyful, and certainly free of pain to others: how fun to be rich! Concealed is the dirty secret that it is the gruelling and distasteful labour of others — many others — usually low paid, that makes that fun possible. Far more people are washing laundry or cleaning the lavatory than being Bill Gates. Yet who gets to write the op-eds in the *New York Times* or speak at Davos? The freedom of the few is bought with the pain of the many.

I feel crass and clumsy, even a bit embarrassed, when I make these points. I worry that I will be attacked as naïve and disingenuous. Once, a diplomat friend from my old days said I was 'immature' to believe in anarchism. He represented a country that pretends to be democratic but imprisons government critics, and where drug dealers are executed by hanging. It is a very wealthy country, whose culture largely amounts to that of an airport shopping arcade. His job, according to his unstated presumption, is of course 'mature'. My hatred of injustice and the denial of freedom to the many, childish. If I, a convinced believer in and advocate for an alternative system, cannot shake off this anxiety and fear of criticism, even ridicule, what hope is there that the rest of us will? Something has to give. Perhaps something has to break.

****

When the farmer sees his neighbour using a new piece of machinery, he wants one too. When one houseowner puts a solar panel on her roof, the incidence of panels in the vicinity rises. This is the engine of imitative spread. When people see the power of taking control and abandoning the hierarchical and oppressive behaviours of capitalism, replacing the unrepresentative decisions taken by 'democratic' government with a system where they are in charge, they will want the same.

This may be the way to cut through the anaesthetic of Mark Fisher's 'capitalist realism', to start *doing* the alternative. By walking through it, we begin to re-align the deep grooves in our brain that tell us that the status quo is unchangeable and eternal (which of course it isn't; nothing is). Somehow it's not enough to know about it. While that education is a necessary precursor, you have to do it, to practice it, what anarchists call *praxis*. Because to do it is to live it. Show, don't tell.

This is the 'prefigurative' politics of France's Situationists. That we enact the political alternative we wish to see. Art could point the way by disrupting the conventional present. Some see Banksy's public art, secretly painted in the dead of night on walls and vacant spaces across the country, as an inheritor of the Situationists' credo. But the popularity and price of his art in the world's auction rooms merely show how this act of resistance has already been appropriated and swallowed up in capitalism's maw. The BBC, hardly the loudspeaker of the coming revolution, happily reports the appearance of his latest artwork. It wasn't long after the occupation of Zuccotti Park began in New York City — the birthplace of Occupy Wall Street — that T-shirts were to appear in shop windows uptown adorned with the slogan Occupy Everything. The rapper Jay-Z marketed his own 'line' of 'Occupy' casual wear.

Art embodies the imagination. But modern art is often reflective merely of the capitalist culture in which it is conceived, mercenary and cynical (skulls coated in diamonds for instance). Such art celebrates both novelty and monetary price, a direct replication of the methods of capitalism. You can now buy shares in valuable artworks which are then stored in vaults as their value increases, never to be seen.

Art, including music and literature, is too often soporific and anaesthetising, helping numb us to the realities of our situation. More thoughtful and evocative art offers criticism of the status quo but fails to elaborate a coherent alternative. And indeed much of mass culture — advertising, the publications or TV series that benefit from it, or 'influencers' — is an intrinsic part of that creation of false demand and consumerism. As the Situationist Guy Debord said, "A society's 'culture' both reflects and prefigures its possible ways of organising life".[39]

The questioning of the status quo that is intrinsic in much art, save the most conservative, needs to perform a more educative service by, for instance, demonstrating the covert absurdity of much of modern 'orthodox' behaviour, including the mouse-wheel soul-lessness of most modern work, or the grotesquerie of distant politicians making decisions for the masses of whom they know nothing but the vaguest and impressions, instead concealing that ignorance with paltry ideology. The Situationists challenged the commodification of art and consumer culture through the creation of 'situations', which by their nature immersed the observer/participant in an alternative reality and illustrated the temporary and grotesque character of the conventional culture.

Maybe we can learn from the Situationists today. We need cultural expression that embodies the possibilities of new realities while rejecting the old. This is beyond the task of the conventional political party or campaign; it must be taken on by artists themselves. This will not be a 'movement', even if it is a conscious departure from current fashions. Anarchist art by its nature must be autonomous, temporary[‡] and self-expressive, reflecting the pluralism and independence, as well as abundant creativity, implicit in the idea. A voice for all. Anarchist art will thereby be inherently more heterodox and variegated, intrinsically more questing and diverse. Ultimately, perhaps, art should not be seen as a 'separate' activity, conducted by a selected group of 'artists'. Instead, art would be intrinsic to everything, an expression of us all. Art, in a sense, would cease to exist. As the biographer of Debord describes:

[‡]   'Our situations will be ephemeral, without a future. Passageways. Our only concern is real life; we care nothing about the permanence of art or of anything else. Eternity is the grossest idea a person can conceive of in connection with his acts' (Guy Debord, "Report on the Construction of Situations, and on the International Situationist Tendency's Conditions of Organization and Action," written in July 1957).

What the world needs more than ever are modern-day Don Quixotes and François Rabelaises, new romantic men and women from La Mancha, defiant dwellers of abbeys of Thélème, wise magicians of laughter and tears, humanists and utopians who reach for the stars because they want to stand upright. Play and laughter can become a revitalised seriousness, no joking matter, things essential and life-enhancing, not sidetracks and diversions to making money and accumulating commodities. Laughter can be therapeutic and political, with positive creative potentiality as well as negative critical power.[40] The Situationists believed in the rupture, the revelation, the moment when the conventional and orthodox are suddenly and violently interrupted and shown to be what they really are. A different reality surfaces. The Hurricane Sandy, for example, that made people see that government wasn't there to protect them but that they could rely on each other. The Grenfell Tower disaster that shows how capitalism and our deeply flawed system (called 'representative democracy') conspire to cause mass death. Or, as it was for me, the Iraq War.

This is the glitch in the matrix of artificial reality when the hero and soon-to-be saviour Neo is shown the bleak 'desert of the real'. But that moment is his starting point for resistance against the machine.

What is holding us back? Perhaps it is our own sense of safety that we must begin to question. In my favourite poem, 'Leap Before You Look', WH Auden, another Englishman who lived in New York, argues that we must leap before we look:

The sense of danger must not disappear:
The way is certainly both short and steep,
However gradual it looks from here;
Look if you like, but you will have to leap.

Tough-minded men get mushy in their sleep
And break the by-laws any fool can keep;

It is not the convention but the fear
That has a tendency to disappear.

The worried efforts of the busy heap,
The dirt, the imprecision, and the beer
Produce a few smart wisecracks every year;
Laugh if you can, but you will have to leap.

The clothes that are considered right to wear
Will not be either sensible or cheap,
So long as we consent to live like sheep
And never mention those who disappear.

Much can be said for social savoir-faire,
But to rejoice when no one else is there
Is even harder than it is to weep;
No one is watching, but you have to leap.

A solitude ten thousand fathoms deep
Sustains the bed on which we lie, my dear:
Although I love you, you will have to leap;
Our dream of safety has to disappear.

Our dream of safety has to disappear.

Aime Césaire used his poetry and essays to inspire a future beyond colonisation. His most well-known poem, 'Cahier d'un retour au pays natal', charts his voyage of self-discovery through examination of his place, the city of Fort-de-France, the capital of Martinique, through changing identities to the revelation of self-empowerment. It is noteworthy that his journey of collective liberation began with the transformation of his own identity (as it does for Neo in *The Matrix*). Resistance comes from self-affirmation; it comes from the rejection of passivity, it comes from action:

Beware, my body and my soul, beware above all of crossing your arms and assuming the sterile attitude of the spectator, for life is not a spectacle, for a sea of pain is not a proscenium [a theatre stage].

There is a deep connection between the personal and collective experience. One role of the poet is to speak out against injustice. In his own case, Césaire finds himself in being a voice:

My mouth shall be the mouth of those calamities that have no mouth, my voice the freedom of those who break down in the prison holes of despair.

Through this liberatory project, he finds his purpose. The struggle to be ourselves — our own self-determination — is the starting point of the broader fight to transform society as a whole.

****

Some point to the coercive powers of the state that keep us in line. After all, the state alone is allowed to use force or, more insidiously, threaten it (for it is more the threat that controls us than the use). The more that freedom is denied, the more coercion the state requires: witness the incredible and pervasive 'Big Brother' power of the Stasi to control the population of East Germany, where family members were employed to spy on each other, friends spied on friends. But in the end, even there, no state is powerful enough on its own to control us all, as the crowds streaming through the breaches of the Berlin Wall proved in 1989. There, the West provided an existing model of a possible alternative. Today, we may need greater powers of imagination and hope: a vision of our own ideal city.

Rebecca Solnit points to the importance of ideas in shaping our reality.

> Once you create a new idea of what is possible and acceptable, the seeds are planted; once it becomes what the majority believes, you've created the conditions in which winning happens. It may be the least tangible, but most important, part of a campaign. Ideas are powerful and dangerous, as their enemies know, and everyone else often forgets.[41]

Ideas, she points out, are often created at the margins, then become mainstream. The press, Solnit observes, tend to see change as coming out of nowhere, suddenly, but in fact it is a function of much longer-term and sustained processes, above all, the propagation of the ideas of change themselves. Ursula Le Guin urges us to use our imagination:

> The exercise of imagination is dangerous to those who profit from the way things are because it has the power to show that the way things are is not permanent, not universal, not necessary.[42]

Imagination can also be applied to our living space, too often today designed by small groups — often men, rarely disabled or marginalised, or even a single man. Architecture can embody and enable this new politics with buildings that are open, transparent, human-centric, with space for meeting and convening. If there are to be monuments, they should be monuments to humanity not to bankers or war. Above all, anarchist architecture should be democratic, though not design-by-committee, in contrast to the architecture created by small groups imposing their design on others, some of whom may live many generations hence. Design justice principles already make clear that design must be facilitative rather than directive and centre those most affected (a principle that more or less applies to any politics).§ Jane Jacobs, who took on and defeated the soul-less and Machiavellian designs of Robert Moses on

---

§   Taken from the Design Justice Principles, a good set of guidelines.

New York City, observed that 'Cities have the capability of providing something for everybody, only because, and only when, they are created by everybody'.[43]

The Situationist Ivan Chtcheglov thought a lot about the future city (notably, not an 'ideal city'). In place of the banal design politics of, say, Richard Rogers, who proposed that the optimal neighbourhood should comprise work, living and leisure space (a reductive triumvirate representative of the dominant cultural ethos), Chtcheglov proposed that,

> The districts of this city could correspond to the whole spectrum of diverse feelings that one encounters by chance in everyday life.

He suggests,

> Bizarre Quarter — Happy Quarter (specially reserved for habitation) — Noble and Tragic Quarter (for good children) — Historical Quarter (museums, schools) — Useful Quarter (hospital, tool shops) — Sinister Quarter, etc. And an Astrolarium ... Indispensable for giving the inhabitants a consciousness of the cosmic. Perhaps also a Death Quarter, not for dying in but so as to have somewhere to live in peace — I'm thinking here of Mexico and of a principle of cruelty in innocence that appeals more to me every day.

Chtcheglov sees much greater possibilities of the city where,

> Everyone will, so to speak, live in their own personal "cathedrals." There will be rooms more conducive to dreams than any drug, and houses where one cannot help but love.[44]

He goes further. Future architecture should bend to our wishes:

> Architectural complexes will be modifiable. Their appearance will change totally or partially in accordance with their inhabitants.

The only limits to the city, as to our very selves, should be our own imagination. Enticingly he imagines a chamber of love where,

> Couples will no longer pass their nights in the home where they live and receive guests, which is nothing but a banal social custom. The chamber of love will be more distant from the centre of the city: it will naturally recreate for the partners a sense of exoticisms(s) in a locale less open to light, more hidden, so as to recover the atmosphere of secrecy.

How does that sound?

It is not only our own imaginations that may inspire us to build an ideal city. Other civilisations have been there before. There is an unfamiliar story of humanity's past to tell, one not of kings, queens and empires but of civilisations which practiced equality, non-hierarchy and self-government.[1] One recent academic study cites the example of Monte Albán, a Mexican city whose ruins lie above the city of Oaxaca.[45] The city was founded in 500BC and flourished and grew, home to seventeen thousand people, despite a lack of water supplies or fertile land. The paper, authored by Linda Nicholas and Gary Feinman, proposes that one explanation of the city's success was equality of power and wealth.[46] The city was governed by collective processes directed from below. The city enjoyed an extraordinary 1,300-year period of relative prosperity, a far longer duration than the vast majority of such single settlements. It seems very unlikely that our own 'civilisation' will last 1,300 years. Indeed, some are predicting its collapse within a few years as the depredations of climate change spread, only exacerbated by the gross inequalities in power and

---

[1]   See, for instance, David Graeber and David Wengrow's *The Dawn of Everything*.

wealth of the current dispensation. In Monte Albán, 'There is very little indication of highly autocratic or concentrated power, nor stark inequalities of wealth', Gary Feinman, the study's co-author, told a newspaper. 'Plus, there are many indications of cooperation between households'. His paper recounts that there was no sign of glorification of leaders; housing was constructed of similar adobe materials, which were solely used in other cities for high-status houses. 'There are no rich tombs, no great caches of household riches or other evidence of extreme wealth differences and no large, ornate palace that is clearly the ruler's residence', the study reports. 'From early in the site's history, the city's core was centred on a large plaza that could have accommodated a significant proportion of the site's population'.[47] A public space for congregation and collective decision-making perhaps. David Graeber and David Wengrow chart a very different history of human politics in *The Dawn of Everything*. They argue against the common assumption that large populations inevitably lead to complex bureaucracies and unequal power structures. They highlight early cities like Taljanky in Ukraine which show no evidence of centralised government, grand buildings or significant wealth disparities. In Mesopotamia's Uruk, popular assemblies governed the city.

The authors cite the example of urban egalitarianism of Teotihuacan, a Mesoamerican city of similar size and magnificence to Rome, its historical contemporary. Once authoritarian, its people started to build public housing instead of monuments and practicing human sacrifice. 'Many citizens', the authors write, 'enjoyed a standard of living that is rarely achieved across such a wide sector of urban society in any period of urban history, including our own'. For most of the past five thousand years, kingdoms and empires were 'exceptional islands of political hierarchy, surrounded by much larger territories whose inhabitants ... systematically avoided fixed, overarching systems of authority'.[48]

Real people once lived like this. The way of a city is not inevitable; the way of a society, indeed the existence of the state itself, is not inevitable.

****

The powers of the state, or indeed economic forces, are far less than the potential power of the masses. But only rarely does the state need to exercise its power because we so willingly abide by its rules; we are self-policing. Just as the unit of labour, namely us who work, unresistingly abides by the 'laws' of the market, by accepting the lowest wage available for the type of work we do, by never questioning the logic whereby the CEO can earn many hundreds of times what the average employee of the company receives, by submitting to the control and self-abnegation of the hierarchy of organisations and institutions.

In effect, as Byung-Chul Han argues, we police ourselves into compliance.

Inasmuch as it expends a great deal of energy to force people into the straitjacket of commandments and prohibitions, disciplinary power proves inefficient. A significantly more efficient technology of power makes sure that people subordinate themselves to power relations on their own. Such a dynamic seeks to activate, motivate and optimise — not to inhibit or repress. It proves so effective because it does not operate by means of forbidding and depriving, but by pleasing and fulfilling. Instead of making people compliant, it seeks to make them dependent.[49] The message here is clear: we are the very system that defines and entraps us; it is a circular and constant process of experience and reaffirmation, by word and deed and mostly unconscious. And there, of course, equally evident, that by changing that behaviour and those words we can change the system itself. In the expression of subjugation lie the seeds of self-liberation, if only we would see it.

The panoply of beliefs that underpin the current system resembles nothing so much as a religion, a deep-seated set of beliefs expressed both externally — by politicians, corporate leaders and commentators — and internally, as a set of behavioural heuristics — to do some things and not others, a moral structure. It is surely no coincidence that as capitalism or 'neoliberalism' has risen to pervade all economics, politics and culture, so has adherence to religion declined. Instead of worshipping a god, we worship the notion of 'freedom'. But it is not real freedom; it is a simulacrum. Neoliberalism has not given us freedom, either political, economic or social. It is more subtle than the overt oppression of, for example, Soviet-style state communism. It is only occasionally required to be coercive, as Han argues. In our minds, power has been disguised as permissivity, indeed freedom itself:

> The greater the power is, the more quietly it works. It just happens: it has no need to draw attention to itself. To be sure, power can express itself as violence or repression. But it is not based on force ... In its permissivity — indeed, in its friendliness — power is shedding its negativity and presenting itself as freedom.[50]

Han argues that we have internalised the neoliberal ideology to such an extent that the world has ceased to be real to us. Neoliberalism has invaded our minds so that politics is, above all, mental or psychological, threatening our ability to be present in our own lives, to think or even — perhaps most shockingly — to love. We are so immersed in a materialist universe, of faked-up claims of meaning and anaesthetised to reality (because realising all this is simply too painful), we have crippled and diminished our greatest source of meaning and humanity — love and the authentic expression of our human-ness through our relationships to one another. If this is right, it means that as long as neoliberalism endures, true love is impossible.

Logical argument, it seems, can only take us so far in ridding ourselves of this monstrous controlling 'other' that dwells within and saturates the fabric between us. You can point out the domination and hollowness intrinsic in the system; its failure to satisfy the hunger for richness of human need and desire; its disastrous environmental consequences. Somehow these logical arguments are not enough. We can sense that something is terribly wrong. Not only is it there in the data of planetary destruction and inequality; there is a deeper hollowness, a spiritual emptiness.

And here we find ourselves again, back to the same questions. Perhaps at our deepest level we are afraid of losing the religion of capitalism. If we don't believe in that materialist and horribly logical belief system, what do we believe in?

Some argue that we need to replace the false gods with new belief systems to replace materialism, and indeed some, like Bernardo Kastrup, reject the notion of the existence of a material reality in itself. Instead we live in a field of consciousness, perhaps even inside God's brain. Some turn to Indigenous beliefs to discover a greater unity between life, meaning and planet, stories that integrate and cherish these three elements. Others consume psychedelics to explore new ontologies of being and believing. After writing the *Tractatus*, and its destruction of logical philosophy, Ludwig Wittgenstein replaced his logic with a more traditional belief system in Christianity. He gave away all his money, apologised to everyone he believed he had ever wronged, and went on to live the humble life of a hospital porter.

But it strikes me that all such philosophies suffer from the same flaw. They all impose a prism on reality, a lens through which we must experience the world. This means *this*, that means *that* (thereby, incidentally, through that act of definition, creating the possibility of conflict). It's like constantly looking at the world through the gap between our fingers.

It would be pleasant for our minds to cease the endless and exhausting hunt for meaning and the tiresome application of abstract structure into which to fit the world. It would offer a kind of perfect mental freedom, the abolition of all filters between us and reality. I suspect, however, that we all need some kind of theory or system to interpret the world. But it seems necessary that at the same time we accept the limits of all theories, all belief systems and philosophies. This too offers some kind of release. Truth and reality are so much greater than how we can describe or understand them through mere terms and axioms. This can be common ground we all can accept and occupy together, regardless of our commitment to separated religions or philosophies.

I suspect that belief — or acknowledgement of the limits of beliefs — is not itself enough either. We have to *feel* the change. We can only reprogram ourselves by replacing old and perhaps comforting emotions with new ones. We can rearrange the neurons and synapses of our brains only by experiencing and perhaps above all *expressing* something new, just as I am learning how to live anew. We change reality through declaration and action.

My intuition is that only by restating an unwanted emotion as something more positive can we really change ourselves. It is not enough to accept that the current system doesn't work. It is not enough to be open to the possibilities of new structures and belief systems. Only through this emotional act of restatement is it possible to really embed the shift to something new.

But how? By surfacing the pain and declaring it, we begin (unconsciously acting it out, as I did as a fascistic school prefect, is *not* the answer). But this too, if performed in isolation, is insufficient. Our pain and our desire for transformation must be heard and seen and acknowledged. It is this connection with other people that may prove our only salvation.

Only through communication and connection, the expression of our very essence as humans, that we can restate our spiritual emptiness as authentic human need. That communication is what creates us as humans. And only through such communication can we have a chance that at last the emptiness is filled.

6
Archetypes of Revolution

A S NEWS spread of the Occupy protests, I began occasionally
to attend the "General Assembly" meetings in Zuccotti Park
in downtown New York City. I found the meetings profoundly
moving, a sentiment that, needless to say, I had never felt at the UN
Security Council a couple of miles to the north (except on one day,
September 12th 2001).

Anyone could speak; hundreds listened to their words echoed by
the extraordinary "human mic", where the crowd would repeat the
words of the speaker so that everyone could hear. In the early weeks,
there was a sense of great excitement and optimism. I was amazed by
the variety of the participants, from students to besuited Wall Street
office workers.

It didn't take long, however, for smaller groups subtly to begin to
assert their authority over others. Like many with small children and
a business to attend to, I could not sleep overnight in the park — in
reality, a rather bleak concrete plaza. Some who did, however, seemed
to feel a certain superiority over part-timers, as if putting in the time
counted the most. What was happening to Occupy Wall Street began

to fulfill the warning of the "tyranny of structurelessness" prophesied by the feminist writer and political theorist Jo Freeman.

Unless great care is taken, Freeman argues, there is a tendency for those with the loudest voices and a sense of entitlement, often born of class, race or gender, to dominate nominally non-hierarchical movements. The early founders of Occupy, some of them anarchists, had attempted to mitigate this danger by the very process of the General Assembly with its various procedures designed to allow all to speak and make decisions on equal terms. But it wasn't enough.

Just as crippling was the absence of a guiding philosophy of the movement. Its loud cries of protest against the inequity and cruelty of the current political and economic dispensation were heard around the world. Its manifesto was not.

The easy criticism, that there was no Occupy "manifesto," carried some truth but missed the point that in a movement of many, it is impossible and indeed wrong to impose a single set of political demands.

Nevertheless, it was striking how little one heard compelling proposals for the way forward. Many Occupiers seemed to believe that petitioning Washington was the answer, even while acknowledging the poisonous corruption of that sick place. Others banged drums. Sometimes, I would look up at the ugly, but towering citadels of capitalism that surround Zuccotti Park and imagined the denizens looking down at the demonstrators far below.

Sealed behind double glazed windows, I doubt that they could even hear the chants from the street.

****

One rash night, I invited the crowd to join a "working group" to consider how to set up an alternative bank.

The 2008 financial crisis had turned my attention, as others', to the banking sector. It didn't take much research to see the utter corruption at the heart of the very nervous system of the contemporary economy.

The sector was dominated by a few massive monopolistic banks which funded literally thousands of lobbyists in Washington. Congressmen openly admit that the lobbyists write banking legislation for them.

"Freshmen" Congressional representatives are quoted saying that the banking committee is the most popular to serve on because it earns them the most campaign contributions — of course, from the banks. Unsurprisingly, the resulting legislation protects the banks' profits and, in its vastness and complexity, amounts to a huge barrier to entry for others to compete in what is, in effect, a closed market.

The banks do not have to comply with rigorous law; the law complies with them. And all the reams of law failed to protect the world from the reckless and irresponsible profit-seeking behaviour — the creation of almost incomprehensibly complicated derivatives, for example — that plunged the world into economic catastrophe in 2008.

Needless to say, that disaster caused the greatest harm to the poorest, some of whom starved in distant countries while in America millions of hardworking people lost their jobs and homes. The bankers were largely unaffected and, as history then demonstrated, immune to any meaningful accountability.

Against all this, it seemed a quixotic gesture to try to build an alternative. But I did not believe that asking Washington to fix the problem would work. My analysis of the hugely overcomplicated Dodd-Frank legislation was that, in fact, it would help protect the power of the big banks but would not prevent — because it could not foresee — the next financial innovation that might wreak havoc on the world's economy.

The financial sector was too complicated and massive; the economy had become "financialised", a place where speculators and quant-trading algorithms could cause disaster in wholly unpredictable yet catastrophic ways. Banks were effectively acting as speculators rather than as safe repositories for our money or responsible providers of credit. The stabilising capital reserves they were legally required to hold were dramatically insufficient (and remain so today). Banks could reap the profits from this risky behaviour but, as the financial crisis so clearly demonstrated, when things go wrong it is the taxpayer who has to bail out the banks and who bears the true cost of this profit-seeking.

It was not that bankers were irredeemably evil people; the system itself encouraged and rewarded their casino behavior. If banks were to escape being taken over by competitors, they had to make profits. To make more profits, they had to innovate new ways to make money, such as the toxic credit default swaps that helped trigger the '08 crisis. The system itself was the problem, not its operators (though some cannot be so lightly excused).

Legislation would not fix this problem; only the creation of new forms — a new system itself — might work. We needed simple banking, a return to the Jimmy Stewart *It's a Wonderful Life* community banking, where capital worked for people, not the other way around.

Scores turned up to our first meeting. As the weeks went by, and once everyone had given their speech about what was wrong, the group dwindled to a few. I was surprised by who kept showing up: often middle aged but also young, many of the group were defectors from banking, themselves disgusted by the practices they had witnessed from the inside. The most dedicated, who put in by far the most labour, was a former commodities trader who wore a pinstripe and trilby, about the last person you would have expected at an Occupy rally.

We met week by week for over two years.

We set up a cooperative company which, we hoped, would eventually be able to offer accounts and other financial services to anyone, and particularly the forty million or so "unbanked" Americans who are denied a foothold in the economy because they cannot get bank accounts or reasonably priced credit, and are instead exploited by loan sharks and banks offering exorbitantly priced tools such as pre-paid cash cards. We negotiated a new low-cost card that would undercut all the banks' cards because it was non-profit and any returns would go back to the co-op and its owners — the customers.

Our company, The Occupy Cooperative, was an attempt to sidestep one of the most outrageous barriers that the big banks have set up to protect their profits: staggeringly, it is against federal law for a non-profit credit union to operate nationally in America and offer its services to anyone.

We failed.

One reason was that setting up a new financial entity is an enormous task that proved beyond a small but dedicated group of volunteers with day jobs. We probably aimed too big; we didn't appreciate that change might need to start small, accumulate and spread.

But one insidious reason illustrates the difficulties of the necessary construction of new and better systems of banking and economic interaction. Our venture was breaking new ground. We were terrified of being sued into penury by litigious banks. We sought legal advice. We visited almost every law firm in the city that practiced banking law. Without exception, every lawyer we met loved our plans. But not one agreed to help us. Every law firm was working for one of the big banks or credit card companies. 'I would love to help you, but I've just had lunch with Citibank', one lawyer told us. It was to be eighteen months before we found *pro-bono* assistance and a green light to proceed, by which time the market had shifted against our planned first offering, the Occupy Card. This is how power works. The banks and their pliant legislators make the law, then exploit it to protect their profits and destroy competition. It's a racket, pure and simple. And it works.

Occupy, however, taught me many things. Protest has limits, particularly in demanding the reform of a sophisticated and highly entrenched system. Those who benefit from that system have great wealth and power, and can hire armies of lawyers and lobbyists to defend their privilege. That system, of corrupted government and iniquitous capitalism, is mutually reinforcing and thus doubly hard to disintegrate. Such reform must come through the hard labour of constructing alternative, better systems. This can be gruelling work, and it can fail.

But Occupy showed me something that touched me to the quick. There are huge numbers of people, from all classes and walks of life, who are appalled by the current system. Occupy helped establish relationships and networks across New York City, the United States and indeed the world, relationships that transcend the petty labels of political parties, ideology or class.

Our group was contacted by those engaged in similar efforts, not just in Rhode Island and San Francisco but also in Germany and Israel. We gave each other strength and ideas. Those networks endure. Thanks to Occupy, I am in touch with a software cooperative in New Zealand and hacker collectives in Barcelona, who work to expose Spain's rampant political corruption.

In New York, groups of Occupiers continue to work on concrete initiatives, such as a debt collective, to address economic injustice. It was Occupiers who marshalled the earliest and most communitarian response to Hurricane Sandy. They have shown me that political change is a collective project that can only work when small efforts combine to produce massive transformation.

Self-government, the abolition of coercive hierarchy and domination, worker-owned cooperatives: this is a philosophy that puts people and our relationships with one another at its centre. There's a name for this philosophy: anarchism. It's striking that this word and this philosophy are so often dismissed as extreme, when all it amounts to is putting people in charge of their own affairs, whether in government or at the workplace. It can be done, but it takes action, not words. This too is long-standing anarchist philosophy.

Anarchism proposes something simple and humble, but also inspiring. That we deal with each other as equals, without coercion or violence and with respect, sharing our decisions, whether in our cities and towns or the workplace. The central argument of this book is that such relationships of equality promote the maximum flourishing of that most important of human qualities and needs — love.

No one pretends that the construction of this new way of doing things is easy, and there are new habits of cooperation, deliberation and consensus to learn, as a deeper, more human order is woven to replace that imposed from above. Perhaps it was always there. The British anarchist Colin Ward argued that a the culture and habits of a cooperative society already exist, but are submerged and repressed, 'like a seed beneath the snow, buried under the weight of the state and its bureaucracy, capitalism and its waste, privilege and its injustices, nationalism and its suicidal loyalties, religious differences and their superstitious separatism'.

There are extreme forms of anarchism where some believe that all institutions and forms of organisation are innately hierarchical and must involve domination. Libertarianism, which is not to be confused with anarchism, puts the individual at the centre, where his or her wishes transcend all others. Anarchism, by contrast, is about community and fostering equality of relations between people.

There's no political party that offers these ideas. Turkeys don't vote for Christmas (or Thanksgiving in the US). You cannot tick a box or click a link and somehow these ideas will come into being. These ideas have to be constructed, brought to life where you are and with those around you. I do not believe in violent revolution but in something more gentle, enduring and fundamental. The necessary transformation of the economy and human society will take a long time, a constant and ongoing process, where the values that we seek are expressed through the very actions that we take. Protest may signal the need for change, but alone it is not enough. As the statement widely attributed to Buckminster Fuller puts it:

> You never change things by fighting the existing reality.
> To change something, build a new model that makes the existing model obsolete.[51]

Reading anarchist history and memoir, I am struck by the enormous energy and sacrifice of the nineteenth-century anarchists — Bakunin, Kropotkin (who once lived down the road from where I sit) and the Lower East Side's own Emma Goldman. Each was imprisoned, vilified and exiled. They did not believe that a petition would change society. They would revile today's online campaigns and "virtual democracy" ("Click on your favourite policy!"), which are heralded as change (but in fact are anything but) and contribute to the perpetuation of the *status quo*, and worse, confuse and drain energy from those who wish for fundamental change.

These anarchists realised that asking others to effect change was futile. It had to come from oneself. And therein lay great liberation and joy.

Some call for "revolution". Roger Hallam, one of the co-founders of Extinction Rebellion, has been sentenced to five years' imprisonment for his part in peacefully blocking the M25 in protest of the government's inaction over the climate catastrophe, sentences far more severe than those handed down to most of the rioters who tried to burn down hostels for asylum seekers and assaulted the police a few months afterwards. Roger and his fellow 'Whole Truth Five' show that there are some who are actively taking on capitalism and its enabler, the state, and they are harshly punished for it. From prison, by blog and podcast, Roger has called for revolution, but like Kropotkin in the nineteenth century, I don't believe that the English will revolt.

Perhaps protest can get us there? While mass protest may have caused the downfall of the Mubarak regime in Egypt, there is little sign of real impact of protest in the deeply entrenched systems of the West. A million people marched against the Iraq War, with nothing to show for it: the invasion went ahead. Extinction Rebellion mustered hundreds of thousands of protestors to its most successful rallies. Perhaps this affected the policies of the forthcoming Labour government, perhaps it didn't. The evidence is scant. In Catalonia, the pro-independence movement celebrated a million people (or so they claimed) demonstrating on the streets of Barcelona on Catalonia's national day. Catalonia today is not independent. Today, I watch tens of thousands protest the slaughter in the Gaza Strip, yet the British government continues to supply Israel with weapons.

Most troublingly, I have a deep suspicion that protest might sometimes, by some unacknowledged mechanism, have the opposite effect to that intended: protest doesn't challenge authority; it reinforces it by reaffirming government's role as 'the decider'. Protestors are appealing to government to do something different, rendering the authorities as the active party with agency, the protestor as passive.[*]

In this way, protest may indeed prove actually counter-productive. As Paul Cudenec notes, Herbert Marcuse suggested, that the traditional forms of protest could actually prove counter-constructive — 'even dangerous' — in that they draw attention away from more significant levels of control and, by implying that there is some point in trying to influence the authorities in any significant way, 'preserve the illusion of popular sovereignty'.[52] Instead, I believe the goal should be the assertion of autonomy, the demonstration of alternatives by building them, the rediscovery of our lost agency and, with that, the glorious invigoration of what it is to be a truly free human being.

****

I have lived in and known societies where power has been overthrown and new states have emerged. Along with everyone else, I watched the Berlin Wall come down, and I have lived with the East Germans who brought it down. I have discussed revolution with democracy activists who occupied Cairo's Tahrir Square, some of whom languish in jails to this day. (And by the way, they told me that they didn't go onto the streets to get 'Western-style' democracy; they were already well aware of what that meant.)

And Britain today does not feel like those places, not at all. In all those places, there was a deep and suppressed hunger for change, rage at long-standing oppression and a desperate need for the control that brings security and safety to individuals and their families. There was a willingness to sacrifice all, including their own lives, for freedom. I admire Roger Hallam and his comrades for sacrificing his liberty for revolution (and I protest the gross

---

[*] This problem is intriguingly explored by Anthea Lawson in *The Entangled Activist*, which suggests that campaigners can become caught up in the very ideologies, systems and assumptions that they seek to change, thereby unwittingly helping perpetuate the *status quo*. See: *The Entangled Activist*, Perspectiva, 2021.

punitiveness of the government's response to non-violent action), but I don't think that most people are willing to do the same, let alone risk their lives.

I have worked for self-determination in six would-be independent states — Somaliland, Western Sahara, Kosovo, South Yemen, South Sudan, and Catalonia — or seven, if I count my sporadic work on Palestine. In the two cases which became independent and — mostly — recognised countries — Kosovo and South Sudan — there was no doubt in anyone's mind that if independence was not granted to those entities and recognised, there would have been war. That was one of the main, if not the most important, reasons they were given independence (for recognition by other states cannot be taken; it must be given).

In Catalonia, none of the politicians I met seeking Catalan independence, including the prime minister, were willing to sacrifice their lives. They hoped to achieve that end politically through protest, referendums, diplomacy and Madrid's acquiescence (a distant prospect). Simply put, the stakes weren't high enough, nor was it clear that the overwhelming majority actually wanted independence. In South Sudan and Kosovo, a referendum would have shown 98% support for independence (indeed, in South Sudan a referendum did show that massive scale of support). In Catalonia, by contrast, the best the pro-independence parties could hope for was a small majority of voters. In South Sudan and Kosovo, those soon-to-be states, young men publicly bragged about taking up arms for the fight against the oppressor that older men had already fought for many years; there were shrines to dead 'martyrs'. When once I mentioned this to the prime minister of Catalonia, he shrugged and grinned. Catalonia remains a subordinate province of the state of Spain to this day. The prime minister may well have noticed that the Basque region of Spain, where the militant group ETA committed multiple acts of violence in the cause of independence — bombings, assassinations, kidnappings — has been granted by Madrid a much greater degree of autonomy than Catalonia.

Hallam has also cited research by Erica Chenoweth and Maria Stephan showing that only 3.5% of the population has to rise up to bring along the others and trigger wholesale revolution. But Maria and Erica, for whom I have the greatest respect, do not claim that this historical observation necessarily applies to today's Western societies. The crucial difference between places like Britain, France or the US and places like communist Romania, Kosovo or Mubarak's Egypt is that the revolution we are seeking is about *many* things, not *one* thing, not the overthrow of a singular dictatorship. We need to revolutionise the whole of society, its political and economic structures, its values and attitudes, its norms of behaviour, the very way it thinks about itself and what it is to be human (its ontology, if you like). Perhaps this might be achieved by some kind of non-violent vanguard movement of a minority of citizens. But I think it's much more likely to be achieved more gradually and thus more widely. This is a gentle revolution, where opponents and doubters are persuaded, not defeated. One by one, and all together, where the mechanism of spread is the uniquely persuasive power of example: moss spreading across a forest floor.

But I am always wary of somebody, often a white middle-aged man like me, proclaiming that there is only one way: a correct method of revolution. And we should be wary. Those who offer one ways are like mini-totalitarians, insisting that their view of events and change is the right and sole method — the Bolsheviks committed this very error from the beginning, dismissing (and sometimes killing) those who disagreed with their method of revolution and thereby laying the foundations for the repressive state that eventually followed the revolution (they were mostly middle-aged men too of course). The now-forgotten anarchist revolution in Kronstadt, by sailors and citizens who wished for genuine people power, not a party that claimed to speak for the people, was viciously and bloodily suppressed.

The essence of anarchism is multiplicity and heterogeneity: there is no singular pathway of revolution. We each have to find our own way. We each have the challenge — and joy — of discovering our own agency and power.

This is not a politically correct statement of the need for diversity. It reflects the core anarchist belief in the self-determination of the individual, but it also parallels the very nature of the system we confront. We need the tools to fit the job. The neoliberal, putatively democratic system of contemporary Western societies is highly adept at resisting change. It is multi-layered and deeply embedded into our laws, institutions, culture and very way of seeing and understanding the world and what it is to be human. It is nothing less than a complete ontology, a system of how to live. That means that it must be tackled in multiple different ways.

The complexity of the system means that we cannot know the state of the system at any one point: there are too many elements, and the second we fix them in place, they will have changed — they are incessantly dynamic. Crucially, this also means that we cannot predict how change will happen. Change is not linear. We cannot say that Input *A* will lead to Output *B*. Encouragingly, such systems are also susceptible to 'phase change', that the whole system can 'tip' from one state to another, triggered by just one input, especially if that system is primed for change — at 'criticality'. I would argue that the current system is very much at that point, where multiple elements are failing and, in totality, is failing to produce its promised outputs.

But despite the inherent impossibility of predicting how change might happen and thus the futility of offering a single pathway to change, there are some principles to bear in mind. Perhaps the most important is this: the means are the ends.

This Gandhi-an (and indeed Kantian)[†] maxim is of essential importance. It is what we do *now* that matters. The methods we use now create a reality. There is no excuse to use violence in order to progress towards a peaceful future (and it doesn't work anyway). Anarchism's rejection of the distinction between means and ends distinguishes it from capitalism and socialism, which both separate means and ends.

[†]   The second part of Kant's categorical imperative states that humans should always be treated as ends, never merely as means.

Capitalism and socialism both demand present sacrifice and injustice in order to build a perfect future, which oddly never comes. Interestingly, the consonance of means and ends manifests a particular concept of time. There is no past and no future: there is only now. *This* is what matters.

What does it mean that the means are the ends? Simply put, it means that the methods we use to change things must embody the change we wish to see. They need to be non-hierarchical and eschew domination. That means that organisation and direction need to be decided collectively by using the methods earlier identified for inclusive democracy. They may need to be adapted to correct for historical injustices produced by racism or sexism.

The French protest movement the Gilet Jaunes, for instance, used participatory assemblies, where anyone could speak to decide their policies. Delegates were elected to represent the decisions of the local assemblies in more central leadership forums — if they diverged from those decisions, they could be recalled. When anyone popped up on national television to declare themselves a leader of the movement, they were denounced.

Such movements are better leaderless. They are more dynamic and inventive. They do not rely on the masculine hero model and do not offer an easy singular target for the regime to pick off and discredit. Those who are currently marginalised in the system by race or gender need to be at the centre, ideally as many, not as one. We are seeking, above all, a truly pluralist, democratic and inclusive kind of politics and economics; these are the values that our actions must embody.

As for violence, there is a clear moral means-end imperative: non-violence. The evidence of the effectiveness of violence is of course disputed. My own experience is mixed.

Do the examples of Kosovo's and South Sudan's struggles for independence prove that only violence (or, in both cases, the threat of violence) works? Violence is the realm and language of the state. History tells us that violence has created the state, and defined its borders, in much if not most of the world. So perhaps we shouldn't be surprised that it is violence, or the threat of it, that has brought about the creation of the two youngest states.[53]

But there is a deeper lesson to these examples suggesting that violence is a failure. South Sudan's history, since its independence, is one of widespread civil war and bloodshed. It has been a rank failure as a state. Kosovo has fared better, but independence cemented in place a political class of former liberation fighters, some of whom descended into corruption and internecine violence. That class was superseded by a more democratic and uncorrupted leadership only twenty years after independence. As I write, the Serbian minority in Kosovo has yet to be integrated successfully into the state. Many Serbs still reject Kosovo's independence, as does Serbia itself, preventing Kosovo's full membership of the international system through membership of the UN, for instance. The Serbs' rejection of the state of Kosovo has led to repeated bouts of violence and instability, which have sometimes come close to direct conflict between Kosovo and Serbia.

In the domestic realm, there is again a problem with violence. Violence plays the state's game. It affirms the state's otherwise bogus claim that it alone can guarantee the population's security and safety. In this sense, violence *relegitimises* the state: it proves *the point* of the state, which according to its own logic is to provide for the security of the population.

The US government used violence — the Global War on Terror — to relegitimise itself after its gross failure to protect its population on 9/11. The nature of that war, in particular the invasion of Iraq in 2003, was not about just defeating the direct threat from Al Qaeda. The Iraq War had nothing to do with Al Qaeda. The US administration needed to prove its utility to its people — to relegitimise itself. Similarly, violence within the state's borders is exploited by the state for the same purpose.

The mechanism of how protest, particularly if violent, reinforces and helps legitimise the already powerful can be seen in taxi company Uber's brazen co-option of protest to further its own ends. The evidence is in the thousands of emails and files leaked by a whistleblower from

Uber. As it introduced its operations in multiple countries around the world, Uber often encountered protests from traditional taxi drivers who stood to lose their livelihoods. Sometimes these protests turned violent, with Uber drivers attacked (and in one or two cases, killed) and cars overturned and torched.

Far from being dissuaded by the unrest, Uber executives *welcomed* the violence. David Plouffe, a former campaign manager to Barack Obama, who was then Uber's vice-president of policy,[‡] was upfront about the company's expectations on a trip to Cairo to defuse growing hostility to the platform there in 2016. "We've seen some violence around the world," he said. "But that usually ends up expediting regulatory reform [that helps Uber] with the government."

At a deeper level, violence helps justify government and authority. Governments claim their ultimate legitimacy from their alleged protection of the population's security. Thus, when violence occurs, governments are swift to claim the mantle of the ultimate guarantor of peace, even when, in historic terms, governments have far more often been the perpetrators of organised violence than ordinary people. Most insidiously, the use of violence against authority justifies government's own use of greater violence.

Chenoweth and Stephan argue that historically non-violent political change has been more successful and enduring than violent revolution. Like all political science, of course, much depends on how you count it (indeed whether you *can* count it). Recent examples of non-violent revolution, in Egypt or Syria, are not encouraging. Here, peaceful mass demonstrations were met either by horrific government repression (Syria) or, by the political vacuum thus opened, exploited by more organised forces, in Egypt by the Muslim Brotherhood, who then took power only to provoke a violent counter-revolution by the military, the true 'deep state', who hold power to this day. By contrast, the non-violent revolution in Ukraine (the Euro Maidan protests) was

---

[‡]   The 'revolving door' between the state and private business is another of the more covert mechanisms of how the one reinforces and enables the other.

successful. Tunisia used to be another example of successful non-violent revolution, but today it is ruled by an increasingly authoritarian government. There are obviously no easy lessons.

In all these cases, protestors were confronting authoritarian anti-democratic regimes. The objective was *singular* — to overthrow and replace that regime. In our current dispensation in the West, in places like Britain or the US, the task is more manifold — it is *plural*. In order to replace the system, we have to do *many* things, not *one* thing. Though I would argue that it is not representative, the *ancien regime* will claim that it is democratic. We have confront this claim of legitimacy at its heart by establishing *more* legitimate forms of democracy through inclusiveness and participation, starting at the communal level. We have to establish more shared forms of enterprise either by establishing new cooperative ventures or by taking over existing ones. But in all cases, this will be achieved not by force but by persuasion. Force will only legitimise those who resist.

In the West, it is the examples of the French, American and Russian revolutions that are perhaps most salient in our consciousness and reinforce an archetype of revolution that is often violent and led by singular vanguard groups. Such an archetype is of a small Castro-led military movement — of the HTS[§] in Syria — that overthrows a regime already on the verge of collapse.

The Italian political thinker Antonio Gramsci contrasted these Leninist techniques of taking on the institutional hegemony head-on, what he called a 'War of Manoeuvre', with the 'War of Position', where we work through and around key institutions, not submitting to them, a slower campaign fought through politics, civil society, cultural spaces and the economy. I prefer a 'War of Replacement' where we don't seek to overthrow or destroy existing institutions but instead seek to replace them with exemplars which prove themselves superior and thus spread organically by imitation and inspiration.

[§]   Hay'at Tahrir al-Sham (HTS) is a coalition of northern Syria-based Sunni Islamist insurgent groups that evolved from Jabhat al-Nusrah, or "Nusrah Front," al-Qa'ida's former branch in Syria.

But perhaps the most relevant example of recent times is the fall of the Berlin Wall and collapse of the Soviet empire. This revolution was characterised by the mass withdrawal of consent. Our current system has no deep materiality: it isn't concrete and iron; it has no ultimate form. It is, as Gustav Landauer says, a 'set of relationships' to which we must consent. Take away that consent and the system collapses or, at least, is unable to continue, opening the space for an alternative. Hannah Arendt, the great theorist of revolution, put it:

> That all authority in the last analysis rests on opinion is never more forcefully demonstrated than when, suddenly and unexpectedly, a universal refusal to obey initiates what then turns into a revolution.[54]

How do we prepare for such moments? Clearly, the first step is to recognise, with an unflinching eye, the situation we're in, ignoring the culture of distraction and denial that suffuses everyday culture. Then, it is to design and, piece by piece, build the alternative.

The poet Rainer Maria Rilke suggested we should start simply *living the question*, absolving ourselves of the immediate dilemma of finding answers:

> Don't search for the answers, which could not be given to you now, because you would not be able to live them. And the point is to live everything. Live the questions now. Perhaps then, someday far in the future, you will gradually, without even noticing it, live your way into the answer.[55]

This tallies with a core principle of anarchism that it is the *praxis* that matters — *how* we pursue the revolution *is* the revolution.

What is indisputable is the urgency. The far-right is well advanced in its 'war of position' across Europe, winning elections and occupying culture with its reactionary assault on 'wokery', its demonizing of immigrants and latent authoritarianism and intolerance of dissent.

The climate crisis needs to be addressed immediately, not by 2050. Most excitingly, the possibility of a far richer, more flourishing dispensation is available right now.

****

The power of one over another, or worse, power of one over the many is one of the prevailing but unquestioned sicknesses of our benighted age. Society is rife with power relationships, overt and hidden, from government's ultimate monopoly of force to the more subtle, but also poisonous, power of a boss over his or her subordinates. Power is expressed in microcosmic and concealed interactions, as well as in the more public and crude threats of the law or military force.

Conventional thinking is that we should overcome powerlessness by obtaining *more* power — climbing up the ladder. This is what I once thought and sought too, and became part of a government elite. But hierarchical power, as I learned, ultimately humiliates and disfigures the powerful.

Rousseau sought the abolition of coercive power for both the dominated and the dominator:

One man thinks himself the master of others, but remains more of a slave than they are.[56]

Nietzsche is often thought of as a philosopher of power and domination, even fascism. But he considered the will to power over others to be the will of the weak: the really strong person seeks power only over herself in order determine her own life and future. The only person one should obey is oneself. Power is found in self-mastery and gives great joy. Seeking power over oneself is in fact seeking freedom, to transcend what one is and become what one can truly be. In his penetrating understanding of power, Nietzsche is thus revealed as a philosopher of anarchism.[57]

The denial of the oppressor's power is itself a liberatory objective.

'This then is the great humanistic and historical task of the oppressed — to liberate themselves and their oppressor as well. The oppressors who oppress, exploit and rape by virtue of their power, cannot find in this power the strength to liberate either the oppressed or themselves. Only power that springs from the weakness of the oppressed will be sufficiently strong to free both.' — Paulo Freire[58]

To be powerful is to be locked into an eternal struggle to maintain that power. The politician humiliates himself through the necessary evasions and elisions of the truth required by the disfiguring practice of 'politics'. They are to be pitied. This is no way to live, as Lao Tsu observed in the *Tao Te Ching*:

> Wise men don't need to prove their point;
> men who need to prove their point aren't wise.
> The Master has no possessions.
> The more she does for others, the happier she is.
> The more she gives to others, the wealthier she is.
> The Tao nourishes by not forcing.

By not dominating, the Master leads.[59]

What we reject is power over others; what we seek is control over our own affairs. Studies indicate that it is *power over* others that brings out the worst in people, aggressiveness and exploitativeness for instance. By contrast, control over our own circumstances foments better behaviours — the very opposite characteristics to those elicited by power over.[60]

Thus, the heart of the task is not only to liberate ourselves but also to liberate the oppressor. It's important not to demonise the enemy. This is the way to accelerate counter-reaction, perhaps violent. We all resist when criticised and attacked. It's more productive and indeed accurate to think of the oppressor and oppression itself as functions of the system. Those who perform the oppression are also victims of that system. Defining them as 'the enemy' will only provoke resistance. But if we replace the system, the oppressor disappears like a wisp of smoke. After the fall of the Berlin Wall, no one wanted to be called out as a member of the Stasi, the huge secret agency that controlled the East German population. At the fall of Assad in Syria, regime soldiers cast off their uniforms.

My intuition is that this revolution will be built not by violence but by persuasion. We need to persuade those who may currently be sceptical or hostile. The changes envisaged in this short book are comprehensive: eventually, we need to win everyone over. The new dispensation cannot be imposed, for that will only sow the seeds of future resistance.

During my first diplomatic posting to the British embassy in Germany, I once spent a few weeks with a family in Dresden, a city situated in what was former East Germany, the German Democratic Republic, communist-ruled for forty years. The purpose of the stay was to improve my German language skills through 'immersion' with actual Germans. My visit took place shortly after the Berlin Wall came down. Relics of the previous order were much in evidence. Little Trabants and Wartburgs, cars that people had to wait years on waiting lists to acquire, rattled over cobbled streets. The family lived in a Plattenbau, the ubiquitous, cheaply constructed concrete tower blocks that now blighted a once-beautiful city that had been flattened by British and American bombers in 1945.

The couple were bitter. The new capitalist dispensation was not suiting them well, in particular the domination and arbitrary bossiness of the 'Wessis' from former West Germany who now, as they saw it, lorded it over the 'Ossis' from the East. But what most bothered them was that people behaved differently now. In the communist days, they told me, there was more solidarity between people. Today, people were more individualist and selfish. One particular example stood out to my hosts. Under communism, although the penalties were less, people did not drink and drive. Under capitalism, they did.

Twenty-five years later, it is the provinces of former East Germany that have witnessed the resurgence of the far-right in Germany, including but not limited to the Alternative für Deutschland (AfD). The seeds of frustration over lack of agency, lack of control, were perhaps sown in Germany's reunification, a dark shadow to a moment of putative liberation. A new order was imposed on the east with no mechanism to secure overt consent.

A sudden complete overturning of the current system would undoubtedly be disruptive and potentially dangerous in a society that is alienated from itself and where the social fabric is ragged. Violence and confrontation may well be the result: Hobbesian anarchy of the worst kind. A more gradual change is more sustainable because, above all, this is about more than inverting the power relationships embodied in existing institutions; it is about changing culture: a gentle anarchy.

And this is perhaps its greatest appeal. It is not only political transformation; it is also social. When people have agency over the affairs that matter to them, they have more life satisfaction and freedom to flourish — to live as they wish to live. Where people negotiate their affairs directly with one another, without domination or hierarchy, there is less tension, less confrontation, less of the humiliation that result from one person's — or an institution's — power over another: people get on better. Where people more intimately understand each other's needs and desires — and above all, when they are included in decisions about their lives — justice and thus stability is the more likely outcome.

****

Today, society has become angry, feckless and sometimes violent. People react with disproportionate rage when provoked. A gang of kids severely beat another child on the streets of a quaint Victorian seaside town where I once lived. In Hexham, a rural town in Northumberland, one teenager stabbed another to death; in London, where I now live, stabbings, often of teenagers, are an almost weekly and barely noted occurrence. The rage and hatred of the internet is for all to witness.

Measures of loneliness are at all-time highs.[1] Why, when according to the capitalist credo, life is supposed to be better?

Mass media abounds with stories of what will happen come the collapse, whether by flood, drought or alien invasion. In all cases, dystopia is the result, a Hobbesian war of all against all — marauding gangs compete for power and scarce resources, using whatever weaponry comes to hand (it's striking that their guns always seem to have plenty of ammunition, their cars enough petrol). Anarchy of the worst kind. Perhaps we are subliminally reassured that things could be so much worse than our current state; it is a way, of course, of lulling ourselves into apathy over the status quo. It is also sustaining a myth. But these myths, of course, secretly perpetuate a negative view of society and, indeed, of each other: that we are not to be trusted without the authority of the state to keep us in line.

The climate crisis has given a whole new lease on life to this dystopian genre. There is now the prospect, and it is a real one, of food running out or widescale floods, reviving the speculation that we are only 'nine meals from anarchy'[**] — of the most violent kind. Some are already predicting collapse of the economy and indeed of society much sooner than once anticipated.

It cannot be ruled out and the science is dismal (we shall return to this). There will be more Hurricane Sandys. In 2023, temperatures hit an unprecedented 40°C in London. There were fires in east London. Predictions suggest a substantial chunk of the city will be regularly under water as soon as 2050. There is more and more flooding across the country, and the world. Pakistan saw a full two-thirds of its habitable land flooded. And it will persist and get worse. Central government is

---

[1] Thirty years ago, 55% of men reported having at least six close friends. In 2022, only 27% of men had six or more close friends. Fifteen percent of men have no close friendships at all, a fivefold increase since 1990. Source: American Perspectives Survey, Survey Center on American Life (May 2021).

[**] Writing for *Cosmopolitan* in 1906, the American lawyer, journalist and short-story writer Alfred Henry Lewis observed: 'There are only nine meals between mankind and anarchy'. Perhaps unsurprisingly, it was a lawyer who predicted chaos without the rule of law.

by all accounts not prepared. More and more flood defences are in disrepair in the UK, just as they become more necessary.[61] I would be sorry that natural disaster be the trigger for self-organised democracy and community action, but that may prove to be the case. As global heating threatens food supplies, power cuts and rising waters, it's obvious that bottom-up, networked communities, where people are more enmeshed together, will be more robust than a fragile top-down hierarchy, where a few take decisions for the many. I fear we have already entered an era of temperature extremes, flooding, drought and food shortages where people need to be more autonomous yet connected and thus resilient in order to survive.

My suspicion is that as one crack appears, the whole monolith might collapse. But it is deeds, not words, that will get us there.

The anarchist and revolutionary Mikhail Bakunin said that 'we must spread our principles, not with words but with deeds, for this is the most popular, the most potent, and the most irresistible form of propaganda'.[62] The rule for the most effective political action is an echo of a crucial rule of theatre: show don't tell. Plant a flag and others will follow.

For Gustav Landauer, 'propaganda of the deed' comprised the construction of social forms and communities which, in turn, would inspire others to transform society. If the state was merely a set of relationships, as he believed, the solution was to establish a new set of relations between each other: the system was not something that 'one can smash in order to destroy. The state is a relationship between human beings ... one destroys it by entering into other relationships'.[63] It is a maxim that should also be invoked in a place of everyday domination, humiliation and indeed our very dehumanisation.

7
Generative Cooperatives

I N 2020, I stepped down after spending sixteen years running an NGO that I founded, Independent Diplomat. I then worked for a private consultancy and other NGOs. Needless to say, I found the transition to being told what to do and how to behave a difficult one, not least because of what it revealed *post hoc* about my own conduct as a manager.

The private consultancy, like the NGO, preached the language of equality. The boss was fond of saying that his company operated non-hierarchically and that everyone contributed on an equal basis. Rather foolishly, I took him at his word, sometimes politely contradicting his views on the subject we were researching and once, most self destructively, calling his attention to the fact that in meetings with our client, where often as many as twenty people were present, he and the client's boss were the only two who seemed permitted to speak. Everyone else was supposed to listen deferentially to the two big bosses. I pointed out that this was not conducive to a rich and productive discussion.

It won't surprise the reader to learn that my contract was not extended when it expired. I was told that I didn't fit in with the organisation's ethos of 'teamwork'. The experience of being fired was one of the more humiliating of my life. It still pains me when I recall it years later.

Nor will it surprise the reader to learn that the NGO wasn't much better. There the hierarchical reality of the organisation was camouflaged in the language of 'values'. The NGO held repeated collective meetings on the organisation's supposed values, such as equality, diversity and inclusion during 'values week'. Not one of these declared values was in fact respected despite the forced atmosphere of 'fun' and 'teamwork' expressed through jokey staff exercises on our secret skills like dancing or sharing cat photographs. Equality was manifested in the fact that it was the head of the organisation who made the ultimate decisions on the others' salaries and work, and indeed, what the organisation worked on. I didn't last long there either.

Both experiences were life low points. Both were profoundly depressing. And of course such experiences are routine for most people. I realised, to my distress, that as boss of my own NGO, I too had preached a good line about non-hierarchy and values while, in fact, presiding over a reality whereby others were highly incentivised to agree with me because I had power over their pay and terms, and indeed, their employment (they were equally incentivised to laugh at my jokes). I fired several people. In the US, where the organisation was headquartered, firing someone also means taking away their health insurance, plunging them into a desperate situation where they must pay exorbitant health costs themselves. So dismissal is a double blow. I once had to fire a man whose wife was receiving treatment for cancer on his employer-provided health insurance. The sacking itself was one of the most painful experiences of my working life, though doubtless worse for the poor man I was firing. His eyes bulged in alarm when I delivered the blow. (I justified it to myself that it was either him or us, given how damaging his conduct was.) And of course it is this unadmitted fear of losing health insurance, and with it bodily security, that only deepens the power imbalance between employer and employee. Invading our very bodies, the coercion could hardly bite deeper.

In the old days, bosses were bosses, and hierarchy was overt, stated in job titles and the size of one's office. Today, it's much more confusing. Everyone works in collective spaces with equal desk space, with bowls of fruit and bouncy balls or in equally sized boxes on video calls. Power is smilingly concealed behind confusing job titles and earnest declarations of the rejection of power, in fact deepening the humiliation as we are all forced to go along with the charade, grinning like idiots as we repeat the mantras of teamwork, 'ownership' and collegiality while secretly fearing the sack. And of course it is worse for those traditionally — and still today — often marginalised in the workplace, women and people of colour. There the power imbalance is only exacerbated by the disguised prejudices against them, the micro-aggressions, subtle discrimination and the drip-drip-drip of institutionalised bias.

In the essay 'What is Human Becomes Animal', from his *Economic and Philosophic Manuscripts of 1844*, Karl Marx described the alienation of work in bleak terms, alleging that work made us less than human, and indeed nothing more than animals. Marx got to the heart of what work is about. It is being paid to do something you would not otherwise do. For Marx, to be made to do something you would not otherwise do is to become less than human, because the fully fledged human is free to choose. To work is to be made less than human; it is therefore to be made animal.

I certainly didn't feel like an animal when I was collaborating in the ghastly fake culture of the workplace, whether the NGO or the private consultancy. But I equally didn't feel myself. Every morning, I had to gee myself up for the Zoom meetings and morning 'check in', pretending that I was continually enthused about the topic of my work, in the NGO the riveting subject of steel decarbonisation. And of course losing my salary was a terrific blow, casting my family into deep worry about paying the mortgage.

It's even more confusing because contemporary culture demands that we seek fulfilment at work, that somehow it be the expression of our deepest wishes for creativity and accomplishment. For most of us, this is a myth, but a myth that suits the purposes of capitalism, because it obscures the reality that we are spending a great deal of time doing things we wouldn't otherwise want to do. Being animals, as Marx would have it.

The two principal expressions of power in the workplace are hierarchy and money. As wage inequality has grown, so has the differential of power. Today, the average CEO of a FTSE 100 company earns eighty-six times the average employee's salary (in the US, the disparity is an incredible 354:1 for CEO pay relative to unskilled workers). This disparity shows no signs of reducing anytime soon, while wealth disparity has accelerated even faster (illustrating Thomas Piketty's analysis about how returns on capital exceed those on labour). And it seems that technological innovation is increasing these inequalities. The US and UK are, in reality, societies of mostly poor people with some very rich people.[*] This is directly contrary to popular desire, where surveys across forty countries indicate that the bulk of people would prefer much lower pay differentials of 7:1 (they moreover tend to underestimate the current degree of inequality, estimating the current ratio at 30:1).[64]

Meanwhile, those lower on the food chain in a company suffer not only from less financial power but also — crucially — from less agency. Naturally, they have less say over what they do. This contributes directly to lower well-being. A recent study argued that if well-being is factored in, income inequality in the UK — already the worst in western Europe — is significantly worse than previously believed, creating a hidden "real income" gap. In a study of the British civil service, a lower ranking on the ladder of authority was a greater predictor of death from heart

---

[*] According to the latest Office for National Statistics (ONS) wealth data (to March 2022), the wealthiest 1 % of households in Great Britain had total household wealth of at least about £3.12 million, while the least wealthy 10 % had £16,500 or less. That means the richest 1 % had roughly 190 times more wealth than the bottom 10 % of households. Source: American Perspectives Survey, May 2021.

disease than commonly listed risk factors such as smoking, cholesterol or hypertension.[65] The rich live significantly longer than the poor. The current economic system fosters uncertainty and insecurity, but stress is also directly correlated with the degree of hierarchy, whether in the workplace or in social status: the less our control, the greater the stress. And needless to say, this gross inequality is exacerbated by other systemic inequalities: 'The people who do worst out of this widening gap tend to be women and ethnic minorities, and the winners tend to be white men.'[66] Employment law has given lawyers a great deal of lucrative work, but it has not changed the basic reality that the boss has the power to take away your livelihood — your very means to live. This is an awesome and terrible power, often so lightly wielded. It lies behind every otherwise innocuous request, "Would you mind taking the notes of this meeting, Linda?" and creates a constant tension, an erosion of the employee's personal sovereignty and sense of autonomy. It creates fear of the worst kind, inadmissible and subterranean, suffusing all experience at the workplace.

Meanwhile, we are ever more monitored and surveilled in the workplace. Technology now enables managers to monitor the precise amount of time a worker is at her desk or is looking at 'non-work' websites.[67] An increasing number of employees is now managed by machines, with algorithms determining their work schedule and monitoring their performance, with punishments and rewards meted out by computed calculation. One software company goes as far as to track employees' keystrokes in order to gauge how committed they are to the company. In many jobs, there is little distinction between a human and machine manager, with the decisions of both determined only by data, not by more humane instincts — again, the immeasurable that, in fact, make up the content of what it is to be human. The human individual has been turned into a thing.

The heart of the matter, and the source of our crisis, both for ourselves and for the planet, is agency, or rather, the lack of it. The ultimate power in the company is the owner, whether the shareholder, to whom the board and CEO are accountable, or the private owner.

The obvious solution is to equalise ownership: give every worker a share, perhaps even every customer too: the cooperative.

Setting up a cooperative is rather different from the hackneyed hero's story of the lone entrepreneur with the brilliant innovation that they build in their garage (if you have one). For one thing, co-ops benefit from the wisdom — and will — of the many. Someone I know from the Occupy days in New York City, Erik Forman, described to me how three people — Erik, a driver and a former Uber employee — built a drivers' cooperative in New York City as 'bricolage' — pulling bits and pieces from other places.

Referring to the exploitation drivers were experiencing while working for Uber or Lyft, Erik commented:

I've never seen this hunger for change that exists with drivers. Every single transaction reveals exploitation. They feel like a way to regain control is to have control and ownership over the platform.[68] Most companies start with financial capital, he commented, but the Drivers Cooperative started with human capital, otherwise known as people, drivers who found that Uber's promises of independence and financial success were proving hollow in the face of low fares and escalating costs. Today, the Drivers Cooperative has seven thousand owner-drivers and is the largest provider of rides for people with disabilities in the city. Raising money wasn't easy (and this is one of the frequent drawbacks critics mention of cooperatives), but they did it by taking loans and crowd funding. The drivers themselves lent money to their company, today returning them 11% on the dollar.

But the Drivers Cooperative faces deeper systemic challenges which illustrate the grip that profit-maximising companies have over the political system. Uber has pursued a monopoly-seeking model whereby, initially financed by venture capital, it invades a market by under-pricing its services in order to destroy the competition. Then, once competitors are annihilated, Uber racks up its prices to maximise its profits. Hubert Horan has been a meticulous analyst of Uber and notes that '[t]oday, Uber is offering much worse service at much higher prices than the traditional taxi industry that it had 'disrupted' ... This is a crappy business', Horan is quoted as saying, '[and t]he only way Uber has ever improved its profit margins is by screwing drivers'. In India, two driver-owners committed suicide after Uber lowered its rates for drivers.[69] You don't need to be an economist to see how this disadvantages both the drivers and the consumers — us — allegedly the ultimate beneficiary of capitalist competition but, in reality, the target for maximum extraction of money.

The cliché of cooperatives is that of a small, local grocery store owned by its employees. Supposed economic experts, like Larry Summers, the former Secretary of the Treasury in the Clinton administration, argue that co-ops cannot expand because they cannot get investment. But Spain's Mondragon Corporation, a kind of cooperative network of co-ops, proves that co-ops don't have to be small. Mondragon is Spain's seventh largest company.

Cooperatives are some of the longest-lasting companies. Worker-owned ventures tend to operate on a longer-term perspective, because workers consider their lifetime, not just this quarter's profit report. In good times, members share the profits; In harder times, the cooperatives support one another and reallocate workers and funds among themselves to preserve jobs. The aim is employment maximisation and worker benefit maximisation rather than profit maximisation.[70] All members of the co-op, from the most junior to senior, have equal votes. During the COVID pandemic, workers at many Mondragon co-ops voted to reduce their own salaries or hours temporarily until the economy recovered.

Cooperatives can also be the foundation of community wealth building. Local councils can choose to spend their money locally, preferencing commonly owned businesses rather than more typical for-profit ventures. 'Anchor' institutions, such as hospitals and schools, can make the same choice. In Preston, UK, local contracting, worker cooperatives, and investment in local businesses have transformed the city's economy. This community wealth building supports political and economic democracy, better pay and local control over wealth, creating a more equitable and sustainable economy.[71] It is the antithesis of the lowest-wage-possible employers of the dominant current capitalist model.

Economic agency is as essential to liberty as political agency. You cannot be free without either. You may work in a cooperatively owned company where you have a stake and a say but without political agency; you will remain far from free. Moreover, the cooperative will itself be subject to laws you have no part in deciding.

Economic empowerment plays into political empowerment. Inspired by Mondragon, in Jackson, Mississippi, the Black majority city in the Deep South, local activists are building a cooperative economy, piece by piece, business by business. Their vision is comprehensively political, social and economic. A network of independent but connected democratic institutions that empower workers and citizens, particularly to address the needs of poor, unemployed Black and Latino residents. An assembly is convened to discuss issues raised by inhabitants, and solutions are found locally. The new dispensation, like Mondragon, is a conglomerate of cooperative businesses, each supporting the others. The members of 'Cooperation Jackson' don't call themselves anarchists, but their ideas of democratic employee ownership and radically inclusive self-government are consistent with this tradition. Labels matter less than the practice.

Without shared ownership — and thus without equal agency over our economic, as well as social and political lives — no one is truly free.

But what happens if you're already working in a typical share-held or privately owned company? When you don't have the freedom to set up your own cooperative or the kind of owners who are willing to hand over ownership to the workers?

In a place I worked at recently, a very 'right-thinking' climate think-tank, it was striking that the management, of which I was part, took on the persona of the institution, quick to dismiss the demands of junior workers for pay rises and clarity about promotion, and instead discussed methods to suppress dissent. In one example, the organisation's collective 'retreat' was expressly designed to avoid what one manager called 'whinging' from the staff; instead, sessions would focus on the dreaded 'organisational values' and 'creativity' with the aim of making the event 'more enjoyable' (for whom, one wonders). This was paradoxical given that members of the management actually shared the same concerns over pay and conditions. But somehow these interests are suppressed as the institutional interest prevails. Hierarchy clearly appeals to people's sense of importance and self-worth. 'Boss' thinking is, unfortunately, contagious.

It's interesting how often management, even though it shares the interests of the workers, starts to embody the interests of the owners. It is a natural function of institutions that those who run them start to ape the interests of the institution — minimising costs, maximising profit — rather than their own. This is why, in class terms, the middle class of management is often the biggest obstacle to change.

Modern management is highly skilled at offering venues for 'listening' or 'consultation'. An NGO I worked at set up an 'employees' forum' for concerns to be vented, usually pointlessly. These are subtle modes to dissipate and, ultimately, extinguish the energy for justice and change. Only through ownership is power genuinely shared, where management is by consent and — ideally — consensus, not by imposition and the ultimate coercion of the sack.

Cooperatives are still little known and often misunderstood. Their value as enduring models of shared agency and ownership is not generally recognised, even though cooperatives have historically enjoyed much greater longevity than privately held companies. They also flourish in an eco-system with other cooperatives, so there will be a catalytic effect once the movement gathers momentum.

In the current eco-system dominated by private models of ownership, the few disadvantages of cooperatives are foregrounded. One alleged disadvantage is the difficulty of cooperatives in raising investment funds — the so-called 'capital conundrum'. Private companies can get funds by offering shares to potential investors, which would then give a return. Cooperatives can also attract funds by offering bonds with either fixed or variable rates of return. Community shares are another option. They can also take on other forms of debt. Cooperatives can offer digital tokens as repositories of value, for instance in return for a contribution in building the cooperative, tokens which can then be used as means of exchange with others involved or for purchases from the cooperative.[72] More interesting, however, is why this is so often raised as a problem. It reveals the mindset that growth is all important and trumps the interests of employees. We will see that at a macro, economy-wide level, growth — or more precisely, unequally shared growth — is not all it's cracked up to be, and it is indeed one of the problems of the current dispensation because the planet cannot sustain the type of growth currently promoted. But at the company level, the growth imperative is a rarely questioned trope of modern micro-economic and cultural thinking. What if we regarded companies instead as guardians of the interests of their employees and customers, and indeed, the environment rather than as enterprises whose priority is profit alone? This does not mean that profit and competitiveness are neglected; the partnership John Lewis has been a successful company for over a century in the most competitive of markets, retail. These imperatives just take their place alongside the other equally important imperatives of real people and the planet: companies that are genuine in attending to the interests and needs of their stakeholders because it is built into their very structure and legal identity ('stakeholder capitalism' is merely voluntary).

Another cliché that supposedly justifies the privately owned model is that only profit-driven companies are motivated to innovate, driven to make more money. Again, this is simply not true. Open source — where discoveries and ideas are transparently shared in the community — has been demonstrated to lead to faster scientific progress than the siloed model of private profit-led innovation. Indeed, there is evidence that in the current profit-led private model innovation is slowing down. The DeSci movement, for instance, aims to facilitate collaboration and release science from the straitjacket of current funding models, ultimately to advance discovery, research and innovation. DeSci is pursuing self-sustaining scientific ecosystems, with communities the new 'shareholders' of scientific knowledge. OpenScience meanwhile seeks the release of scientific research and data from behind private ownership and paywalls. These movements see science and knowledge as a public good, whose practices and structures need to promote sharing and accessibility in order to maximise progress. Openness and transparency rather than proprietary and closed.

Some claim that inequality itself spurs innovation. The argument goes that without the incentive to increase relative income or wealth, entrepreneurs will not be driven to develop new products or services. This argument is easily dismissed. Historically, inequality does not correlate with growth. Growth is not a primary indicator of productivity and innovation. Unequal societies do not grow faster than more equal societies. Indeed, the very opposite may be true. One study shows that investors benefit when they pay employees more generously. Over a three-year period, companies that invested in their employees were associated with a 4% higher return on invested capital compared to competitors who did not.[73] Of course, a traditional method to secure greater workers' rights and benefits is through the trades union. Union membership has however declined in the modern economy. Unions were much more powerful in the days of 'heavy', large-scale industry with discrete bodies of workers of common interests, like coal or steel workers. But as these industries have declined in the West, outcompeted by the industries of the likes of China and India, so have the unions diminished.

But there are signs of a revival. As young people are realising that the dream of a steady job, predictable career and decent pay is evaporating, they are turning to unions. There is evidence of middle-class mobilisation — young, educated people both joining unions and recruiting for them. In the US, one Rhodes scholar ignored the traditional route of entering a high-status, high-pay profession and instead went to work for Starbucks in order to help the unionisation effort.[74] Notably, she and her fellow workers did not dislike their workplace, but chose to unionise because it gave collective power to their individual voices and a coherent mechanism to discuss their needs and concerns. In Starbucks, the CEO has vigorously opposed unionisation because, he alleges, it impedes that very conversation (troublingly, he has publicly mooted running for President).[75] Starbucks the company has organised against unionisation, deploying managers to lobby staff against voting for a union. His covert interests are self-evident.

In the past, unions were often regarded as the engines of broader change. Anarcho-syndicalism is a school of thought that sees the union as the wellspring of political organisation and power, that industrial unions should be the main vehicle to end the wage system and capitalism itself. Anarcho-syndicalism has a rich history. Perhaps its heyday was the Spanish revolution in 1936 when the unions were the prime movers in establishing an anarchist society. Unions were crucial in spreading the ideas of anarchism and educating workers in the years preceding the revolution. Indeed, the unions were important vehicles of military mobilisation in the fight against fascism; an image of the united front of the National Confederation of Workers (CNT) in alliance with the National Anarchist Federation hangs (FAI) on my wall.

My preferred model of change is an inclusive one, where all are convinced of the virtues of a new economic and political settlement. Persuasion rather than coercion. But the vision of the anarcho-syndicalists remains relevant: the empowerment of the employee or worker. Unions can be the vehicle not only for improvements in wages and terms and conditions in specific workplaces or companies. They can also be the avenue for campaigns and new behaviours in terms of racism and sexism. Unions can help set up housing cooperatives and networks of new cooperative businesses by providing finance and action. In other words, they can be instigators and facilitators of broader political and economic change.[76] There is one clear requirement: that unions embody the type of democracy they wish to see instituted, or in other words, egalitarian, inclusive and participatory. There is an inevitable tendency for long-lived institutions, such as unions, to develop hierarchies and cadres of officials who run the institutions in their own interests. Likewise, they can often start to embody and replicate deep-seated and broader imbalances, already manifested in society at large, over race and gender, for instance.

This is a deep-seated characteristic of all institutions: that in the long run and without corrective strategies, they will develop their own sets of interests which diverge from their declared ostensible purpose, in this case the inclusive representation of workers. The only way truly to avoid this is to run unions according to inclusive, participatory practice — facilitated meetings — where union representatives, who are ideally temporary, only represent decisions made by these meetings. The techniques of so-called 'Sociocracy' offer well-proven methods to ensure workplace democracy: an equal voice for all.

Indeed, we need to excavate a deeper layer of what's going on in organisations. The institution where people work, of course, is often much more to its employees and other associates than merely a source of wages and benefits. It is how its employees spend much of their lives. It is thus supposed to be an expression of meaning and even identity — how we see ourselves as people, individual and together. It is no surprise that the most heavily controlled, hierarchical and ordered forms of organisation (for instance, the army) has fetishised identity the most, through uniforms, insignia and the celebration of tradition.

In turn, the promotion of institutional identity comes at the price of the individual's own separate identity. We all know soldiers who identify themselves as, above all, soldiers or members of their regiment or unit. I do not decry their choice, but note the transaction. In becoming a diplomat, a profession with its own distinct culture and codes, I sacrificed my own identity. But more broadly, the proliferation of institutions as organising units of our existence and, indeed, often the means of our survival must be seen as a broader erosion of our individuality and freedom of self-expression.

The disappearance of the suit and tie in the office has only been replaced by other symbols of corporate belonging and obedience, the 'casual' clothes of shirts and chinos, the constant 'positive attitude' required in the modern workplace, which in its own way constitutes a much more insidious version of mind control than the pin-striped suit and bowler hat. In JP Morgan Chase, the employees at the counter of the high-street bank are forced to wear identical blue shirts, marked with an embroidered Chase insignia, almost like cattle branded with their owner's initials. The chief executive, Jamie Dimon, is not so obliged.

Institutions are thus expressive of particular notions of what it is to be human. The institution embodies the economic needs and identities of its employees, but it is a top-down process: the market-driven requirements of the company dictate everything else, from the terms of employment to the culture of the office. Be aware that the true aims of an organisation are invariably concealed within the disguises of 'mission statements' or corporate goals: the secret, inadmissible but over-riding goal is always the institution's self-perpetuation. Never does an institution propose its own abolition.

Thus are our lives shaped and directed. Thus is our individuality suppressed. Thus is our humanity diminished.

****

Thomas Piketty has told us that the main driver of current inequality is that growth increases faster than wages; wealth inequality is accelerating faster than income inequality. The current dispensation is one where workers are systematically exploited by capital. The returns on labour are not given to the workers but to the owners. If you own shares in a successful company, you will enjoy much greater returns in terms of dividends and share-price rises than the workers who make it happen. This is one of the main drivers of wealth inequality (today, automation and technology are the others). We need to equalise the relationship between capital and labour: the only means is through the transfer of ownership itself, not to the state but to the worker-employee. If we do this, company by company, workplace by workplace, then a broader society-wide change will come into being.

Inevitably, forcing this transfer involves confrontation. The owners of capital will not give up their advantages lightly. But in truth, it is labour that enjoys the power, if only workers would realise it. Without them and their consent, as we have seen, the system ceases to function (and consumers, too, enjoy a certain power: the act of purchase is their vote). This may require strikes. It may require other manifestations of worker power, such as works to rule. There are many ways to threaten and actualise the withdrawal of consent.

Occupation is one method. A notable example was the occupation of the Zanon ceramics factory in Argentina in 2001, part of the 'recovered factories' movement, which began when the owner attempted to lock out the existing workforce in order to replace them with a more docile staff — they were owed large amounts of back pay. The owner was well-connected in national and local politics, and had been a sympathiser of Argentina's military junta. In desperation to keep their jobs, the Zanon workforce occupied the factory. Interestingly, they organised themselves spontaneously through worker assemblies rather than through their union, which was corrupt and in cahoots with the employer. After camping at the factory for many weeks without pay, the workers eventually resumed production. One justification for their action was that the factory was built with public funds, including from the World Bank. The renamed factory became a successful worker-owned cooperative which substantially increased its workforce. It also built a local health clinic and in other ways contributes to the local society. Meanwhile, the regional government continues to represent the owner's interest, seeking to recoup loans for which he was the beneficiary. It also refuses to buy the factory's product.[77] The Zanon transformation was part of a much wider movement of worker takeovers in Argentina. The worker-recovered enterprise movement was a reaction to the country's economic depression and financial collapse. The movement involved the non-violent occupation of hundreds of closed factories by thousands of former workers in an attempt to reclaim their sources of employment and to push for self-ownership. There was a shared vision of solidarity, embodied in the establishment of worker-owned cooperative enterprises (*empresas recuperadas por sus trabajadores,* or ERT), based on horizontal authority, collective decision-making, and shared returns.[78] The act of occupation was central to achieving the movement's goals: by occupying and, in some cases, re-starting production, workers forced former employers to negotiate.

But there is something more here. Modern culture celebrates the notion of work, that we should be always busy, making 'more' of ourselves and, of course, maximising our money. But is this what we were really put on the planet to do? Is it what we want to do? Well, like so much of what we're discovering here, we don't really know because we've never tried.

To escape the tyranny of the workplace, it has always been an option simply to spend less time there or to leave it altogether. This is the motive of the Lying Flat movement in China where young people have been rejecting the Stakhanovite[†] model of Chinese capitalism and its '996' culture (twelve hours a day, six days a week) in order to work as little as possible. The same trend is perceptible in the US, that cradle of capitalism:

For ten years, Doreen Ford worked in retail stores in Boston and hated it. So at the suggestion of her grandmother, she gave up her job and looked to exploit her love of dogs to make ends meet. Doreen now walks dogs part-time. She has not held a traditional job since 2017. She says she's never been happier. Quoted in the *Financial Times,* she said, 'Usually, at best, [working was] pointless, and at worst it was degrading, humiliating and exploitative'.

'I think there's a lot of positions that just don't make any sense, that do not have to exist', Doreen said. 'You're just pushing around papers for no good reason. It doesn't really help anybody'.[79] Reporting

---

[†]   The Stakhanovites was a government-ordained propaganda movement in the Soviet bloc which celebrated the superhuman accomplishments of individual workers such as Alexey Stakhanov, who mined vast quantities of coal per shift by many multiples greater than the average.

on the impact of the anti-work movement, Goldman Sachs warned that it posed a 'long run risk' to labour force participation. A risk to whom, one wonders.

This is the kind of subterranean trend that might fail to attract headlines but can in fact fundamentally change the dynamics of labour. For every worker who drops out of the conventional job market will push wages higher for those who remain, as labour supply drops. So there is a benefit to others, not only to oneself, by 'lying flat'.

It's no surprise that polls demonstrate that most people would prefer to work less. There is, moreover, a powerful ecological argument. Working less is consistent with the degrowth — or rather deGreed — necessary to keep the planet within its ecological boundaries. We need to produce sufficient public services and goods for public well-being. We do not need SUVs, fast fashion and the arms industry — and workers with true agency in their workplaces do not want to produce these things. This implies less overall production, requiring less labour. So it's possible to imagine an economy that is producing sufficient goods for everyone's well-being, where time, energy and resources are not wasted on benefit-less industry, but where everyone has a job — when employment is prioritised over profit — and actually, overall, work less. Some see central government providing this guarantee: I prefer to see it coming as a natural outcome of the cooperative type of business. Models show that in a post-growth global economy, where the rich countries produce less, the Paris target of 1.5°C temperature rise becomes once again plausible.

Perhaps the problem is not so much work in-itself but the jobs that we are made to do. Few argue that we should avoid work so that others should do it instead. What we resist is the alienating, exploitative and humiliating nature of many current workplaces. If we were working towards an ideal — a place that is inclusive, where people feel valued and where they can express themselves fully — I doubt that people would resist work *per se*. It seems self-evident, therefore, that the only workplace where such conditions can exist is where workers have agency, which in turn requires that they have power. Equality maximises agency. Equality of power requires equality of ownership.

Looking at more extreme forms of the exertion of power over others, the historian Robin D.G. Kelley has written of the Black 'anti-work' movement which sought to resist the racism and exploitation of America's Jim Crow South through the established tactic of withdrawal of labour and also other creative tactics. For the enslaved and the discriminated against, the workplace was a major locus of their oppression. Kelley argues that Black anti-work politics emerged as a response to the harsh realities of racialised labour exploitation. African Americans have long been stereotyped as 'lazy' or 'shiftless', which paradoxically coexisted with their exploitation for hard labour.

Kelley identifies various forms of Black anti-work resistance including engaging in acts of sabotage, slowdowns and theft as ways to resist exploitation and mitigate the impact of work. Some workers chose to participate in the informal economy, including both legal and illegal activities, as an alternative to traditional wage labour. And some Black workers avoided low-wage labour by starting their own enterprises. Today, those politics of resistance to wage and thus to very personal exploitation can be seen in workplaces such as the Evergreen Cooperative Laundry in Cleveland, Ohio, which is 90% owned by its workers. It aims not only to flourish as a business but also to build wealth and careers for its owner-workers. In Detroit, new cultures of cooperative business and community wealth are flourishing. It is a mistake to regard cooperatives as merely vehicles for shared ownership. They are much more than that. They can also be delivery mechanisms for personal and social freedom, where different values govern lives rather than the arid and inhuman calculus of profit.

In his seminal 1932 essay, 'In Praise of Idleness', Bertrand Russell attacks the modern conception of work. He argued that society places too much emphasis on work, often to the detriment of personal fulfilment and social progress. In other words, conventional work is in fact holding back the necessary transformation of society. Belief in the virtue of hard work is largely a product of the industrial revolution and serves to maintain the existing social order. Russell criticised the capitalist system for creating unnecessary work and perpetuating inequality. He argued that technological advancements should lead to reduced working hours for all rather than unemployment for some and overwork for others, which is of course exactly what we see today. For Russell, leisure time was vital to encourage personal growth, creativity and society's progress. Many of humanity's greatest achievements in science, philosophy and the arts have come from people with ample leisure time (and often expensive educations). With more leisure time, Russell argued, society would be more culturally rich and intellectually vibrant, less prone to conflict and social unrest, more equitable with a fairer distribution of work and resources, better equipped to address social and environmental issues.

****

Our culture is obsessed with being productive: each of us has to have a purpose, ideally measured in output and accomplishment, a fortune, a new app or a new company. We have internalised this idea so that the boss now lives inside us. As Byung-Chul Han puts it, we are 'master and slave in one. Even class struggle has transformed into an inner struggle against oneself'.[80] The ancient practice of Daoism may have something to teach us. Meaning and purpose may be found not in their pursuit but in giving them up (just as we gain personal power by giving up power over others). In the ancient Daoist masterpiece, the *Zhuang*, it is suggested that we should not always aim to be useful. *Zhuangzi* argued that escaping the notion of usefulness would help us live happier, more fulfilling lives:[81]

By letting go of our concern over whether we (or things in our lives) are useful, we can become happier by being more in line with nature, we can celebrate the wondrous diversity and difference of people and of things as good in their own right, without thinking of some bottom line. You are not a mere tool, but a glorious part of a wild and diverse Universe.[82] We return to the — crucial — means-end distinction, a cardinal element of anarchist thinking (perhaps first expressed by the Daoists). If work is a means to leisure and liberty, why not engage in leisure and liberty without work? Why suffer present hardship in order to gain an uncertain future benefit? According to Zhuangzei, we don't really need to strive to strike a balance between usefulness and uselessness. We need to reject the idea of use altogether. Societies based on usefulness do not make us happier or more in harmony with nature.'[83] This is hard to take on board when we are so brainwashed by the gods of production and productivity, endlessly badgered to make more of ourselves, to get up earlier and work harder. Efficiency is vaunted, and things and people are measured by their usefulness: I heard a defender of refugees argue that refugees are economically valuable before he used the humanitarian argument for asylum, a classic case of neo-classical utilitarianism. Even the desperate fleeing from oppression and human misery must first prove their economic worth. You can see insidious utilitarianism, too, in the argument against arts education, that instead subjects like computing or business studies should be promoted in their place. The arts are not 'useful'. People have become tools.

This seems a profoundly anti-human argument. The arts are the realm of the ineffable, wherein, as we have seen, there may reside what is most important — and certainly most beautiful — to humankind. At funerals, we do not read spreadsheets but poetry. We do not recite company mottos; we sing hymns.

Are the Daoists right? Is doing less the pathway to fulfilment and happiness? We can test this hypothesis only by experiencing it — less work or, at least, less work of the humiliating and pointless kind. And again, we come up to the deeper spiritual question: How should we spend our lives? What indeed is it all for? It's strange that deep interrogation of political or economic structures ultimately keeps bumping up against this question.

The irony of so many contemporary companies, businesses and, yes, NGOs is that the bosses cling on to the hierarchical power that they 'enjoy'. A greater flourishing is available for them and for those they currently 'manage', aka command, if they were to give it up. Being the boss humiliated and constrained me within prescribed behaviours that were ultimately inhuman. Being bossed imposed different constraints — and humiliations. In both situations, I was less than what I could truly be. I am less than human. I am animal.

8
After Consumerism

OR MONTHS before my fiftieth birthday, I dropped repeated hints to my long-suffering wife that I wanted a watch for my birthday. I even told her what type of watch I wanted, an expensive Swiss watch called an IWC pilot's watch, and I sent her the link to buy it. I would gaze longingly at the watch on the internet. IWC was made for suckers like me. Its site included a video of vintage aircraft swooping and soaring: the watch was designed to evoke the dials and knobs of a mid twentieth-century aircraft. I felt that such a watch not only conjured my childhood piloting fantasies and love of aircraft but also was appropriate for a man of my age and accomplishments. Serious people had watches like this.

So I was disappointed when my birthday came around and she presented me with my gift. I could see from the wrapping that it was a watch case. My heart lifted, but as I unwrapped it, it sank when I saw that it wasn't the IWC I had wanted but a much cheaper manufacturer. 'Sorry, darling', my wife had said, 'but the other watch was just too expensive'. And of course she was entirely right. There was no way we could afford the IWC watch which cost thousands of pounds. It was ridiculous of me to think so. 'But this watch really suits you', she commented as I tried it on.

The watch is still on my wrist, years later, though battered and scratched after a bike accident in New York City. I have come to treasure this watch and regard it lovingly. Why? Because she gave it to me. Even its scratches remind me of how I enjoyed my bike ride back from my daughter's school, spinning along over my favourite bridge in the city, the Williamsburg Bridge.

What makes the watch so valuable to me is that it is imbued with something far beyond its materiality and ability to tell the time (it's a quartz, which are much more accurate than fancy handmade mechanical watches). It carries the memories of the moment she gave it to me, the birthday celebrations she had organised for me, a wonderful day, and my profound connection to this person, the love of my life. Even now, when I think of it, tears spring to my eyes.

****

When I was a boy, I used to go fishing to find peace and solitude. I learned to fly fish, a sport where the angler uses a bait of a hook dressed up to look like a tiny insect that the fish like to eat. The angler must 'present' the fly to the fish by delicately casting his line onto the water so as to replicate the behaviour of the insect as it lands upon the water's surface. It is a gentle, quiet art. Fly fishing produced in me a kind of mesmerism where I became at one with my watery surroundings, a lake or a river, watching its rhythms and trying to sense the movement of the fish. On one blissful occasion, I was fishing a bend in the River Exe in west Somerset, when I looked up to see an otter gambolling along the river bank opposite me. On another occasion, this time in Montana in America's west, I was standing ankle-deep in a slow-flowing river. I heard a slight splash behind me and turned to see a small deer only a few yards away. We both stopped and looked at each other, and the deer went on its way. These were some of the most beautiful moments of my life.

Rachel Carson, author of the seminal environmental text, *Silent Spring*, found a deep sense of meaning and rhythm in nature:

> There is symbolic as well as actual beauty in the migration of the birds, the ebb and flow of the tides, the folded bud ready for the spring. There is something infinitely healing in the repeated refrains of nature — the assurance that dawn comes after night, and spring after the winter.[84]

That assurance is now under grave threat. I did not think about whether the scenes of my boyhood would endure, whether the river would stop flowing. I thought that nature was as enduring as a mountain. I made no connection between the nature I enjoyed and my own impact upon it — the food I ate or the emissions from the aircraft that flew me to Montana. These were distinct and separated phenomena. It would not have occurred to me to think that the nature I so loved was slowly but surely being destroyed.

I am lucky enough to look out over the sea as I write this book. It's a tranquil view of the Conwy estuary as it flows into the Irish Sea. But the view conceals menace. Already, waves splash the windows during storms. Within a few decades, the sea will have risen enough to make my house uninhabitable. The streets by the beach in the village where I live will all soon be underwater — forever.

We had assumed that nature would endure. Now it won't — at least not in its current form. This is a seismic change in our worldview and our sense of safety.

But today, the data are as terrifying as they are relentless. During the 2022 Antarctic summer, temperatures during a heat wave rose by an incredible 70°F (40°C). This has never happened since records began. Since 1970, there has been on average almost a 70% decline in the populations of mammals, birds, fish, reptiles and amphibians.

Britain has less than half its biodiversity left. Unbearably hot heat waves are now a hundred times more likely. Eleven major cities are forecast to become unlivably hot. And as the heat increases to levels that humans cannot endure, a massive migration will take place as many hundreds of millions of 'climate refugees' — a term not yet recognised in international law (thus the title carries no rights) — will move to cooler climes. They will have no choice.

I feel a great sense of fear and despair at these data. I worry deeply about how my children, let alone their children, will fare in this dangerous and uncharted world.

Until recently, I worked for a climate 'think-tank' that is attempting to advance the fight against climate change. Like many NGOs it follows a kind of campaign model whereby it seeks to persuade governments to be more progressive and ambitious, a kind of incrementalism.

But there are deep tensions within the organisation. The fact is that this approach is failing. I worked to study and shape international policy to mitigate climate change — the COPs, the UN climate process, etc. These processes rest on a deep belief that governments will take care of the problem.

The science is abundantly clear. They are not taking care of it. Governments are doing nothing like enough to limit warming to the supposedly 'safe' level of 1.5°C or even the far riskier 2°C. Note too that there is no scientific basis to these targets. They are the entirely arbitrary choices of collected governments at the Paris climate talks of 2016, chosen to represent the best guess of those governments of an acceptable limit to warming. The disasters that are already happening, such as the unprecedented drought of 2022 in China or the vast flooding of Pakistan, where fully a third of the habitable land was under water, demonstrate that these targets are already too conservative.

The UN-convened panel of climate scientists, the Intergovernmental Panel on Climate Change (IPCC), in their last report confirmed that current government policies to reduce greenhouse gases —

even if implemented — will lead to 2.8°C of warming. This too is a conservative view: the IPCC offers the most cautious and 'lowest common denominator' estimates of the world's climate scientists. Its conclusions have to be agreed by every UN member state, including the likes of Saudi Arabia and Russia, petro-states which are notorious for watering down climate forecasts.

A more accurate view of the true nature of climate scientists' views is to be found in a *Nature* survey which asked IPCC scientists for their private — i.e. honest — views about global warming. Six of ten IPCC scientists who responded to *Nature*'s survey believe that the world will in fact warm by at least 3°C by 2100.[85] These predictions are not idle speculation. Shockingly, just under half of these same scientists said that global warming has caused them to reconsider major life decisions, such as where to live or whether to have children. More than 60% said that they experience anxiety, grief or other distress because of concerns over climate change.

3°C would be an epic catastrophe where large tracts of Earth would be rendered uninhabitable. Sea level rise would inundate huge areas of low-lying land. This disaster would potentially end human civilisation as we know it. This is what most scientists believe is coming. According to the UN Environment Programme's 2021 Emissions Gap report, to limit global heating to 1.5°C, the world must halve greenhouse gas emissions in just eight years. This is not going to happen.

Most of us prefer not to think about these imminent horrors. I constantly oscillate between denial and dread. Why isn't there a greater sense of shared panic? There should be. But if others are not panicking, why should we? Are we no more than lemmings barrelling over the cliff edge to our doom?

A crucial driver of this denial mechanism is that governments claim that they have the major responsibility to fix it. Plenty of governments, particularly those most at risk of sea level rise or other disastrous climate events, are explicit that not enough is being done. But there are many others, like Britain's, where the governments pretend that their policies will ensure that by 2050 carbon emissions will equal the carbon removed from the atmosphere, the famous 'net zero' — notably another totally arbitrary and unscientific target.

There is a self-reinforcing circle of argument going on between the population and governments — governments want us to believe that they are fixing it, and we want to believe them. This goes to the heart of our dangerous and confusing relationship with government. Government claims to take care of our security. It's the ubiquitous 'they' again. 'They', we assume, must know what they're doing about climate. We renege on our own responsibilities, even our own consciousness, as government encourages us to do.

But the problem goes deeper than merely government policy, much as that matters.

Intriguingly, it all seems to start at the same place. What is our point? What is our goal as human beings? What do we want? Because, of course, the modern economy and government policy to facilitate it rests on one massive assumption — that what we want is more goods and services, more stuff. Growth! As we have seen earlier, this is not a safe assumption, at all. But it remains the guiding and unquestioned principle of government policy, the god to which all else is subordinated.

Things begin to fall into place. A false presumption of our own desires and objectives is propagated by an unrepresentative political system that has been co-opted by those who benefit from that false presumption — they make money from it (and indeed they seek money because it offers them the fool's gold of fulfilment and power). That false presumption is contributing to planetary destruction. It's a system.

But we have seen earlier that human desires and needs are much more varied and sometimes immaterial; above all, they seem to be about relationships, the very thing that makes us human. If these, rather than economic growth, were centred in society's objectives — and government policy — material growth would become less important (like the expensive watch I once desired). This in turn has profound implications for the planet.

Most governments are very far from abandoning the god of growth, though some, like Costa Rica and New Zealand, have begun to do so. In Britain, both government and opposition hew to the theory that growth can be 'greened', the tempting narrative that our economies can continue to grow while getting rid of greenhouse gases. This is largely to be achieved through technology, by shifting to renewable energy and electric vehicles.

Governments claim that their policies — subsidies, taxes and rules — will decarbonise the economy quickly enough to keep emissions down so that the 1.5°C target remains possible. The British government likes to hold itself up as one of the most progressive governments in the world in decarbonising its economy, an example that others should follow, a 'climate leader'.

Sceptical as I am of government in general, I would like to believe the government. I want to believe that they are decarbonising our economy fast enough and will help drag along the rest of the world toward faster decarbonisation. Of the opposition parties, only the Green Party questions this narrative. All the others maintain that green growth is possible. They take this position, not because this is what the science demands, but because it is what they think voters want to hear.

Unfortunately for all of us, it isn't true.

****

The argument that arrives at this conclusion rests on the notion of 'decoupling', namely, that growth can be achieved at the same time as reducing total emissions. The goal here is so-called 'absolute decoupling', that you can continue producing more while reducing carbon emissions to zero. In other words, as growth increases, emissions decline in *absolute* terms.

Instead, what's really happening is that growth goes up, but so do emissions, albeit more slowly: emissions decline only in *relative* terms.[*] This is called 'relative decoupling', i.e. that less carbon is being produced for every unit of production, which is progress, but it's not enough. Sometimes, economies do 'absolutely decouple' and reduce emissions overall as growth continues. But the evidence suggests that this is only temporary — for example, when Britain replaced coal-fired power stations with gas-fired power. But this gain does not endure as long as growth continues and electricity use rises in absolute terms. Jason Hickel, one of the leading thinkers in this field, concludes that 'at current rates, the countries that have achieved absolute decoupling of GDP from CO_2 will take on average more than 220 years to decarbonise'.[86] The arguments around decoupling are complex and technical, but a recent review of the available evidence came to the conclusion that there is no evidence to suggest that absolute decoupling is taking place, and moreover, there are considerable grounds for doubting that it will.[†]

There is a simple logic at work here: How is it possible to keep producing more stuff without using resources? Until every element of the supply chain is totally decarbonised, it is literally impossible to produce goods without emitting more carbon. Theoretical pathways that allow the world to keep to 1.5°C warming, promoted by the IPCC for instance, rely on both carbon capture, an unproven and expensive technology, and as yet unproven and unprecedented

---

[*] 'The validity of the green growth discourse relies on the assumption of an absolute, permanent, global, large and fast enough decoupling of economic growth from all critical environmental pressures. The literature reviewed clearly shows that there is no empirical evidence for such a decoupling currently happening ... In most cases, decoupling is relative. When absolute decoupling occurs, it is observed only during rather short periods of time, concerning only certain resources or forms of impact, for specific locations, and with very small rates of mitigation', Source: 2019 report "Decoupling Debunked: Evidence and Arguments Against Green Growth as a Sole Strategy for Sustainability," published by the European Environmental Bureau (EEB).

[†]

advances in energy technology.[87] In other words, more hope than proof.‡

Moreover, no one has successfully decoupled GDP growth with the overall material 'footprint', i.e. the consumption of all resources, including biodiversity, which remains tightly coupled to growth. We are a long way from creating a successfully 'circular' economy which recycles all the material goods, whether buildings, cars or shoes, it produces: I am not sure that this is possible. Instead, the more our economy grows, the more of the natural world it devours. This cannot go on indefinitely.

Some countries are successfully reducing their carbon emissions while continuing to grow, but the question is speed. Is it happening fast enough? And here the answer is clear. It is not. Emissions need to fall by 50% by 2030 and to zero net emissions by 2050 if there is to be any hope of keeping to the 1.5°C limit set by the Paris Agreement. As I write, emissions continue to rise. Despite the undoubted progress in decarbonisation in some countries, there is no country currently on track to achieve the Paris targets.

Techno-optimists argue that new technology will achieve absolute decoupling. Perhaps, eventually, AI will find a solution that humans cannot yet imagine. I would like to believe them too. The trouble is that the evidence, so far, isn't there. Technological change has not achieved absolute decoupling. In other words, it is not bringing emissions down fast enough.

Given its central importance of this question — essentially, will technology save us? — there is a great deal of debate. Some contend that technology is advancing at an exponential rate. A recent paper suggested that, extrapolating from historic examples of technological

---

‡ 'The voice of careful, rigorous science has spoken against the feasibility of green growth as a mitigation strategy ... But there is also another dangerous voice. It is the one of cherry-picked statements that give the illusion that developed nations have gotten green and that further economic growth is compatible with climate targets. This voice is made of vague claims and fuzzy definitions which can neither be proven true nor false. It is a pat on the back for regions, countries, and industries who use these arguments to turn a blind eye to the necessary degrowth of their economic activities'. Source: *Decoupling in the IPCC AR6 WGIII*, Timothée Parrique.

take-up, the rate of take-up of renewable energy technologies would be far faster — and far cheaper — than hitherto predicted.[88] But notably, both of these views are hypothetical. The hard data of recent technological advance point to a slower and not exponential progression. One paper, for instance, measured the growth in the number of patents as an indicator of progress.[89] It did not find exponential growth. It also found that progress is variously distributed across technologies. The fastest growth was in software development, when in fact what we need is progress in *hardware* — the machines that produce energy and products, electricity and steel or that can remove carbon from the atmosphere. Meanwhile, for every 'eco-innovation' that comes along, even more patents are being filed for traditional or extractive technologies. And so far, AI is not the salvation: its deployment is instead massively increasing energy consumption.

Interestingly, a group of scientists who have come to this conclusion is the IPCC, the UN's own climate monitor. Here, 234 climate scientists nominated by their governments reviewed over 14,000 papers. Unnoticed in their 2023 report, because it is so opaquely written and buried within its hundreds of pages, are littered various observations which affirm the 'degrowth' hypothesis, namely, that rich countries will have to consume less if carbon emissions are to fall fast enough to keep us to the 1.5°–2°C pathway.[90] This is dramatic stuff — and the first time the IPCC has ever mentioned degrowth. In other words, 234 internationally renowned climate scientists, peer reviewing each other and working to consensus, have come to the conclusion that the *only* way to keep Earth's temperature at or below 2°C is for the rich societies, which consume and emit by far the most, to consume less.[91]

****

So how do we achieve the necessary speed of decarbonisation, in addition to pursuing technological innovation? The answer is staring us in the face: produce less, which means use less — consume less.

The good news is that most of the population, and indeed most countries, won't have to worry about this: they already are using a lot less than average. This policy does *not* mean that poorer countries should stop developing as fast as they can. It means instead that the richest countries, and to be precise the richest people in those countries, should consume less. This is because of a simple economic law: the rich consume — and therefore emit — more, in fact, far more.[§] The world's wealthiest 5% use more energy than the poorest half of the global population combined.[¶]

Many call this policy 'degrowth'. I think this term might mislead because it suggests to some, especially the sceptical, that everyone will get poorer. It doesn't in fact mean that because the bulk of the population, and the bulk of countries, will carry on as they are now — trying to get richer so that they can have a decent life with *sufficient* housing, food, education and other basic needs met. Instead, the richest 10% who emit a grossly disproportionate share of global emissions will have to consume less. This means fewer cars, smaller houses (and thus smaller energy bills) and fewer flights. It is essentially a reprioritisation of the economy away from growth at all costs, which benefits a few, to sufficiency — and well-being — for all, inside and between countries.

Big cars, advertising, multiple houses and lots of flying: these goods are well in excess of those necessary for a good life — sufficiency. What is consuming more than you need? Greed. So this strategy might be better called 'de-greed' than degrowth. As Kate Raworth, the author of *Doughnut Economics*, says: we should escape the paradigm of growth altogether and talking about more or less of it. Instead, we should

---

[§] The bottom 50% of the world population emitted 12% of global emissions in 2019, whereas the top 10% emitted 48% of the total. Since 1990, the bottom 50% of the world population has been responsible for only 16% of all emissions growth, whereas the top 1% has been responsible for 23% of the total. See: 'Global Carbon Inequality over 1990–2019', Lucas Chancel: *Nature*.

[¶] Extraordinarily, the richest 1% produced as much carbon pollution in one year as the 5 billion people who make up the poorest two-thirds of humanity. Source: Oxfam International: "Climate Equality: A Planet for the 99%"; *Dispatches from an Unaccountable Elite*, Ross, Carne. Cornell University Press, 2007, p. 179.

talk about how to thrive within the planetary boundaries (identified by Johan Rockström) and how to achieve well-being for all. Raworth talks about thriving, but we need to be clear what that means. Perhaps this is only for us to determine: how best we can live, our choices, expressed. Obviously, we have material needs, but beyond that, it is for us to decide, perhaps by the *doing* more than the declaration.

The issue is of priorities. How do we de-prioritise material growth, as defined by GDP for instance, so that we stop destroying the planet through carbon emissions and ever-increasing consumption and instead prioritise sufficiency, justice and human well-being as both the planet and, indeed, the bulk of its population demand?** The results of successful participatory processes, such as that in Porto Alegre, have demonstrated it is precisely these priorities that emerge from such collective, inclusive decision-making. When properly and fully consulted, people prefer equity, sufficient public services and ecological sustainability (of the genuine, not rhetorical kind). Polls indicate that the large majority of the population favour an economy that preserves planetary resources within the planet's ecological limits. A recent study, moreover, found that 70% of people preferred to sustain a particular resource for future generations, even if it meant a present cost for themselves.[92] Poll data also make clear that the bulk prefers a more equitable economy and society, where the minority are still rewarded, but not to the extent that today's gross inequities have created. In her book *Global Spin: The Corporate Assault on Environmentalism*, Sharon Beder cites evidence that the majority of people in most countries regard the protection of nature as *more* important than economic growth.[93] Immediately a chorus can be heard: it is not possible; no one will accept degrowth! This only demonstrates the obsession with growth as the metric of 'progress', that in order to be happier, people have to be richer and that growth therefore must remain the top political priority. It also reflects the fact that the priorities of the modern capitalist economy are not set democratically, but by the tiny minority

---

**

who own the bulk of the shares in the companies that determine what is produced and how, and whose over-riding objective is not human well-being but, simply, profit. That is the very nature of the system.

There are in fact reams of data that demonstrate that wealth makes people happier only up to a certain point, confirming Max-Neef's hypothesis, described earlier. After that, increases in wealth only make people marginally happier.[94] Instead, what really seems to affect well-being is inequality. The more unequal a society, the less happy it is — the more riven by crime, depression and other social ills[95] — a psychic reaction to fundamental injustice.

In any case, the data are also clear that growth tends to benefit only a minority — those who are already rich. In the US, mean incomes have flatlined for at least two decades. In other words, the bulk of the population are not getting any better off. In Britain, wages are in real terms lower than they were before the financial crash of 2008. Globally, the benefits of growth accrue to a tiny minority. So abandoning growth as the target will only, in reality, significantly affect the minority who are already wealthy. Indeed, we can see it this way: we need to shift the burden of degrowth from the masses who are already experiencing it, when their incomes need to rise, to those whose incomes are already way above sufficient.

There are already economies and societies that have shifted their focus away from growth to well-being as a broader and richer measure of what matters to people. Costa Rica demonstrates that a country can achieve high levels of social progress while enjoying relatively modest levels of economic growth.[96] Societies such as Finland have shown that growth and social well-being do not correlate. Finland is one of the happiest countries in the world, yet it does not have the largest GDP. Instead, notably, it enjoys very high levels of trust in other people and in government and in institutions (and this is one reason we need to rebuild democracy at the same time as change our economic foci).

Everyone globally can enjoy Finland's levels of well-being with energy consumption at 1960 levels.[97] The climate problem would be solved. The UK for, instance, can reduce energy demand by 50%

and still enjoy comparable standards of living.[98] The key to all this is sufficiency. As Max-Neef contended, it is entirely possible for everyone to have 'enough' — to have a decent standard of living — while using far fewer natural resources than we do today. Such an approach would also help promote climate justice. Currently, the global North consumes far more energy than required for human needs. The three billion people of the global South far less. Current decarbonisation trajectories proposed by governments of the global North to meet their Paris targets, manifested for instance by the IPCC, presume that developed countries will continue to use energy at two or three times the rate of the global South — the developing world. What's needed instead is true climate justice: that the global North uses less energy and the global South uses more,[99] a kind of energy convergence — reducing energy use in wealthy countries to achieve rapid emissions reductions, and ensuring sufficient energy for development in the rest of the world.[100] It is not enough simply to demand that government shifts resource consumption, essentially by making the rich consume less — taxes on big cars, houses or flying. Our political system is captured by the wealthy. Very wealthy men buy access to government ministers by joining exclusive 'donor clubs' — if they don't have access already. Fantastically wealthy men decide what's in our newspapers or on social media. The news' 'agenda' is largely set by people whose incomes put them in the top 5% or 10% (witness, for instance, the preponderance of second homes owned by senior journalists). Our culture gives much greater prominence to the views of the super-wealthy (the op-eds by Soros or Gates, the tweets by Musk) than it does to others more ordinary. In Britain and the US, none of the major political parties have the courage or imagination to call for degrowth, or simply give priority to well-being over growth. The growth paradigm has thoroughly captured the mainstream.

There is no sign, for instance, that governments are willing to put taxes on carbon-producing consumption and redistribute the revenue to the poorest. This would be a simple and just way to reduce both consumption and inequality. There is no sign that governments are prepared to institute the kind of wealth tax that Thomas Piketty has proposed in order to render society more equal. And in think-tanks, like where I worked, degrowth is simply dismissed as 'unrealistic', a term I have come to detest.

(There is a longer essay to be written on how think-tanks and NGOs, funded by the mega wealthy through opaque and unaccountable foundations, often reflect and reaffirm the political economic status quo, offering mere tinkering when fundamental re-engineering is required.)

There is another problem with redistribution by government decree. It is the implication of coercion — that wealth would be removed from the very rich to be redistributed to the poorest so as to achieve more well-being for all (since the utility gained from one extra unit of consumption is greater for the poorer). This transfer is absolutely necessary, but coercion should be minimised. I would prefer a more natural and perhaps gradual process of redistribution through the sharing of ownership of production and enterprise (cooperatives), instead of the private or state model of ownership. Cooperative businesses do not prioritise growth but instead foreground the needs and welfare of their worker-owners and, ideally, the environment. Cooperatives prioritise employment and sustainability — endurance and resilience over profit. They are not driven to produce more and more, for more and more profit; they don't ceaselessly create demand through planned obsolescence or advertising — or sponsor celebrities and influencers — that make us feel inadequate without the latest fashion or gadget.

Moreover, when workers are given a choice over what to produce, they will choose not to produce armaments or luxury cars and other ornaments of wasteful consumption. They will choose, as all of us would prefer, to be socially useful. No longer driven by the gods of profit and production, businesses have less need to drive endless and ever greater consumption.

Instead, these shifts can only be achieved by making democracy truly more representative — and that does not mean 'representative democracy'. It means, as we have seen, *inclusive* participatory democracy where everyone has a say in the decisions that most affect them. Only in this way is it possible to ensure that the interests of the bulk and breadth of the population are given due weight. As observed in Porto Alegre, when the mass of the population get to decide priorities, they are very different from the results of typical machine politics — they favour the measures of well-being: schools, hospitals, social care. They do not place economic growth at the top of the list.

So the conclusion surfaces: the only way to de-centre growth as the 'point' of society and, indeed, as the goal of government is to shift to a different kind of democracy which includes everyone and which, thereby, will decide that it is *not* growth that matters most but *other* priorities like social solidarity, justice, provision of basic services to live. If we had mass, direct democracy of the kind I have proposed, we would find that a different direction and goal of society would naturally emerge. By the very process of direct democracy, community and trust within society would be rebuilt. Because people would be free to express their views, away from the reductive and antagonistic forms of party politics, we would find that choices would be very different: away from the material and towards the things that make life worthwhile — which include the immaterial and metaphysical. We would find that government, once in our own hands, would start to orient around the things we truly want, the things that truly matter.

The obsession with growth and economic consumption is clearly also, in a more subterranean fashion, a fear about control and indeed social stability itself. Without the carrot of consumerism and more things, would the donkey keep walking forward? Without forward motion, would the bicycle topple over? What then would stabilise society? Hence the need for new generators of social cohesion — self-government — alongside the economic shifts that are ecologically necessary.

****

The components of this new and necessary dispensation emerge — a new comprehensive concept: a different kind of economy requires a different kind of politics, and indeed, vice versa. A new, superior form of human flourishing becomes available. It is also the means of our own and the planet's preservation. By allowing our survival, agency and self-expression, and by prioritising our relationships and the things without names beyond the material, it becomes a means of at last becoming our most human. In this sense, the whole is different from and indeed greater than the sum of its parts: the Germans have a word for this (the English don't), a *Gestalt*.

But there may be something more to it still. Truly inclusive democracy may indeed deprioritise material growth. However, we might need a deeper transformation to change our relationship to consumption and, indeed, to nature itself. It comes back to who/whom and to the subject-object relationship itself: a manufactured separation. In the case of the world's natural 'resources' (itself a somewhat reductive and utilitarian terminology, implying consumption rather than respect, coexistence or preservation), that who/whom equation has been clear: humans have been ruthlessly and heedlessly exploiting and consuming 'it' — nature — causing the out-of-control destruction we witness today.

Suzanne Simard points out that the idea of nature as an object separated from humans (where humans invariably sit above it) is a modern Western construct reflective of a colonial mindset. Indigenous people had a symbiotic relationship with the land and existed *within* nature rather than viewing it from outside. Clearly, we in the West need to revise our own view of this separation and replace it with a notion of mutual dependence (though clearly nature would survive well enough, indeed rather better without humans around; it is more us who rely on nature: our lives indeed depend upon it).

Amitav Ghosh also locates this drive for destruction in colonialism. 'Why has this crisis come about?' he asks,

> Because for two centuries, European colonists tore across the world, viewing nature and land as something inert to be conquered and consumed without limits and the indigenous

people as savages whose knowledge of nature was worthless and who needed to be erased. It was this settler colonial worldview — of just accumulate, accumulate, accumulate, consume, consume, consume — that has got us where we are now.

The planet's survival, says Ghosh, depends on a return to an ancient and long-tested perspective: seeing Earth as a living being to be listened to, understood and respected. 'The indigenous peoples of the Americas have been saying for decades that our past is your future and now that's exactly what's proving to be the case'.[101] So we should refer to Indigenous knowledge to renegotiate our relationship with the natural world, recovering the belief that humans are one with nature, inseparable. This takes us back to the fundamental understanding of what it is to exist: that there is no who/whom, no subject/object; there is just the relationship itself in order for existence to ... exist.

Murray Bookchin believed that the desire for domination lies at the heart of the problem. He argued that man's domination of nature would not cease until we had ceased to dominate one another.

As long as hierarchy persists, as long as domination organises humanity around a system of elites, the project of dominating nature will continue to exist and inevitably lead our planet to ecological extinction.[102]

In his essay, 'A Philosophical Naturalism', Bookchin explained why there is a directionality in nature that tends toward freedom; he even suggested that we can derive an ethics from nature, and in this we hear an echo of Kropotkin's voice. Like Kropotkin, Bookchin asserted that in nature we can find an objective basis for why concepts such as mutual aid are not just arbitrary choices we make; rather, there is an imperative for them within nature itself. In *A Vindication of Natural Society* (1756), even the conservative Edmund Burke proposed that nature 'if left to itself were the best and surest Guide'. Not only should we cease our domination of 'nature', we should let it guide us.

It is often the poets and artists who must argue the 'incontestable' verity of the inseparability of the human and the natural. As my friend, the poet John Burnside put it, 'we must realise that nature is not elsewhere ... but here and everywhere.' He describes how in childhood his job was to go to the garden shed to fill the coal scuttle for his family's house. Because it was cold and he wanted to get back in the warm house, he used to rush to the shed. Then, thanks to a fall, he stopped and realised something powerfully elemental:

I became aware of something I had missed before in my hurry to be done. To name it was beyond my vocabulary then (and even now, I cannot say that I know what it was) but after a while I had the sense, every time I went out, that something was there. It was something felt rather than seen, something intuited, even, but it was real. It was present, as I was present — and yet, as I looked around, it was nowhere to be found. Or rather, it was so everywhere that it seemed to be nowhere at all ... I must confess that the idea of God never once entered my head. Instead what occurred to me, if only in the vaguest terms, was that this everywhere-and-nowhere thing was what most people meant when they talked about "nature".[103] This unity of the human and the 'natural' world clearly does not fit into the narrow linguistic and terminological ranges of those who, instead of co-existence and mutual dependence, see mere 'resources' waiting to be exploited. John would lament the tragedy of language and terminology that we cannot put words to this fundamental of our very existence. He was an author of the ineffable, aware that the space between words said as much as the words themselves.

So, as Bookchin proposed, we need to eradicate the notion of domination itself. This is where it fits in with the new *Gestalt*. A society and economy characterised by equality and inclusion, *ipso facto*, makes domination impossible. We cease to look at one another as factors of production to be exploited at the lowest possible wage, or as mere producers or consumers, but as fully rounded humans. We no longer think of using other things, separate from us, for our own benefit. We realise that we are indeed inseparable.

Where does this desire to dominate and exploit come from? How do we enact this new politics of non-domination?

Today, the instinct to dominate is given ideological cover not by colonialism but by the neoliberal ideology that the market will preserve and provide, an assumption that has proven to be hopelessly naïve. A central pillar of the ideology is the argument that if ownership is clear, owners will be incentivised to protect their resource — land or water — and its price shall be determined by its scarcity which, as it rises, will preserve the resource. This simplistic application of theory to the planet has been disastrous — who owns the climate? How do you account for waste and pollution caused by production?

Elinor Ostrom was awarded the Nobel Prize for economics for her work on the commons. Reviewing thousands of economics papers, a meta-analysis, she showed that natural resources are better preserved when they are shared and managed by all those who cultivate them and benefit from them. She emphatically refuted the lazy yet commonplace assumption that a shared resource will be selfishly exploited by individuals until there's nothing left: the so-called 'tragedy of the commons'. She believed that democratic management of the commons only works, however, when *all* concerned are included in the governance of the resource, whether it's a field, a river or a lake. We have encountered this requirement before, of course.

Ostrom cites examples of groups of fishermen self-organising to agree and self-police catch limits to preserve a fish stock, or farmers managing the grazing rights of a piece of common land, ensuring that the land is not depleted by overgrazing. Ostrom's work proposes a different kind of ownership and a different kind of self-government, but one that tallies with our earlier findings about democracy and agency. Inclusive systems of self-government produce outcomes that are fairer but also more sustainable.

As with democracy and the business, ownership is key. Or, more specifically, control (which is often synonymous with ownership). The record of large private landowners in Britain in protecting the land they control, whether agricultural or 'wild', is abysmal. The biodiversity of the UK has plummeted over the last decades. Britain is 'one of the most nature-depleted countries in the world'.[104] Why, when Britain is a country of nature-lovers? Simply, they do not have control.

More than 50% of Britain is owned by less than 1% of its population — aristocrats who benefited from seizing land that was once shared, the innocently named 'enclosures' in England, which were in fact theft by a few of what once belonged to all, the thieves including the Church of England, an astonishingly wealthy and iniquitous institution and, of course, the royal family itself (I refuse to capitalise this inherited and parasitical absurdity). As the poet John Clare put it: 'All sighed, when lawless law's enclosure came'. Marx attributed the creation of the proletariat to the enclosures. This makes sense: in the act of enclosure (i.e.,theft), capital — land — was put in the hands of the few; the rest remained landless to be exploited as labour by the capital owners, all sanctified by law controlled by the beneficiaries of the theft. As one nameless poet lyrically described:

> The law locks up the man or woman
> Who steals the goose from off the common,
> But lets the greater villain loose
> Who steals the common from the goose.

Enclosure begat capital-owners, which in turn begat feudalism, which in turn begat class hierarchy. In Scotland, huge tracts of land are still held by descendants of those who stole the land from small crofters and smallholders in the infamous 'Highland Clearances' of the eighteenth and nineteenth centuries (an innocuous term for an egregious crime, yet another example of terminology being decided by the powerful)[††]. And of course the enclosure — or rather appropriation - of America's land by immigrants from Europe was an epic example of the same phenomenon — taking what was once commonly held and turning it

---

[††]   Interestingly, the name for the clearances in the Scottish language, Gaelic, i.e. the language of the victims, is more accurate: they were called *Fuadaichean nan Gàidheal*, which translates to 'the eviction of the Gaels'.

into private property. As Eula Biss writes, John Clare lamented how taking the land made slaves of those who once owned it: 'There was a time my bit of ground / Made freemen of the slave' — the land feels the loss of the people who lost their rights to the land.[105] Joel Scott-Halkes of WildCard convincingly argues that we cannot expect successful management of the land unless we *control* the land. He proposes the radical re-democratisation of common land and, when necessary, citizens' takeovers. But the notion that every square foot of land must be owned by someone has been beaten into us over centuries. The idea that land can be owned in common seems almost fanciful, but it was once the norm, and happens still. Indeed, commoners had rights over that land — to graze their animals, to cultivate crops or collect wood.

In a remarkable village called Marinaleda in southern Spain, the local people fought for the under- and poorly used land of the local aristocratic landlord. They simply marched onto it. The police — and this was under General Franco's fascist rule — tried to evict them, but they resisted (peacefully). When the police laboriously removed them, they simply returned and occupied the land again, over and over. Eventually, the local authorities gave in. The land is now owned and farmed collectively. Notably, when the marches began, no one, including those participating, believed they would succeed.

Talking to the farmers when I visited Marinaleda, I was very moved by their evident joy in the land and commitment to cultivation that preserved it — a relationship of mutuality ignored in the dominant narratives of agricultural exploitation. When they were mere labourers employed by the landlord, they didn't feel this way. It only changed when they had a stake. In Marinaleda, farming decisions, including who farms which bit, are taken collectively in a dusty village hall. The meeting I attended wasn't very dramatic and was somewhat monotonous, but in its way, it was revolutionary. The village applies the principles of mutuality and collectivism to other areas of life. The villagers build houses together. They are, of course, therefore much cheaper than dwellings built by developers out to maximise profit. Which villager gets the best-positioned house is decided by lottery.

In Rojava, in parallel with bottom-up democracy, there is a movement to build new forms of agriculture and land use, a revolution described in 'Make Rojava green again'. There too it is recognised that who controls the land is intrinsically connected to its management, whether to preserve it or to exploit it. The philosophy of 'social ecology' manifested in Rojava's 'green' revolution sees society's structure and the relationship to the environment as intrinsically connected. You cannot reform humanity's relationship to nature without transforming relationships between humans themselves: the removal of domination in all relationships. Social ecology emphasises the importance of direct democracy and community participation in decision-making processes. Thus, what is going on politically in Rojava is deeply connected to what is going on with the land. Without social justice, it is impossible to relate to nature in a sustainable way. It is no surprise that episodes of grotesque domination of humans by humans, such as colonialism, are also characterised by rapacious exploitation of the natural world. The psychology is essentially the same.

Now to turn to the harder question — Where does this need for domination come from? There is no question that the desire to acquire and accumulate — and dominate — is at least in part a consequence of the prevailing culture. There's a self-reinforcing loop at work. A vicious spiral, if you like. If I don't take it, someone else will. If I don't dominate them, they will dominate me. When greed and selfishness are celebrated, not only is our own moral system deformed, but also, more perniciously, we believe that others' are too. So culture must be tackled in tandem with the re-engineering of the mechanics of the system. Telling by showing (or indeed singing, dancing, painting, acting), etc.

But I cannot help but think that the desire to acquire and dominate is driven not only by the self-reinforcement of culture but also by a fundamental absence in our lives — of control, of agency, of power over our own lives. We do not have control over the things that matter most to us. Indeed, things feel very out of control. This means that when the opportunity presents itself to control something or somebody — a person, an animal, a plot of land — we take it, if only to experience the fleeting satisfaction of for once being *in* control. I cringe at the shameful moments in my life when I have exerted petty control over someone — a taxi driver, a waiter, an employee — simply because I *could*.

In the longer run, we are deeply incentivised to seek the permanence of control by gaining power, whether political or economic, through wealth or hierarchy, even when this experience is ultimately itself hollow. Rank and money. The power to get other people to do what we want, not what they want (Bertrand Russell's very definition of power). It's a way of avoiding our pain by inflicting it on others, for all domination is pain, whether psychic within ourselves or physical upon the planet.

Our loss of control provokes a hunger for that control. These phenomena are ultimately the products of a system, both political and economic. The combination of allegedly 'representative' democracy and capitalism has taken control from us. This system has become so deeply rooted within us that we no longer see it and no longer question it. This is the heart of anarchism — the struggle, peaceful but determined, in actions embodying its principles of justice and inclusion, to take control back. It is a struggle for freedom and sovereignty over our own and collective affairs. In ending the domination of nature, it is also a struggle for the very means of our survival.

9
Beyond the State

IN SEPTEMBER 2023, I began working with a small consultancy to attempt to improve the outcomes from the UN's Summit of the Future which was to take place a year later. Though it was supposed to be a landmark event, the reader probably wouldn't have heard of it. The UN Secretary-General called the summit to address and decide future 'governance' for the world for the 21st century, correctly identifying that the world's existing system is not working well in stopping war, ending poverty or mitigating climate heating. His office produced reams of recommendations for the UN member states. They mostly ignored them. Instead, the 193 UN member states spent many months negotiating a long and wordy text that said almost nothing. So paltry was the ambition of the negotiators that they claimed that it was a victory merely to agree on *anything* in times when the world was divided by war and injustice. And they had a point. This was probably the best that the world could hope for.

I spent months with my colleagues cajoling member states in private meetings and convenings. I myself wrote various textual proposals of new norms and ideas that might improve world 'governance'. One was that the UN and other multilateral bodies should agree and implement the principle of 'nothing about us, without us' — a principle from the disability rights movement (and others) that those most affected should always be at the table where decisions about them are made. Of course, in a text that had to be agreed by China, North Korea and Iran, or indeed the UK, such a principle was unlikely to be agreed. So the failure to include my proposal was no great surprise. Another idea was that the needs and rights of future generations should be acknowledged and addressed in multilateral decision-making. This proposal fared better but was considerably watered down before the text, the so-called Pact of the Future, was adopted into a series of vague aspirations to consider the needs of the young and those not yet born.

The diplomats I worked with were well-intentioned but weary. They realised how small were the chances of agreement to anything meaningful. There was no vision, no real leadership. Governments in capitals, obsessed with their own short-term problems, failed to engage on the summit, leaving the negotiation to diplomats in UN missions. Those diplomats were well aware that failure to produce an agreement would mark another waypoint in the slow decline of the UN and the international system of rules. The negotiation was a dispiriting exercise of ploughing through long and tedious texts, dense with wordy reaffirmations of past agreements and light on actual decisions to change anything. Meanwhile, in the real world outside the negotiating chamber, Palestinians were being slaughtered in the tens of thousands in the Gaza Strip; Russian missiles rained down on Ukrainian cities.

When I was a diplomat, I too believed in the state-based order, that what mattered was what states decided and how they interacted and reached, or didn't reach, agreements, a world symbolised by the photos that so often adorn books on international relations, of chessmen and chessboards, something one-dimensional, if complicated, but predictable according to an agreed set of rules.

The systems and rules that ordered the world of the past are less and less effective in the world of today. Those systems were at their heart based on the state, or system of states, an order manifested in organisations like the UN whose membership is confined to states alone, yet which makes decisions and rules that aim to govern the whole world. It is a system that embodies and perpetuates a profound and enduring fallacy: that the world can be managed, and its problems solved, by top-down authority.

There is a category mismatch between the reality of the world and the structure that is supposed to govern it. The system of states which we inherited is not suited to the needs of the 21st century. The problems of the world transcend borders. Climate change is negotiated in a state-to-state process, where states pressurise and bargain with each other over their 'commitments' to reduce carbon emissions, which most closely resembles the arms control processes of the twentieth century, a different problem both in type and in scale. In the UN climate process, formally known as the Framework Convention on Climate Change (UNFCCC), there is a lowest-common-denominator logic whereby, for instance, the collected predictions of UN scientists are framed as only what everyone can accept.

The world in reality is not in fact a system of discrete, individuated entities negotiating with each other over issues that they alone control. Or, rather, it is — but at only one level. Instead, it is a *complex* system, a system of billions of actors in constant, dynamic interaction, whose condition at any one time is impossible to 'freeze' or determine. A system that is neither chaotic nor stable but something in between, where linear chains of cause and effect — of action A leading directly to outcome B — no longer apply. In such systems, the idea that control can be exerted from above, by authority, is a fallacy.

As I have said before, the world in reality is not the chessboard that so misleadingly adorns textbooks or journals about 'international relations' but a Jackson Pollock painting, for despite its appearance, a Pollock carries a certain order and balance beneath its otherwise chaotic loops, swirls and drips.* In complex systems, we cannot predict what interventions will lead to change; the system is inherently unpredictable. Yet we remain saddled with a system and, crucially, ways of thought that claim an impossible knowledge and unattainable expertise. Governments repeatedly claim to know what's going on in the world, but their knowledge can only be limited and deeply imperfect, because that is the nature of the system.

The obvious conclusion is that we need to move beyond the state, and its systems, to arbitrate and manage our world. A better system will not come about without changing the nature of the state itself. One day, I hope, states will be like Rojava, a kind of non-state governed from the bottom outwards, a very different kind of beast to the conventional and familiar top-down authority. A community of communes engaging with other communities of communes, a kind of meta-commune.

A confederation of such entities would arrange and negotiate the world in very different ways. There would be no more Putins launching wars to fulfil a fantasy of a glorious Empire of Russia. There would be no more manufacture of 'interests', the artificial hierarchy of what is important to states. There would only be representatives talking about the diverse and authentic needs of their peoples, expressed from the ground of human experience and reality, not invented according to antiquated logic by well-dressed diplomats behind the high walls of government ministries. There would be disputes, no doubt, but such entities would be inherently collaborative in relations with others of their kind. Meanwhile, the idea of homogeneous, discrete entities known as the nation state would slowly but inevitably evaporate as peoples intermingle, migrate and become ever more heterogeneous. 'Them' and 'Us' would become absurd. Attacking 'them' for the sake of 'us' becomes ridiculous and obscene, unthinkable. In this way, the arguments for the utility, for instance, of nuclear weapons would

---

* I analysed the many deficits of modern diplomacy in my book *Independent Diplomat: Dispatches from an Unaccountable Elite.*

be ultimately eroded. The husks of ballistic missiles, submarines and strategic bombers would transform into monuments to a less enlightened and backward age, like the ruined medieval castle I can see from my window as I write.

We are some way off from that happy condition. In the meantime, we must struggle with the archaic and ineffective architecture of states inherited from previous generations, which only seems to suit the Putins and Trumps, who use their vetoes in the UN Security Council to protect themselves and their allies from consequence for their war crimes. Thus do war crimes persist, flourishing when accountability is non-existent.

But we can change the way we think about international relations. The names and terms, the assumptions, the hierarchies of knowledge and authority. And since any system of knowledge or heuristic rules must inherently carry a content of moral judgement of what is acceptable, what is important, etc, then, if you like, we need a new morality of international engagement and relations. For one question has always bothered me in the game of states: why are states permitted to behave in ways that individuals are not? Why should their morality and thus their rules and systems be any different to those that apply to us?

I once practiced the morality of the state, in fact, its amorality. And to my enduring shame I did terrible things. I helped perpetrate sanctions on Iraq, measures that did enormous damage to the innocent civilian population (one notorious statistic, from UNICEF's Iraq Child and Maternal Mortality in 1999, estimated the number of child deaths resulting from sanctions at 500,000). I negotiated the UN resolutions that imposed and perpetuated those sanctions. I didn't decide the policy, but I enacted it. I was responsible. But I was never held accountable. My actions were normalised by the culture's amorality that suffused my diplomatic work. None of us working on Iraq thought we were doing anything morally wrong. States are entitled to kill. According to Weber, the monopoly on the use of violence is what defines the state. Killing is what states *do*.

The state system is also *stupid*: it is not adapted to the world as it actually is. It is a rigid system imposed upon a more complicated, dynamic and richer reality. The imposed simplification of complex heterogeneity is an act of force or violence — required to force a complex world into the categories that suit those in authority. Indeed, it is authority that simplifies reality into hierarchies and comprehensible patterns. Authority and the state have every interest in portraying what is complex as simple, because this affirms their power — that they alone have the power to understand, order and control events. The desire to order is in kinship with the desire to control. The denial of complexity is in its way a denial of the possibility of freedom ('Domination is the outcome of responding to complexity through simplification', as Murray Bookchin put it). We must learn to live, therefore, with complexity and, with that, uncertainty. As Montgomery and Bergman noted, 'uncertainty is where we need to begin, because experimentation and curiosity is part of what has been stolen from us. Empire works in part by making us feel impotent, corroding our abilities to shape worlds together'.[106] The words *state, borders, institution*, even *diplomacy* describe a superstructure which is not reality and, increasingly, does not reflect reality. (All terms are less than reality.) They also create a way of thinking about 'international relations', itself a term compromised by its implication of a world of states or countries in relation to one another — a presumption of an over-arching system.

Others have suggested different ways of thinking about the world. Gandhi and Nehru proposed the idea of 'One world or none', a belief system that all humans are essentially one family whose needs must be attended to as a whole, not as separated entities. This informed the Indian national policy around the time of the establishment of the UN, which advocated a kind of world government.

I do not think this is the answer, even if the core philosophy is appealing. World government will be inevitably distant from the people whose needs it will arbitrate; it will be un-transparent and unavoidably unaccountable. National governments are already too removed from the people. Above all, it would not be legitimate — it's totally implausible that it could be elected.

Some friends of mine have proposed a 'Global Citizens' Assembly', composed of a representative sample of the human family, chosen by random selection but in a way that embodies representativeness, i.e. fair proportions of countries, wealth, race, etc., a process: sortition. The idea is that this would deliberate the crises confronting humanity — conflict, climate, inequality, etc. But this too would suffer the legitimacy problem — is it plausible that a group of, say, 400 people could claim to represent the world's populace? Wouldn't it be dismissed as some kind of elaborate focus group? And who gets to decide the process of selection itself? Who decides the decision-making process? Inevitably, there are dangers of Western bias in the design process itself and thereby of replicating the existing imbalances in today's structures.

Indeed, I'm not convinced that the issue is structural or institutional at all. Such an assumption only encourages institutional tinkering when the core problem is the way we *think*. Adding India, Nigeria or Japan to the UN Security Council's membership will not make it more just or effective at ending wars. It may well make it worse (even if it might be — sort of — more fairly representative).

So what would be a better way of thinking about the world? To start, I don't think *my* way of thinking should be at the centre at all; instead, people are best qualified to express their own needs and desires. The imposition of Western moral rules rather than the wishes of those most affected is a kind of arrogance. Take the so-called Golden Rule: 'Treat others as we would be treated'. But who decides this treatment? The subject not the object. The Golden Rule implies 'we know best'.

The Golden Rule, at its most extreme, leads to disasters like the 2003 Iraq War which were, in part, justified by the belief among the war's instigators that the people of Iraq 'wanted democracy'. The people of Iraq were, of course, never asked; the half million who died

in the war among them, unconsulted. There is a superior maxim —
ask other people first, put their desires and requirements first.

It follows that those people should be part of decisions about them,
Nothing About Us Without Us. There is an additional benefit here.
People from a place will know that place best. They will already know
the solution. They don't need other people — usually white — to
tell them. I am heartily sick of the media inviting former Western
ambassadors to explain places like Palestine or Lebanon to the general
public, often when they haven't been posted there for decades and
whose status, even when they were there, separated them from the
reality of those places. It seems too obvious to state that Lebanese or
Palestinians know their circumstances much better; they speak with
the authority of experience and legitimacy — their truth *should* be for
them, not for others to declare.

Another simple moral maxim is that people have equal status
and an equal right to be respected and valued. Again, this should be
unarguably true, but it is evidently not in the dehumanised rhetoric
of 'refugees', 'asylum seekers' or 'economic migrants' who are all
doing exactly what we would do in their circumstances. Yet they
are objectified and, of course, often demonised. They are treated as
lesser beings with lesser rights than those of us lucky enough to have
been born into peace and comfort. The objects of foreign policy —
foreigners — are similarly reduced, just as I was part of a policy that
reduced the Iraqi people to mere adjuncts to our superior practice of
statecraft. Thus we were able to ignore their suffering.

This simple rule should also take us past the racism so often
evident in today's practice of 'international relations'. Israeli victims
of Hamas are given names, histories and photographs in the press, as
they should be. But Palestinian victims of Israeli attacks are nameless,
history-less and reduced to mere statistics of dead and wounded,
just as Iraqis were nameless and even numberless and thus could be
ignored, as we arbitrated sanctions. Bloody civil wars in Sudan are
given far less attention, both by media and by government, than wars

in Europe. The colonial history of almost all the world is ignored in current decisions about debt, aid or responsibility for the climate disaster. Historic injustices, and the obligation of reparation, are simply ignored, consigned to 'the past' when the once-colonised or enslaved live with so many present consequences, from debt to rising oceans.

These maxims seem to me unarguable and indeed we accept them, if not practice them, in our own societies, yet in the 'international' realm they are relegated. This is because the logic and unstated moral rules of the state system have infiltrated our brains, replacing the more accurate and morally defensible logic of our common humanity. Just like the declaration that love should be our supreme goal, the declaration of our common humanity and moral obligation to one another, wherever we live, seems naïve and 'immature' (as my condescending ambassador friend might put it). Somehow we have to make this superior logic as predominant and pervasive as the current inhumane ontologies. How do we get there?

Like capitalism, the state-based system seems immutable and eternal. It is not. It will be replaced, as all systems eventually are. If not by a better human-based way of thinking and doing, then by tyranny, violence and the catastrophe of climate disaster, whose effects will be suffered separately, not in solidarity together. As long as states maintain the false notions of impermeable borders and singular identities and not a more generous, heterogeneous and flexible posture, the billions-strong migrations of climate 'refugees' — people escaping insufferable heat — will destabilise countries and trigger conflict, both within and between nations.

At worst, the dangerous logic of states and separation will end in a nuclear conflagration. Even now, China, Russia, the US and UK are spending hundreds of billions on modernising and expanding their nuclear arsenals. This does not augur well. But if we imagine our personal response to a horribly burned victim of nuclear inferno, regardless of their nationality (could we even tell?), the moral imperative and reality of innate human compassion becomes clear.

The absurdity of our situation is all too evident. That absurdity urgently needs to be exposed.

I've searched in the experience of my own journey. Perhaps it lies in my marriage to a Croatian American and living in several foreign countries, perhaps the generosity of hospitality I received in Kosovo, a country once patronisingly characterised as 'teenaged' by Samantha Power, a senior American diplomat, generosity I have never experienced in a Western country. Albanian culture also taught me about loyalty. Once declared an ally, you are always an ally, a dedication and commitment I have not experienced in my own selfish bourgeois culture. I know that I could call a Kosovar friend, even those I may not have spoken to for decades, and they would help me without hesitation. My greatest intellectual heroes — Wittgenstein, Berlin, Arendt, Said, Benjamin, Le Guin, Fanon, Derrida, Lao Tsu — are all (but for Berlin) foreign. I am sure I have not fully escaped the inherited racism of my background and upbringing, the ridiculous notion of British superiority, but these experiences have diminished it.

Perhaps it is, above all, the experience of meeting people, whether in warzones, refugee camps or poverty, and discovering that their needs for security, for tolerable conditions of life, are the same, to witness their solidarity with each other (and sometimes me) as their predominant characteristic. I am not naïve enough to think that all people are always good, but I do believe that we are pretty much the same and that this reality has obvious and inescapable moral consequences. Our cultural differences are diminishing with travel, tourism and the globalisation of music, art and Tik-Tok — and there is a grief to this loss too — but what is revealed as they subside is commonality, not difference. When I sit on the bus in London, I hear Urdu, Polish, Arabic, Chinese, broken English and other languages I cannot recognise. But we're all going in the same direction.

The name for this approach to shared humanity, to treating each other as of equal worth and rights, is *cosmopolitanism*, an ancient philosophy that long predates most of today's nation states and is ever more pertinent in an increasingly connected and intermingled world.

But perhaps we should go further. We need at last just let each other *be*, and to see each other be, not disfigured by labels and nationalities.

Some argue that we should reject the notion of race itself, that to seek to eradicate racism without expunging race is like pouring petrol on a fire. It is commonly accepted among scientists that race has no biological basis. The Human Genome Project showed that there are no distinct genetic markers that correspond to traditional racial categories. The American Association of Physical Anthropologists issued a statement in 2019 concluding that 'pure races, in the sense of genetically homogenous populations, do not exist in the human species today, nor is there any evidence that they have ever existed in the past'. Philosophers Anthony Appiah and Naomi Zack contend that the term *race* cannot refer to anything real in the world, since discrete, essentialist, biological races have been proven not to exist. The mixed-race couple, Subrena E. Smith and David Livingstone Smith, both academics of philosophy, argue that the notion of race itself perpetuates racism by perpetuating the notion of difference.[107]

The Black American writer Ta-Nehisi Coates agrees: 'Race is the child of racism, not the father' — the very concept of race is a product of the imagination of the racist. The idea of race arose from Europe's capitalist drive for greater wealth, a goal pursued through the domination, enslavement and destruction of Indigenous peoples on other continents.[108] It was presumably awkward to baldly confess the true motives, colonialism therefore required the depiction of Indigenous peoples as savage and inferior, in need of civilising. Indeed, the term 'race' as a way to distinguish groups of humans was created in the late eighteenth century.

Again, we come back to the origins of these sentiments, the deficit within ourselves. Like the instinct for domination, the need to feel superior is not innate but comes from our own pain and anxieties, that we are in fact the inferior. As Jean-Paul Sartre put it,

> The anti-Semite is a man who is afraid. Not of the Jews, to be sure, but of himself and his own consciousness, of his liberty, of

his instincts, of his responsibilities, of solitariness, of change, of society, and of the world ... The existence of the Jew merely permits the anti-Semite to stifle his anxieties.[109]

As James Baldwin once said, it's imperative to excavate the origin of these instincts.

What white people have to do is try and find out in their own hearts why it was necessary to have a n– in the first place, because I'm not a n–. I'm a man, but if you think I'm a n–, it means you need it... If I'm not a n– and you invented him — you, the white people, invented him — then you've got to find out why.[110]

The use of distinct racial identity is, arguably, like the creation of all distinctions, a method of control. The Afro-American thinker bell hooks suggests maintaining a distance from claiming any particular identity, to avoid engaging 'in the either/or dualistic thinking that is the central ideological component of all systems of domination in Western society'.

The absence of all filter and indeed theories of difference offers a return to the 'real', an abandonment of the confusion, provocations and distortions of inherited institutions, theories, norms and names. We weak, vulnerable, needy humans are all experiencing the same reality. Words and descriptions can be acts of violence that slice up a shared, rich and un-worded reality. While they are a necessity for communication, they also separate us from that common experience.

Jacques Lacan argued that there is a reality 'underneath' all the terms we use in an always futile attempt to capture it through description: it lies beyond the symbolic and cannot be fully integrated into our understanding and thus can be traumatic, distressing, disruptive. But without words, we are unable to think. So the loss of our proximity to and experience of this 'reality' is inevitable as soon as we learn words and mental structures to emplace upon the world.

Only a baby is truly present to the Real, and this is a loss we all must suffer. Perhaps we can somehow recover it. It is one reason the shared wordless experience — perhaps of peril or joy — is so much more powerful than the words we might use to describe it.

I experienced this after 9/11 when, for many weeks afterward, New Yorkers did not find a word for 'it', as we called the catastrophe; any words seemed insufficient to convey the grief, the shock, the fear, the compassion. Only outsiders called 'it' names — '9/11', 'Ground Zero' — and thereby attempted to define what it meant. Only someone who wasn't there could describe it, as Slavoj Žižek once did, as 'the desert of the real'. I know what he meant, but by naming it, he only demonstrated how little he understood it, how one-dimensional was his claim to interpret and fit it into — needless to say, his own — theory. What Žižek was trying to get at was that, for once, America could see reality stripped of the self-serving claims of US government policy and categorisations. In a sense, the violent and bloody reality of the Middle East — and the consequences of US policy there — were visited upon Manhattan. And this was precisely the reality that was then re-camouflaged and manipulated by the names '9/11' and the 'War on Terror'. '9/11' was misleadingly rendered as an attack on America, what it stood for and its 'way of life', obscuring the purpose and aims of the hijackers, whose declarations were ignored in the mainstream discourse. Who gets to name and frame things has the power.

But there is something more here. The attacks on the World Trade Center did indeed transport New Yorkers into a shared and very stark and present reality, where for once we were not individuals selfishly seeking our own goals, obsessing about our own lives, but we were experiencing something extraordinary together. A glib term for this might be 'bonding experience', but it was much more than that. It was something more which, of course, I am struggling to put into words: an intensity of being. This sensation (an inadequate word) was *created* together, as we at last encountered 'the real'. It was beautiful and sad, forged by the all-too-tangible experience that we shared, but also otherworldly, ineffable, immeasurable, ethereal ... essential. Strangely, I miss it now. Why did it require mass death to transport us into that limitless dimension? Why can we not dwell in it all the time?

No fewer than 102 nationalities were among the dead of 9/11. After the attacks, desperate family members posted photo-copied portraits of their loved ones on lamp-posts and sidewalks all over lower Manhattan: 'Missing'. In the following weeks, as no one returned from the pyre, those signs became unintended memorials. Though you could have noticed the race, religion or nationality from those notices signifying thousands of dead, you didn't care.

10
A New Gestalt

I T TOOK me a while to realise that the current system is much more than a machine by which to organise society, our political and economic affairs. Rather, it offers a complete and intimidating account of what it is to be human and how to maximise our 'utility' or, put better, our satisfaction in life. In other words, it offers a 'total concept'. An answer for everything. It is rational, coherent and embodies its own kind of morality. It works at several different levels. It is thus impregnable to all but the most powerful counter-theses.

To offer a convincing alternative, we must build our own comprehensive concept. One which has an answer to the common concerns, criticisms and misconceptions of how to organise our affairs together and indeed how to live. The new concept we see emerging is one where the whole is greater than the sum of its parts and, indeed, expresses something beyond its mere quantitative elements. It enables something more than merely the method of arbitrating our affairs or running our economy; something great, something ineffable. The word that comes closest to this is the German the *Gestalt*. I've come to believe that anarchism, and indeed only anarchism, offers such a *Gestalt*.

Its parts lock together: to give priority to what matters most, people must decide their own affairs themselves, in equality, a process that by its very action binds us together, a process that, by generating a richer set of needs and desires beyond the merely material, removes consumption from its unmerited primacy in the hierarchy of needs, replacing it with something else — meaning, compassion, community, love, the immaterial, the ineffable.

Only by that shift is it possible for humanity to live within its planetary limits and preserve the planet on which it depends. And all this exists within a different kind of ontology of what matters and what deserves names and distinctions — who/whom, subject/object, them/us — that distort and manipulate us into opposition and antagonism, where the common experience of reality is far more resonant of what it really is to be human.

Above all, this different way of doing things (which in reality is not that new, though we must learn it anew) puts what matters most to us, our relationship to each other, at its centre, the very thing without which we would not even exist.

This wordy summary is the *Gestalt* of anarchism, a philosophy that gives the greatest space for human expression, for us to find our own path to flourishing and fulfilment, which are things not necessarily measurable or composed of material acquisition.

That offers a way of negotiating our affairs with one another in equality of power, which is the only way to guarantee an outcome that takes all needs into account and is thereby stable, peaceful and enduring.

That satisfies one of our fundamental needs, for control over our own lives. Agency.

That contributes to the cohesive and collaborative function of society, where people's opportunity and propensity to cooperate rather than compete is maximised. Indeed, it offers a way to repair a society that has become dangerously fractured.

That offers a model of society deeply and intrinsically resilient, a mesh of dense human connection and cooperation, a resilience that may become more and more necessary as the damage and disruption of climate heating grows.

And, perhaps most importantly, that offers a framework of equality, mutual aid and reciprocity that is political, economic and social, in which love can maximally flourish.

I resist tying this all up into a neat whole, all ambiguities removed, a *Gestalt* that echoes the false if logically constructed certainties of capitalism and indeed socialism, the forever unfulfilled promise of a better future for all. When you have a hammer, everything starts to look like a nail. Likewise, I resist the drawing of certain unambiguous lessons from the messy experience of my life. For what I see, there is both good and bad, things I can be proud and ashamed of and many other things I don't understand. We are human, after all.

Most anarchists do not claim that humans are perfect. Mistakes will be made. They do not pretend to know the ideal design of society. But it is the *process* — what anarchists call 'praxis' — as well as the principles and values that imbue it, that matters. Among those principles are the constant rejection of coercion of one over another, the constant moral struggle for equality and justice. For it is context and circumstance — the system itself — that bring out the worst and best in us, not merely our innate qualities. Obviously, both can be at play at once. And in anarchism I see a system and the creation of circumstances that, I hope and believe (with passion), will bring out the best.

I have been surprised by my own beliefs. It's become clear to me that anarchism is the only logical system if you believe that only through the freedom to express ourselves and be connected to other people can we be what we truly are, our essence perhaps (though anarchists would resist the certainty of there being any single essential feature). From my own experience, I've come to believe it is our essence; but it's neither my right, nor is it necessarily correct, to universalise my declaration.

Anarchism is the only logical system if you want to maximise human flourishing rather than prioritise material consumption.

Paradoxically, it is also a logical system that works to engender the illogical, the ineffable and the transcendent just as Wittgenstein's *Tractatus* constructs a stairway of logic only to kick the stairs from under him by concluding that what matters most cannot be expressed through logic or symbols, and therein is most important. It is a logical system that ultimately promotes that most irrational and illogical of human essences — love.

It is the very rationality of the current system that is perhaps its greatest flaw, its interlocking logics of market economics and allegedly representative democracy. This challenges our deepest assumptions — I would call them mental rigidities — about the status quo. It takes no account of the irrational, the metaphysical, that essential and inescapable element of what it is to be human. Any political and economic philosophy must find space for this, as I believe anarchism does.

Perhaps here we can see the dialectic of history at work. We are transitioning from a period dominated and shaped by rationalist ideas of economics and human purpose, ideas spawned by the Enlightenment and the Industrial Revolution when empiricism dominated, when positivism ruled: only what can be measured and witnessed matter, ideas which were then exploited by those who benefited most. But the dominance of the rational has come at a great cost, both to ourselves and to the planet. Jung again:

> The more the critical reason dominates, the more impoverished life becomes; but the more of the unconscious, and the more of the myth we are capable of making conscious, the more of life we integrate. Overvalued reason has this in common with political absolutism: under its dominion the individual is pauperised.[111]

Perhaps now is the time for humanity to find a more balanced philosophy, poised between the rational and irrational, reflecting our true natures, where the left hemisphere of the brain — the more fine-grained, analytical and instrumental — is in balance with the right — the more holistic, aesthetic and appreciative, as Iain McGilchrist might put it. A similar pattern of balance between the qualities seen, in reductive binary terms, as male and female, the sun and the moon. It may be a narrow path to tread. As the Nobel Prize-winning physicist Wolfgang Pauli said in a letter to Jung:

> It would be most satisfactory of all if physics and psyche could be seen as complementary aspects of the same reality. […] the only acceptable point of view appears to be one that recognises *both* sides of reality — the quantitative and the qualitative, the physical and the psychical — as compatible with each other, and can embrace them simultaneously.

But, he adds,

> In my own view it is only a *narrow* passage of truth (no matter whether scientific or other truth) that passes between the Scylla of a blue fog of mysticism and the Charybdis of a sterile rationalism. This will always be full of pitfalls and one can fall down on both sides.[112] Ultimately, perhaps, we should choose to reject the binary itself, the rejection of the necessity of division, even definition. Perhaps we should dispose of the 'bourgeois fetish' of the individual, as Alexander Bodganov proposed, in favour of the network, the community. We create reality not alone but together. Perhaps we should dispose of the distinction between individual — the one — and community — the many, altogether, indeed abolish who/whom, the subject-object separation. For, arguably, we can only express our true individuality as part of a group by creating ourselves through our relationships to others, where one riffs off the other and then back again in a constant dynamic. Pure individualism, practiced in a vacuum, is by contrast a kind of nightmare.

The *Gestalt* is of course for now a hypothesis. The only current proof of the concept lies in the past and in the present in Rojava and in Zapatista-controlled areas of Mexico, societies and situations different from our own, about which we have limited empirical data and impartial studies (for sympathisers, including me, do not make the most objective observers). The hypothesis can only be tested by bringing it to life.

But how can we conjure the *Gestalt* into existence? It requires that we recapture agency in all areas of our life, introduce new ways of operating and, indeed, *being*. It could be — it should be — a joyful discovery of what it is to be truly human.

11
Finding the Lost Soul

N THE early 2020's, I suffered what can best be described as a collapse of the spirit. The engine inside me stuttered to a halt. I was depressed and often monosyllabic. I slept a great deal and cherished the liminal space just before falling asleep when I knew, for sure, that oblivion was only a moment away.

I gave up communication with my friends. I found talking a strain, even to my wife. I fell into myself. I imagined committing suicide, dissuading myself only by the needs of my family. I felt that my life was in any case coming to an end. I had lost my point. I fantasised about my funeral, in my self-pity imagining how few people would show up. More prosaically, I would eat entire packets of chocolate Hobnobs on my way back from the supermarket. I gained thirty pounds.

This crisis coincided with the ending of my tenure running an NGO, Independent Diplomat, that I had founded sixteen years earlier. Clearly, I was mourning the loss of my purpose and indeed my status as the founder of a successful and innovative NGO. But it troubled me that the foundation of my mental well-being was so shallow. Once

I had lost this, in part, ego-driven enterprise, I had nothing to fall back on.

I had long been proud of my atheism. I saw myself as a rigorous kind of scientific atheist. One could only believe in what had been scientifically proven. Like Christopher Hitchens, I looked down on those who relied on religion or belief to prop up their weak psyches. Belief was merely a crutch in the face of a pitiless and meaningless universe. To find meaning in such a desert, I relied on a kind of circular logic: meaning could be found in what you do. We, the human, and what we do were the only sources of meaning.

But in my mid-life depression, this logical reasoning was scant reassurance. A good friend had recently died, and I found myself dwelling on the dread prospect of the void after death. If there was nothing after death, all that my life would add up to was the scanty accomplishments of my few short decades on the planet. Denied much affirmation as a child, I was quick to denigrate and devalue my achievements.

My political belief system only reinforced my arid life-view. Anarchism has long rejected religion, 'No gods, no masters', correctly regarding organised religion as a source of repression, hierarchy and domination, usually perpetrated by men. Religion and the church were human constructs, where power hungry men used God and liturgy as a stick to beat and control others. But, crucially, I failed to see that rejection of religion does not necessarily mean rejection of belief.

Then something changed.

One trigger was an article that I was asked to write about spiritualism and anarchism. I'd thought I was, in many ways, the last person to write such an article, but the editor insisted I have a go.[113] I talked about my anarchist friends who saw their 'spirituality' as an intrinsic part of their politics. I expressed polite scepticism, but, in reflection on the topic, I realised that there was an element of my anarchism, my politics, that I could describe as spiritual. Anarchism was not only, I realised, a philosophy of political and economic systems, of how humans transact their affairs free from violence and hierarchy. It is something much, much more.

This something is about connection. In its core, anarchism is about humans connecting to one another without structure and without power relations, as equals. In its essence, it was about the one thing that sustained me in the dark and dangerous hours of my depression, and that was love: love for my wife and children, the one thing that kept my fingers gripping the ledge from which I was hanging.

There had long been a Wittgenstein-sized hole in my belief in logic and rationalism. As I had discovered that day in the NYU library, Wittgenstein, in his *Tractatus*, proved that there were limits to all logical forms of expression, indeed to logic itself; rationalism too was limited to the terms that could be used to describe it. Logic was ultimately circular — it can only be proven by its own terms. Kurt Gödel had come to a similar conclusion with his famous incompleteness theorem: any mathematical — or indeed philosophical system, as Wittgenstein believed — can't be proven only by using its own terms alone. It is literally impossible to prove the coherence and validity of a system by using its native terms.

It is odd that I needed a philosopher and a mathematician to prove that the ineffable and metaphysical exist.

Wittgenstein had opened the door, but I had yet to walk through it. He proved to me, incontrovertibly, that there exists a realm beyond all language, all numbers and all terms themselves. This is the ineffable, the metaphysical and transcendental, and for Wittgenstein this was the only territory that really mattered. As he famously said of it, 'Whereof one cannot speak, thereof one must be silent' (in German, '*Wovon man nicht sprechen kann, darüber muss man schweigen*'). I realised that Wittgenstein had proven that all rational, quantitative systems, such as economics, were intrinsically limited and rational only in their own terms (some of which were invented). These theories didn't describe, because they couldn't, the things that really mattered to mankind.

This revelation led me to question the logical systems that had until then framed my world, the neo-classical economics that purported to describe society and the needs and behaviours of the individual within it. That helped me see that our contemporary society was oriented towards the wrong things — consumption, materials, 'stuff' — when our true needs lay in the immaterial. But at that point it didn't lead me to explore the immaterial itself. Only my mid-life depression somehow initiated that journey.

I cannot put my finger on what it was that led me to spiritual revelation, but I think it may have begun with the dreams that accompanied my deep and much-desired sleep. Despite my desperation for oblivion, my dreams were rich and varied, speaking of another world beyond, populated by signs and symbols — circles, spirals, forests — whose significance I could not interpret.

As Jung believed, dreams are the 'emissary of the unconscious, whose task it is to reveal the secrets that are hidden from the conscious mind'.

What my dreams certainly indicated was that beneath my blank and beaten-down conscious depression there lay an unconscious seam that was vital and vivid, a bubbling lava that was struggling for an outlet from beneath the dead granite. This was perhaps a suppressed essence, a life force that had survived and indeed needed to escape my bleak ennui.

Carl Jung was the shaman of dreams. He believed that dreams are indicators not only of the individual psyche but also of the collective unconscious, a shared stratum that connects humanity, populated by the myths and signifiers that join humankind with its past and, indeed, with visions of its future. Jung believed that once humanity abandoned the spiritual, it was doomed. The pursuit of the scientific and rational alone would lead to disaster:

[S]piritually impoverished, and technologically obsessed. Collectively we were perpetuating the mistake of the alchemists, projecting our spiritual aspirations into material things in the delusion that we were pursuing the highest value. This had encouraged us to treat each other as economic commodities and exploit the physical resources of the planet while neglecting, to our own detriment, the spiritual resources of the Self. The only remedy for our civilization's 'loss of soul' was a massive reinvestment in the inner life of the individual, so as to re-establish a personal connection with 'the mythic world in which we were once at home by right of birth'. Deprived of the symbolism of myth and religion, people were cut off from meaning, and society was doomed to die.[114]

I began to read Jung and in particular his extraordinary memoir, *Memories, Dreams, Reflections*. In the same dark period, I also read a modern philosopher, Barnard Kastrup. Kastrup is what is known as an idealist. Not a political idealist, but someone who believes that there is no material reality to the world at all. His books are devoted to debunking the alleged proof that material reality exists. Instead, he believes that we live in a kind of network of pure consciousness, that all the phenomena we experience are manifestations of this single immaterial reality.

Something Kastrup wrote connected with me. He argued that we could experience religious myth but without believing that myth. Indeed, to believe it is to believe in something almost absurd, not least because transcendence can never be captured in written liturgy that claims to convey 'the truth'. But without having to believe in the alleged myth or miracle, we can nevertheless feel the emotional truth of that belief.*

Something in that resonated with me. Indeed it proved something of a salvation. I don't accept all of Kastrup's belief system. I do believe that there is a material reality, but it is plausible and indeed welcome

---

*   'My proposal is that you allow your chosen religious myth to inform your emotional life as though it were literally true. However, I am not suggesting that you intellectually take it to be the literal truth. Doing so is tantamount to denying transcendence altogether, since it implicitly assumes that the corresponding truths can be accurately, unambiguously and completely captured in a language-based narrative. Moreover, taking a religious myth to be the literal truth at an intellectual level plants the seed of fundamentalism. This has been the source of unimaginable suffering and destruction throughout history' (*More Than Allegory: On Religious Myth, Truth and Belief* by Bernardo Kastrup, Iff Books, 2016).

to me that one can believe the emotional truth of religion without necessarily accepting that religion itself. Experiences I had had earlier in my life suddenly made sense to me.

Once I had been sitting in the so-called Rothko Room in the Tate gallery in London. I was alone in the room, surrounded by Rothko's extraordinary paintings which blended dark colours into one another. Engrossed in the art, I suddenly had a feeling of absolute transcendence; my brain buzzed in a kind of ecstasy. This was a kind of religious experience. It was an acquaintance with the transcendent and ineffable. This was the feeling I continue to seek today. It is the realm that Wittgenstein was talking of. It is the realm of unmediated religion, for, as Wittgenstein believed, no one should get between you and your god.

I began dimly to grasp what Jung and Kastrup were on about. This was the stuff that connects all humans to one another. My exploration continues, and I am unwilling to label or define what I am searching for precisely because it is indefinable. But that it exists now seems to me beyond doubt.

Some believe that our salvation lies in recovery of our spirituality, our sense of the infinite. Hegel believed that the world was moving toward an ultimate spiritual concrescence: the self-realisation of 'the Absolute'. Marx prophesied this endpoint as a post-political condition, a collective emancipation from private property, hierarchy and alienated labour. I don't really believe in ultimate ends, a teleology that frames everything as a journey towards a fixed point — that usually lies in the future. I instead believe in what happens now, in what we *do* now.

For me, we find the absolute, the transcendent, in human connection. This is what creates our reality itself. This is not a philosophy of individualism; it is one of community. It tallies with the findings of quantum physics. As Carlo Rovelli observes in his marvellous explanation, *Helgoland:* 'I believe that in order to understand reality, we have to keep in mind that reality is this network of relations, of reciprocal information, that weaves the world'. In the quantum world, particles only exist when observed, i.e. when a relationship exists between one thing and another. This is what I have come to believe about humanity, too. Without connection, we cease to be truly human. We only truly exist in terms of one another.

What does this mean? It means that we are nothing as isolated atoms. That the individualism that dominates our society, leading us endlessly to satisfy an unsatisfiable urge, is a dead end. We can only find meaning in each other. We are nothing but the sum of our relationships. For me, in my mid-life depression, as I gave up on my relationships with others, I was becoming less human; I was dying. But I was saved by the relationships that cut to my very core, those with my closest family, my most intimate and beloved. These relationships saved me from the end.

Some believe that without a kind of collective society-wide spiritual renaissance, the necessary recovery of society — its democracy, its justice, its sustainability — is unlikely. As long as society is attached to arid materialism rather than, say, idealism (of the Kastrup kind), it is doomed, as Jung too had suggested.

I am not sure, though I do see signs in the revival of Buddhism, yoga or even the shared 'spiritual' experience of a music festival. I believe that the necessary changes in society — towards a cooperative economy and genuinely participatory democracy — can be effected now, and the logical arguments for them are persuasive. But it may be that logical arguments are not enough. We have to feel them in our soul.

This craving for meaning, Jung believed, was an essential part of what it is to be human. It cannot be found in status or material consumption, much as social media influencers and advertisers wish to pretend otherwise. I do not claim that I know the answers for this quest. But I do believe that our needs are to a large extent met in the experience of each other, in community, in the profundity of our interactions with other people. Social science has already demonstrated that happiness lies in the wealth of social relations, not so much in money. It is notable the extent to which capitalism, in its terrible intelligence, has already figured out that people are desperate for that ineffable something. As one marketing expert put it to me, people want to buy meaning. The trouble is, of course, that it cannot be bought.

For young people, the capitalist dream is already dying. They are realising that they will not be better off than their parents. In fact, they will likely be worse off, condemned to a lifetime of debt, first for education, then for housing. Secure jobs and homes are, for many, an ever-distant mirage, never to be attained. Meanwhile, climate heating threatens global catastrophe. As the promise of material success evaporates, perhaps at last the new generation will seek fulfilment elsewhere, where indeed it always lay. My generation bought the lie, and only now in mid-life many are realising the unsatisfying reality of perpetual financial anxiety, boring, unfulfilling work and broken marriages. For others, the only thing to look forward to is the 'freedom' of not doing it anymore, retirement. What a paltry goal. We can surely do better.

Space must therefore be made for the sacred and the infinite, whether in a room full of paintings, a dance club or a quiet meeting hall. Indeed these spaces should be celebrated and preserved, much as cathedrals once were. But above all, we should strive to build a society which promotes the sacred source of meaning, to escape the aridity of the bleak materialist desert, namely, the connection with other people. This connection can be meaningful only when it is *equal*. Loving human relationships are undermined and ultimately destroyed by hierarchy and social division, whether of wealth or class.

Love was my salvation in the depths of my depression, the thing that saved me from self-annihilation. Love is society's salvation that can lead us from the wasteland of individualist meaninglessness, where we currently dwell. The vision of a society built around love, where love is the goal, can animate and motivate us in place of the empty promises of capitalism.

But it is not enough simply to demand change and point to the disastrous future that confronts us. We have to be driven by a vision of a place that is better, where we will flourish in ways that seem unimaginable in the vacuity and superficiality of capitalist culture, where work and society are oriented around the one thing that truly matters — our relations with others.

How do we build a Republic of Love?

12
Declare Your Utopia

'When we are dreaming alone it is only a dream. When
we are dreaming with others, it is the beginning of reality.'
— *Dom Helder Camara*

UTOPIAS HAVE become unfashionable. Perhaps unsurprising after
the disastrous utopian schemes — both fascist and communist
— imposed upon European society in the twentieth century.
Utopias have become synonymous with an unrealistic and unrealisable
dream, a fantasy. Anarchists, too, have resisted utopianism, believing
with some reason that people should find their own way and build
a new society through their collective autonomous actions: no one
should prescribe what this should resemble. Indeed, we *cannot* know
what it should look like.

But it is hard to get motivated by something invisible. Part of the
terrible success of capitalism is that it presents itself as inevitable and
immutable, for Fukuyama, nothing less than the 'end of history'. Or, at
a minimum, that through the fake science of neo-classical economics,
capitalism presents itself as the ultimate and unquestionable fulfilment

of humanity's collected wants and needs, as expressed through acquisition.

But there is nothing inevitable about it. As the writer Ursula le Guin once famously commented in her speech at the National Book Awards in 2014:

'We live in capitalism. Its power seems inescapable. So did the divine right of kings. Any human power can be resisted and changed by human beings. Resistance and change often begin in art, and very often in our art, the art of words.

So we are beginning to change it right now, author and reader together (though I don't claim my words are art). Le Guin's own novels, in particular *The Dispossessed*, depict a vision of an anarchist society. It's one vision, her vision, of course, not *the vision*.

The capitalist system is fundamentally misaligned with the human: it therefore cannot last. By centring and promoting the material, capitalism misses the target of what matters most — the immaterial and ineffable, the something that arises between each other, the reality we create together.

Capitalism nevertheless has a way of seeming permanent. In this way, capitalism defeats the imagination. Dreaming of an alternative has become *infra dig*, almost silly. How foolish to believe that anything can change.

But philosopher Judith Butler suggests we take this fallacy head on:

To stay within the framework of Realpolitik is, I think, to accept a closing down of horizons, a way to seem 'cool' and sceptical at the expense of radical hope and aspiration. Sometimes you have to imagine in a radical way that makes you seem a little crazy, that puts you in an embarrassing light, in order to open up a possibility that others have already closed down with their knowing realism.[115]

I know this embarrassment. People sometimes giggle when I say I'm an anarchist. Sometimes I giggle too, to make them feel more comfortable. But this is my belief to my core, now even my life's purpose. One should not apologise.

Oscar Wilde believed we need a vision to galvanise us, writing:

> A map of the world that does not include Utopia is not worth even glancing at, for it leaves out the one country at which Humanity is always landing. And when Humanity lands there, it looks out, and, seeing a better country, sets sail. Progress is the realisation of utopias.[*]

Notably, Thomas More's original *Utopia* was written as a political critique of the enclosure of common land. He imagined a place where property was held in common, as it had been before that theft. As William Paris writes, More's *Utopia* was neither a denial of nor a flight from social reality but its very depiction: 'The question guiding *Utopia* is whether it was reasonable to expect peasants who have been dispossessed to resist committing the crime of stealing in order to survive. For More, it was the non-utopians who had misjudged reality, and so it was not only their priorities that had to be challenged, but their overall conception of reality'.[116] More's story therefore was not an idealistic fantasy but a polemic against a great crime. It was a profoundly political statement of what had been destroyed.

It's time to declare our utopias. We need loudly and unashamedly to assert that there are better alternatives to the current dispensation. Only such declarations create the possibility of making our utopias real, because only through declaration can other people join.

---

[*]   Wilde also argued for the necessity of disobedience: 'Disobedience, in the eyes of anyone who has read history, is man's original virtue. It is through disobedience that progress has been made, through disobedience and through rebellion'. "The Soul of Man under Socialism," first published in 1891 by The Fortnightly Review.

We cannot let our imaginations be defeated. We must map out and colour in the kingdom of the possible. With such visions, we will find the energy and motivation to build them. We will recruit others.

Victoria W. Wolcott suggests that the idealism and pragmatism of the civil rights movement were grounded in nothing less than an intensely utopian yearning.[117] Its leaders, from Martin Luther King Jr. and Pauli Murray to Father Divine and Howard Thurman, all shared a belief in a radical pacificism that was both specifically utopian and deeply engaged in the contemporary struggle. You can dream and act at the same time; indeed, some would claim that you need dreams in order to act.

For the British anarchist Colin Ward, we do not need utopias but simply to re-discover what was already there. Anarchism was not about fantasies of the future but comprises a 'description of a mode of human organisation, rooted in the experience of everyday life, which operates side by side with, and in spite of, the dominant authoritarian trends of our society'.[118] In other words, we need only expand upon our own experiences, the everyday revelation of the power of cooperation and joy of agency over our common life.

A utopia can be personal. It doesn't have to be universal. Indeed, there is something inherently fascistic about universalist visions. Like other anarchists, I believe that people themselves should be the sole authors of their fate, and the sole architects of their future. So please don't take what follows as a prescription for everyone else. I do however believe that it is possible.

It began with a flood in a small Welsh town. Blaenau Ffestiniog lies in the hills of Eyri, the national park once known as Snowdonia, which had long been threatened by an overflowing river. One winter's night, unusually heavy rain launched waves over the barriers that had hitherto kept the waters at bay.

Though long predicted, the flood was unprecedented. Water inundated streets and houses, causing widespread damage. But from the onset of the flood, people reached out to one another to help, whether to barricade their houses with sandbags or evacuate flooded buildings. When the waters finally receded, neighbours cleaned up the mud and debris together. They wondered why that spirit of mutual aid couldn't endure. The floods had engendered a sense of community and solidarity that they wanted to preserve.

Meanwhile, the feeling grew that 'government', both local and central, had not responded adequately. Apart from the local volunteer fire brigade, help had been slow in coming if it indeed came at all. Food and shelter was provided by neighbours rather than by the state. The flood had been foreseen, but instead of building defences, the council had urged the townspeople to leave, arguing that parts of the village were indefensible. Naturally, the local people didn't see it like that.

The flood had caused immense damage. There was talk of compensation from the government, but this seemed a long way off. It was more urgent and seemed more plausible for the community to start rebuilding itself. And so the townspeople began to meet, daily at the height of the crisis, then weekly as the task ahead became clearer. There was a precedent: there had been 'climate assemblies' in the region of Gwynedd, before the floods, to start discussing what to do about the growing impacts of climate change.

The town meetings now discussed priorities, how to spend what reconstruction money might come, how to plan the town's defences against future floods, how to rehouse those now in temporary housing first with other inhabitants of the town and then into more permanent dwellings. They learned about cooperative models of funding, how investment by the many enabled houses to be built that once seemed unaffordable.

The townspeople insisted that their plans were more legitimate than the local or county council's. Theirs had been made through the participation of everyone, not an allegedly representative few whom many of the townspeople didn't know and anyhow didn't trust: they were mostly not local. So when it came to start building, the townspeople refused to apply for planning permission: it would take far too long. They simply started building. The council sent inspectors and issued prevention notices, but they were politely ignored. The building went ahead. Next were the flood barriers to protect the town from the rivers. Hydrologists were consulted on how to build channels and outlets to prevent the waters from building up again.

The press heard of the Blaenau Forum, as the town meetings began to be known. Some questioned the Forum's assumption of authority, but reporters who visited learned that the Forum was overwhelmingly supported by the local people. Some commentators were at first sceptical and critical. But it was difficult to present the Blaenau population as radical or revolutionary. Sometimes retired, often middle-aged, they didn't fit the image of disruptors. And their message of inclusion of all was one to which many were receptive. Nothing about us without us, they said.

The Forum began to take decisions that went beyond dealing with the consequences of the flood. Sanitation was an immediate issue, but so was the future of the local school and small hospital. The local people demanded that they stay open, but the central government refused, claiming that the town's very existence was unsustainable. So the townspeople withheld their taxes in protest and instead saved them in a fund for the maintenance of the local facilities.

At first, the Forum didn't make any demands. They just started discussing the issues that concerned them — the local schools, hospitals and roads. With growing skills of managing such gatherings, the meetings became a place where anyone could speak, without an agenda. Attendees enjoyed the meetings and found that they liked getting to know their neighbours. People who had seemed strangers were becoming real. The meetings weren't really 'political' in that political party affiliations didn't seem relevant. Attendance grew. After a while, the Blaenau Forum invited their local MP to attend. Always eager to show up for his constituents, upon whose votes he relied, he accepted.

But when he came to the meeting, he found that he was only one of the many voices who spoke. He was expected to listen more than speak. Once or twice, he was asked to communicate views to 'the government', but others at the meeting dismissed this request — what difference would it make? The government wouldn't listen to one MP any more than it would listen to their meeting. Local councillors were invited too. Some of the councillors announced that as elected representatives they could ignore the wishes of the meeting. They were shunned. And through listening to the gatherings, which were growing in size, it became clear to them that these local people were articulating needs and choices that would be impossible for them to ignore. At a meeting about the local hospital, nurses, doctors and patients and their families were all given the floor — practical proposals were made and debated. Solutions were found which were then implemented.

One facilitator proposed that there be five minutes of silence at the end of each meeting. The idea caught on. There was something about the intimacy and community of silence that people found affecting, even moving. Somehow they felt more bound together. At other times, there were dance parties.

Somewhere along the way, and no one could quite be sure the precise moment this took place, the Blaenau meeting became the primary place where local issues were discussed and sorted out. Participants found that when they listened to one another, they found the other's views largely reasonable — others were patients or parents or pensioners, too. Trouble-makers at first succeeded in disrupting meetings, but soon they realised that the social cost was too high. The large majority wanted peaceful, polite discussion. A new culture of discussion and listening began to take life. People noticed that there was less hostility, more courtesy, more willingness to help one another without payment — what some knew to be called mutual aid.

The 'Blaenau Revolution' inspired others. A political uprising caught fire. People began to wonder why all the decisions that mattered to them were taken by a tiny group of politicians in Westminster. Across the country, groups of people met to establish their own local forums. The 'Blaenau Model' spread to other towns, patchily at first, then it began in the bigger towns and cities. A new cohort of councillors emerged, who sought election only to give over their power to the communal assemblies. One or two mayors organised their own meetings, but once established, it was the voices at the meetings, not the 'higher ups', which held sway.

Eventually, of course, came the confrontation with central authority. Sometimes it was over a planning decision — a new bypass, perhaps, or a demand for extra health or education spending — the central government in Westminster or, perhaps, the regional county council — insisted that its laws and decisions be obeyed. The confrontation played out in different ways. Sometimes there were negotiations and compromises were reached. Sometimes more direct action was needed. Once the government tried to use heavily armoured police to force access to the building site of a planned new coal mine, but their attempt failed when several of the police joined the protesters who blocked the route. Over time, the political culture of the country changed as it became clear to everyone that the Blaenau meetings could not legitimately be ignored.

Meanwhile, the Blaenau group reached out to groups in nearby towns and villages. These informal discussions led to the formation of a regional group to coordinate the larger scale decisions that affected a broader area. But these councils were different from the regional authorities that they eventually were to replace. They didn't comprise elected officials who served for a particular term between elections and who made their own decisions. Instead they were delegates who represented their various local groups. They could only represent positions that had been agreed by the local communal groups. If they didn't, they could immediately be recalled. Eventually, and following the same principles, the regional groups aggregated to yet bigger groups, and the network of groups of varying scales spread across the country like a moss spreading over the forest floor, forming what some called a confederation but others simply called the new way of doing things, or the new democracy. Somehow, the baroque but decaying buildings and pretentious terms of the old way — parliamentary democracy — seemed inappropriate for the new dispensation which was simpler, messier but altogether better. People ceased complaining about 'politics' because politics had effectively ceased to exist.

These arrangements were always fluid. They never settled into a fixed pattern of institutions. The decision-making organisations — the communal or regional level councils — were temporary. They didn't have a permanent existence; they existed only by the regular giving of consent by those whose affairs they arbitrated. In this way, these new organisations didn't evolve to have their own sets of interests in self-perpetuation and their own elites who populated the institutions. People took it in turns to participate. In some cases, mass meetings decided priorities, and smaller groups worked through the detailed decisions for approval by the whole. In other cases, 'sortition' was used to select representative groups of citizens who could fairly speak for the whole. In others yet, citizens simply took it in turns to participate in decision-making, like those in ancient Greece, though this time women took an equal place and there were, of course, no enslaved people.

****

Meanwhile, the demand for democracy and control spread across society, seeping into all places, including where people spent most of their days. Why was it necessary to tolerate the overt hierarchy of the workplace and the inequality of rewards from shared labour, when those who did no work enjoyed all the benefits? It was simply unfair and humiliating. In one large corporation, at a 'staff forum' at a large tech company in London, the fire of change was lit.

The staff forum had been used to discuss things like leave allowances and working from home. But one young programmer put up her hand one week and asked what share she and other employees would enjoy of the enormous wealth of the company, counted in many billions of pounds. From the 'management', who attended the work forums dressed in jeans and t-shirts just like the staff, answer came there none. Of course, it barely needed to be said that the employees did not receive any benefit from the company's capital.

The programmer began an email chain with other young employees. They compared their wages to the many millions paid to the CEO and other senior management. The difference was many hundreds of orders of magnitude. The employees were also concerned by the eroding value of their wages, as high inflation ravaged the economy and cut living standards. Rents in London were becoming more and more unaffordable. Another employee, this time a 'customer experience designer', suggested a walk-out in protest.

So began what later became known as the 'Great Awakening'.

The employees chose May Day, the traditional day of celebrating labour, for the walk-out. At first, only a couple of dozen staff members refused to show up to work. They were duly threatened by the management with losing their jobs. The threats, written in aggressive emails, backfired. Some of them were leaked to the press and held up as a crass example of 'boss' behaviour. The following week, the day for the next walk-out, saw hundreds of employees join the action. This time management took a subtler response. They offered a 5% pay increase, phased in over the next few months.

But as the strikers realised their power, they upped their demands. Nothing less than an ownership share of the company would suffice. After all, they, the employees, created most of the company's value through their programming and designs. The employees organised themselves through leaderless meetings, where they worked out their positions. The next week's walk-out saw almost all the London office staff participate. Some groups began to occupy the office itself. Management floundered. Some suggested that employees be granted a few shares in the company, to give them 'ownership'. Some suggested a bigger pay rise. Some suggested sacking all the strikers and hiring in agency workers to cover their work. But the shareholders, mostly big investment and pension funds, warned management that the company risked its future by not ceding to more of the workers' demands. Its share price had fallen precipitously. Its very survival was at stake.

Instead, the strikes spread to other companies. The young programmer wrote a cogent blog post arguing that only ownership would fairly recompense the workers for their contribution to the value of the company. Her blog resonated with a large community of other workers, in industries ranging from tech to manufacturing and transport. She became the informal voice of a generation of young people who felt cheated by the current economic dispensation. Calm, coherent and articulate, her arguments were difficult to dismiss — much as politicians and media commentators tried. She communicated directly with her followers by videos on social media platforms. She had no need for the mainstream press to get her message across. Soon she was joined by others, from various sectors, who articulated the same demands: Ownership now!

With the walkouts and occupations continuing, the company's production was stymied by regular strikes; the management of the tech company was under pressure. Negotiating with the employees, they eventually conceded that all employees of the company would be granted an ownership share. The company's management would be elected by the employee-owners, who would thenceforth be known as partners. One of their first decisions was that no one in the company should be paid more than five times the wages of the lowest paid, including the cleaners and catering staff. The May Day strikers, as they had become known, prevailed.

This victory lit a fuse across the economy. In company after company and industry after industry, the same demand rang out. One by one, company owners and shareholders conceded in the face of repeated, paralysing strikes and occupations. After centuries of domination and exploitation, capital was at last ceding to labour, allowing a fairer bargain between the two.

Meanwhile, as part of the action against management, one of the programmers leaked the code of the company's software product onto a pirate site. Though he was immediately threatened with firing and prosecution, his work colleagues backed him. Others in other companies followed. So began the 'FreeTech' movement where intellectual property, hitherto a preserve of private ownership for profit, was shared for the benefit of all. Its principles became codified in the so-called 'FreeTech charter', principles derived from the pre-revolution Open Source movement — above all, the principle of sharing for mutual benefit — based on the idea that transparency promotes greater innovation. The tools produced by these methods began to be shaped by the needs of the communities who were now controlling their own affairs, rather than the needs of the manufacturers to continue to extract profit from their products, selling users' personal data to advertisers and others eager to exploit them, including political parties. These tools, in turn, were not proprietary but adaptable and scalable, appropriate to the specific needs of local towns and cities and, ultimately, the confederation of self-governing communities.

FreeTech became one of the pillars of the new movement for democracy. And in sector after sector, transparency of technology became the norm. Cooperatives saw their goals in terms of the sector — the needs of all the cooperatives, since they were all serving the same purpose — the needs of their worker-owners, the environment and the common good. These goals were best pursued in a culture of collaboration and partnership rather than competition. Maximum profit and maximum production were no longer the goals. A new economic model came gradually to life, one that was more about meeting human needs and less about creating human wants. Eventually, this entailed less actual production. Jobs without coercion, more free time.

Across the country, the local Forums and their federations produced a novel sense of empowerment and agency. The same was happening in the workplace. It took time for the new arrangements to settle down; circumstances were different in every company and every city. No one pretended that this was a flawless state of affairs. There were still disputes and tensions and mistakes. After all, nothing made by humans is perfect. But it was the process of doing things that changed fundamentally. Participatory, truly democratic, fair because all could participate — it was simply a better way.

Over time, these arrangements settled down into what some people light-heartedly called the Republic of Love. The culture reflected the values of the whole and, in turn, contributed to the change of affairs. Artists responded to the new mood of democracy and transparency. Art became less cynical, less motivated by the big sale and instead became more populist, less elitist, shared, organic, spontaneous, the realm of the many rather than the few. Collective art, whether murals or music, began to populate public spaces, artefacts neither selected nor controlled by bureaucrats or politicians, but by the people together. Cultural debates became less about toxic difference and more about how to promote love or other ineffable human values such as community, mutual aid and social peace or, simply, who had the best tunes.

The architecture of cities slowly changed. The massive, characterless and faceless skyscrapers of the big banks and finance houses were eventually repurposed as apartment blocks and universities. Over time, they were knocked down and replaced with buildings whose design reflected their social purpose — they were open, adorned with greenery, accessible and diverse in colour and design. The private gardens of Buckingham Palace were opened for public use, as the monarchy was abolished and the royal family joined the 'commoners'. The Houses of Parliament became a kind of church to the new dispensation, where regular celebrations of the new democracy rang out in the Great Hall, the magnificent space first built in 1097. Poetry readings, debating clubs and music recitals replaced partisan bickering and nugatory debate.

And in the centre of the city, where the City of London once stood, a massive and magnificent tower was consecrated. Built by many craftsmen and women over a century, baroquely decorated with gargoyles and soaring buttresses, it was called the New Temple to Humanity. With scores of floors devoted to education, meetings, the arts, worship (of whatever god you chose) or simply public space for whatever purpose, governed by an elected committee of those who used it, it represented the diversity and cosmopolitanism of the city where it stood. It became a beloved public symbol, where almost every citizen shared a memory.

The confederation was for a while still called the United Kingdom, but after a while it became clear that this nomenclature no longer reflected the true nature of the country. It became, simply, 'The Peoples United'. It wasn't really a country as they had once been known, more a collection of different communes, regions and peoples who chose their own paths and fates, united in their practices of freedom, true democracy and self-determination. Vestiges of the old order remained — flags, anthems and sentimental hymns — but more as a way of keeping memories alive than reaffirming something extant. In place of the unity, a cacophonous diversity flourished, a hybrid mixture of cultures, old and new, what once had been called 'foreign'. As the false pretences of national identity evaporated, this new land welcomed peoples from all over the world who needed refuge, not least from the climatic disasters that had befallen their own lands.

Work became a matter of choice. Most chose to work enough to get by, and nothing more. In any case, the divide between paid and unpaid work disappeared. If you didn't formally receive pay, you would still be clothed, fed and housed but expected to contribute in some way to the needs of your fellow humans. The shallow values of status and financial success came to be despised as artefacts of a backward past. It became deeply unfashionable to be rich, to own big houses or drive expensive cars. Likewise, professions of class allegiance or preference became a thing of the past, like the divisions of kings, knights and serfs of an earlier era. In all realms, women took a role at least as preeminent as men: in its earlier phases, it was called a feminist republic, but after a while, this name dropped away: it was simply the way things were. As the priorities of society changed, people no longer talked of economic growth as the goal, and indeed production sometimes dropped entirely. Instead, any sense of a collective aim was submerged in a creative diversity of different aims — indeed the notion that 'society', a unitary thing, existed came to be questioned, just as was the notion that 'society' might want one thing rather than many.

Over time, other countries followed the lead of the People's United. The United Nations became truly a body of peoples and not of states, as the different confederations sent delegates to confer over matters of common concern. There was mass disarmament. In the great mixing of peoples and cultures, occasioned by the mass migration from climate chaos, the notion of nuclear weapons as a means to deter war became absurd. If I attack you, I am also attacking me. The world of nation states took its place in history alongside the rule of popes and monarchs. Of course, there were still conflicts. These could not be avoided in a world of dwindling resources, floods, wildfires and unliveable temperatures. But no longer did nationalism or the pathetic ambitions of dictators and despots dominate. As nation states declined, wars became smaller scale and less devastating. The ethnic or linguistic divisions that had hitherto provided convenient dividing lines had ceased to exist. The common interest of peace and collaboration had greater sway in a world where the temptations of nationalism and sentimental patriotism had diminished. Simply put, it became harder to delineate Them from Us, whatever the efforts of self-serving little men to make it otherwise. Their day was done.

Instead, new bonds of international solidarity grew up — between women, people of colour or the autistic — these new loose federations deepened and cemented transnational ties in ways that transcended borders and led to new forms of international collaboration. People realised that they were not only of their country but also of many countries, identities and allegiances. They became truly cosmopolitan.

When sometimes a dictator did rise, or a fascist ideology, and these could not be totally eradicated (the internet concealed various dark corners, after all), the people did not rely on a professional army to defend them. These had become obsolete and unnecessary. Instead, they formed spontaneous militias, women and men fighting side by side, resilient, innovative and diverse in ways that proved impossible to defeat. Using techniques of guerrilla resistance — and homemade drone swarms — they made any invasion untenable. When a threat arose, people from around the world united in providing assistance to the threatened, whether through volunteers or matèriel. 'International Brigades' sprang up. Indeed, a vast network of anti-fascist militias grew, who could be called upon whenever a threat arose. This became its own kind of deterrent to would-be despots, celebrated with new songs and flags.

No one spoke anymore of the end of history. In fact, they talked of a new beginning, a new era in human affairs. An era challenged by the climate crisis, but one where crisis was the catalyst for the birth of a new society. An era where somehow along the way people had learned how to flourish more richly, to enjoy one another more deeply and, ultimately, to find full expression of what it means to be human.

Epilogue:
The Future Is the Present

'To change everything, start anywhere. The secret is to begin'.
Origin unknown.

FIRST started learning and writing about anarchism more than twenty years ago. At that time, there was a great sense of complacency about the world and the future. The US — the West — was the global hegemon imposing its own version of a 'world of rules'. Capitalism was the dominant credo. So-called 'representative' democracy was the ideal political system.

Fewer and fewer today believe this. Disillusionment with 'the system' is mounting; disenchantment with 'democracy' — the supposedly 'representative' kind currently practiced — is rising across the world.[119] The indices of collapse are multiplying. Fires in LA, devastating floods across a third of Pakistan. War crimes proliferate unpunished. Might is right, and rules are trampled underfoot. And beneath it all remains the soul's fathomless emptiness that capitalism can never fill.

As I contemplate what's going on, I have felt great despair. And yet I still feel hope.

That hope lies in the sentences that begin this book, 'I was born into chaos. I live in chaos', a young Californian woman told me just a few days before I wrote these words. She gets it, and her generation gets it. Twenty years ago, I argued that the system would break down and fascism would emerge; I warned of grinning dictators in well-tailored suits. It felt like screaming in an empty room. People laughed. Today, the evidence is all around us. The worst kind of anarchy is upon us. It lies not in the future, but now.

The first step to change, then, has taken place. Realisation. I see it in the understandable despair and disillusionment of young people. I see it in the handwringing in the 'mainstream media' and in those who choose to 'switch off' from all the bad news. I see it in the pathetic complaints that 'no one' has any answers: the feeble, self-serving choice of learned impotence, passivity and, indeed, political ignorance. Examples of alternatives are all around, in the present and past, if you only care to look.

At these times, I am inspired by the bravery and persistence of early anarchists, the Russian Pyotr Kropotkin, the American Emma Goldman, Louise Michel of the Paris Commune or the Spanish anarchists of the Republic. In their days, capitalism and authoritarianism were savage. Factory conditions were bestial. Government enforcement of the demands of capital — the government-sanctioned robber barons who seized land across America; the czarist authorities who maintained serfdom — was brutal. In response, the anarchists acted; they paid a heavy price in imprisonment, exile, penury and public abuse. But they acted. They believed, above all, in action.

I am inspired by the words and bravery of dead friends, authors and poets who lived precariously by their pens and who were thus, unlike most of us, truly free to respond to the world as they saw it. I am inspired by the founders of Strike Debt, a tiny group who met in Zuccotti Park in New York City and began, with small and persistent actions, a movement that changed the debate and ultimately government policy about the crippling, life-altering burden of debt on both young people and the sick in the US. I am inspired by the builders of Cooperation Jackson in Mississippi, who are constructing a cooperative, self-governing society from the ground up. I am inspired, of course, by Rojava. And today, I am glad to be involved in their cause.

In action I find relief from the despair. I find it in new colleagues and friends — young women who travelled to Syria to fight ISIS on Rojava's side; the small group humbly guiding the huge movement of children's parliaments in India; unknown and unrecognised activists here in Britain, who are trying to build new forms of democracy as they witness old forms decay; a young woman who quit her prestigious government job because she could see where it was heading.

'My people' were once 'middle-class professionals', as I was in the Foreign Office. Invariably white, solicitors, civil servants, TV producers, journalists: these were my tribe. I suspect that many were my friends *because* I was in the foreign office, and thus a kind of trophy. Either way, we were the fragile beneficiaries of 'the system', wealthy enough to buy decent houses and sup in moderately priced restaurants, comfortable knowing that the misery of unpayable debt or outright poverty would never be our own. We talked of movies, TV and, less often, books. We debated party politics and personalities, not fundamental reconstruction.

Today, I feel more and more alienated in these conversations. Missing is not only acknowledgement of the disaster we're in but also passion — not just for change but for life itself. Among those of my — middle — age, the cynicism and disillusionment of bourgeois life can barely be concealed. Perhaps a career that has failed or an ambition thwarted. The lesser evil that has been settled for. While for those who 'succeed' by the paltry measures of status or wealth, success and ambition prove hollow.

There is a great urgency to the current moment. The seismic turbulence that we are so uncomfortably feeling also offers opportunity. We have shifted from the rigid complacency of earlier in the century into something more fluid and unstable. Change, bad or good, might happen fast. We cannot be bystanders, for the worst are already on the warpath, already constructing their dystopian vision, already dominating 'social' media (in fact, very anti-social). They must be combatted by resistance, by ferocious and original argument, not by tired clichés of the same old bromides, but above all, by building a better alternative, always peacefully, the promotion by demonstration and construction of a better way. Maybe it will one day require bodies on the line: some are already losing their lives and their homes.

The reason the current dispensation is collapsing is that it doesn't meet true human needs: its foundations do not even encompass the very nature of reality (for it misses out all — the vastness, the infinite — that cannot be measured). It denies our fundamental need for agency — control — over our own lives. In its dry, logical but thus inhuman economics, it renders us into mere consumers or units of labour; it makes us less than human.

Political philosophies such as socialism or capitalism rest on the notion of the future, where everything will be fairer or richer — *better* — for everyone. Henri Bergson believed that time was not hours and minutes and clock time. That was time measured merely by planetary movement, of Earth's rotation around the sun. This was not how we actually *experience* time, Bergson argued. Instead, there is no future, only a past that disappears and the eternal present. Pierre Bourdieu believed that capitalism, itself, with its obsession with the future, dictated our experience of time. Agrarian societies, such as Algerian peasants, experienced time very differently: more as circadian and seasonal rhythms, or ritual. In our current circumstance, the future is no longer a coherent and plausible vision of well-being. Instead the future appears at odds, contested, violent; in many ways, it bodes disaster. Though always distant, but once vivid, the promise of the future is evaporating.

Love flourishes in conditions of equality — of respect, shared power and common well-being (this is why we love friends but not bosses or subordinates). We can be truly free only in such conditions, when we are liberated from the control of the state and social coercion. When we rule only ourselves. The fulfilment of this dream is perhaps the true end of history, a dispensation when humans finally live as humans, not as the diminished functionaries of someone else's petty theories. Peter Marshall, in his brilliant history of anarchism, cites the Christian existentialist Nikolai Berdyaev, who emphasised freedom's metaphysical aspect. He believed that the truly free human is freed from psychological and physical violence, from the State and social pressures, to be entirely self-governing. As a complete person, she is creative in the 'ecstasy of the moment', which is outside time. It is only 'the gathering together of freedom, truth and love which realises personality, free and creative personality'. Berdyaev finally envisages the end of history, which for him is marked by the victory of 'existential time' over historical time, as the complete liberation of humanity.[120] In a modern turn of phrase, we become truly 'present' to our full selves, existing not in the past or future but now.

It feels scary and decidedly unfashionable to use words of great ambition and aspiration. But I believe that something magnificent is available, if only we see it, if only we have the courage to build it. A world where at last we can find fulfilment, meaning and purpose through the practice of intimate cooperation and mutual aid, an environment propitious for that most vital and epic of human needs, wants and joys — love itself. I have no words adequately to convey its gravity or its qualities except to say that it is the most important thing of all.

Carne Ross, February 2025

Acknowledgements

I AM very grateful to Jonathan Rowson at Perspectiva Press for taking the risk to publish this book and for his finely-tuned advice to improve the book, a rare thing in our hasty world. I thank Indra Adnan for first introducing me to Perspectiva.

Special thanks to my dear friend Alnoor Ladha for his constant encouragement and guidance, and for sticking with me during my dark days. It has been a joy and inspiration to discuss ideas and life with you.

John Burnside read at least two drafts and gave me extensive, detailed and invaluable comments. I thank you and miss you, John. Another anarchist poet, Benjamin Zephaniah, who has also sadly left us, encouraged and inspired me: thank you, Benjamin. This book is dedicated to you both, poets of beauty, revolution and freedom.

Alexandra Mills gave me very helpful comments and welcome encouragement. Several others read the book and gave me excellent advice including Jenny Nicholson, Matthew Porges, Kate Whittle, Elaine Nicholson, Gerald Mitchell, Morgan Phillips, Manuel Toscano, Leo Roberts, Indigo Rumbelow, Hendrik Bernhard, Melissa Rice, Mardy Jase, Rita Ashworth, Jenni Crockett, Patricia Mary Lewis, Ian Robertson, Kent Smith, Bojan Francuz, Robert Macmillan, Paul Macdonald, Anka Zawiślak, Lee David, Corey Herrman and Diego de la Rocha. It seems inadequate to thank you like this for the major effort of reading and commenting on my book, but please know that I am more than grateful. You are part of this story.

Thanks to Erik Forman for allowing me to interview him about the Drivers Cooperative.

And particular thanks to my comrade Debbie Bookchin (daughter of Murray) for sharing her extensive knowledge, for our collaboration in support of Rojava and for her unceasing encouragement, advice and friendship.

Any remaining mistakes are mine alone.

And, finally, my thanks and love to Karmen and the twins, who make my world.

Endnotes

1   'Can quantum mechanics explain consciousness?', Marcelo Gleiser, *Big Think*, 24 November 2021.

2   See https://jakeseliger.com/.

3   Quoted from *Right Here, Right Now: Life Stories from America's Death Row*, ed. Lynden Harris, Duke University Press, 2021.

4   Quoted from *Memories, Dreams, Reflections: An Autobiography* by Carl Gustav Jung, trs. Anelia Jaffe, Richard Winston, William Collins, 2019.

5   'Income Inequality and Happiness: An Inverted U-shaped Curve', Zonghu Yu and Fei Wang, *Frontiers in Psychology*, 24 November 2017.

6   'Forget regret! How to have a happy life' interview with Robert Waldinger by Emine Saner, *The Guardian*, 6 February 2023.

7   'Carlo Rovelli on the bizarre world of relational quantum mechanics', Michael Brooks, *NewScientist*, 10 October 2022.

8   Quoted from *The New Possible: Visions of Our World beyond Crisis* ed. Philip Clayton et al, Wipf & Stock Publishers, 2021.

9   'Friendship Is a Root of Freedom' in *Joyful Militancy* by Nick Montgomery & Carla Bergman, Institute for Anarchist Studies, 18 December 2017.

10   Ibid.

11   Quoted from *The Promise of an Anarchist Sociological Imagination*, Erwin F. Rafael, The Anarchist Library, 2018.

12   'British political giving is increasingly dominated by the rich — it's a system ripe for abuse' by Peter Geoghegan, *The Guardian*, 10 July 2023.

13   'Grenfell Tower: the fire, the findings, who's to blame and what happens next', *The Guardian*, 5 September 2024.

14   Ibid.

15   'The people of Grenfell knew the truth before the fire. It's we who must learn from them now'. Gillian Slovo, *The Guardian*, 7 September 2024.

16   Grenfell Tower Inquiry: Statement on Publication of Phase 2 Report, September 2024.

17   *Demanding the Impossible: A History of Anarchism*, Peter Marshall, Harper Perennial, 2007.

18   *The Kurdish Women's Movement*, Dilar Dirik, Pluto Press, 2021.

19   *Surmounting the Barricades: Women in the Paris Commune*, Carolyn Eichner, Indiana University Press, 2004.

20   From the documentary film, Accidental Anarchist (Hopscotch Productions, 2017).

21   'Zapatistas: Lessons in community self-organisation in Mexico', Anna Rebrii, Open Democracy, 25 June 2020.

22   'How non-expertise becomes a strength' Hugh Pope, DemocracyNext, 23 January 2023.

23   'Why did PB decline in Brazil and will Lula revive it?' People Powered website, 7 November 2022.

24   From DemoLab: Concejo Abierto Facebook page.

25   'Why the world can benefit from contact theory' Simon Kuper, Financial Times, 26 January 2023.

26   'Now the Work Begins: Lessons in a New Kind of Democracy with Audrey Tang', Demos YouTube account.

27   'What are the key issues in Taiwan's 2024 presidential election?' Ching-hsin Yu, Brookings Institute, 20 December, 2023.

28   Solonian Democracy Institute 'Digital Democracy Report 2024'.

29   'AI can help humans find common ground in democratic deliberation' Tessler et al, Science, vol. 386, 18 October 2024.

30   'Collapse won't reset society', Adam van Buskirk, Palladium, 11 April 2022.

31   'Why knowing your neighbours could save you in the next climate disaster', Yvonne Marquez, *The Guardian*, 8 December 2022.

32   Ibid.

33   "Never again a Mexico without us": Gender, indigenous autonomy, and multiculturalism in neoliberal Mexico', Melissa Marie Forbis, University of Texas, 2008.

34   Quoted by Anna Rebrii, ibid.

35   For more on Kropotkin, see 'The Ants Have Not Read Kant: Petr Kropotkin and Mutual Aid', *Aereo* magazine, 1 December 2022.

36   'Against school', John Burnside, *New Statesman*, 28 July 2022.

37   *Dialectic of Enlightenment* Theodor Adorno and Max Horkheimer, Institute for Social Research, 1944.

38   *Psychopolitics: Neoliberalism and New Technologies of Power*, Byung-Chul Han, trans. Erik Butler, London: Verso Books, 2017.

39   'Report on the Construction of Situations and on the International Situationist Tendency's Conditions of Organization and Action', Guy Debord, tr. Ken Knabb, Situationist International Anthology, PM Press, 2024.

40   From *Guy Debord (Critical Lives)*, Andy Merrifield, Reaktion Books, 2005.

41   'Want to see political change? Look to the margins', Rebecca Solnit, *The Guardian*, 14 September 2022.

42   "The Operating Instructions." Ursula K. Le Guin, '*The Left Hand of Darkness*', Ace, n, 1999.

43   From *The Death and Life of Great American Cities*, Jane Jacobs, Penguin, 1994.

44   From *Situationism: A Compendium*, Guy Debord, Ivan Chtcheglov, Asger Jorn, Raoul Vaneigem, Mustapha Khayati, Bread and Circuses, 2014.

45   See 'Equality was the key to ancient Mexican city's success, study suggests', Mattha Busby, *The Guardian*, 16 March 2022.

46   'The Foundation of Monte Albán, Intensification, and Growth: Coactive Processes and Joint Production' Linda Nicholas, Gary Feinman, Frontiers in Political Science, 8 March 2022.

47   See 'Equality was the key to ancient Mexican city's success, study suggests', Mattha Busby, *The Guardian*, 16 March 2022.

48   'Human History Gets a Rewrite', William Deresiewicz, *The Atlantic*, 18 October 2021.

49   *Psychopolitics: Neoliberalism and New Technologies of Power*, Byung-Chul Han, trans. Erik Butler, London: Verso Books, 2017.

50   Ibid.

51   *Ideas and Integrities: A Spontaneous Autobiographical Disclosure* (1969), Buckminster Fuller, Estate of R. Buckminster Fuller, 2009.

52   Quoted in *The Anarchist Revelation*, Paul Cudenec, Winter Oak Press, 2013.

53   This article explains my lessons learned about self-determination: 'From conflict to compromise, lessons in creating a state', Carne Ross, *The Independent*, 25 June 2019.

54   *On Revolution*, Hannah Arendt, Faber Modern Classics, 2016

55   *Letters to a Young Poet*, Letter Four, July 16, 1903, Rainer Maria Rilke, Penguin Classics, 2016.

56   *The Social Contract* Jean-Jacques Rousseau, Penguin Books, 2004.

57   *Demanding the Impossible: A History of Anarchism*, Peter Marshall, Harper Perennial, 2007.

58   From *Pedagogy of the Oppressed*, Paulo Freire, Penguin, 2017.

59   *Tao Te Ching*. tr. Stephen Micthell, Perennial Classics, 1999.

60   *Power Corrupts, but Control Does Not: What Stands Behind the Effects of Holding High Positions*, Aleksandra Cislek et al, Pers Soc Psychol Bull, 2018.

61   'Growing proportion of England's flood defences in disrepair, analysis finds' Josh Halliday and Carmen Aguilar García, *The Guardian*, 1 January 2024.

62   'Letters to a Frenchman on the Present Crisis' (1870)' in 'Bakunin on Anarchy' Mikhail Bakunin, ed. Sam Dolgoff, 1971.

63   In *Weak Statesmen, Weaker People*, Gustav Landauer, The Anarchist Library, 1910.

64   'How Much (More) Should CEOs Make? A Universal Desire for More Equal Pay' Sorapop Kiatpongsan and Michael I. Norton, Perspectives on Psychological Science, Vol 9, Issue 6.

65   *The Myth of Normal: Trauma, Illness & Healing in a Toxic Culture*, Gabor Maté, Daniel Maté, Vermilion, 2024.

66   Andrew Clark, Professor at the Paris School of Economics.

67   'How a new age of surveillance is changing work', *The Economist*, 13 May 2022.

68   'A Worker-Owned Cooperative Tries to Compete with Uber and Lyft', *New York Times*, 28 May 2021.

69   'Meet the most powerful Uber driver in India' Varsha Bansal, Rest of World, 4 January 2023.

70   'How Mondragon Became the World's Largest Co-op', Nick Romeo, *The New Yorker*, 27 August 2022.

71   'How worker ownership builds community wealth and a more just society', Pamela Haines, Waging Nonviolence, 3 February 2023.

72   For more about this, read 'What Co-ops and DAOs Can Learn from One Another', Austin Robey, FWB, 13 January, 2022.

73   *The People Factor: Why Investing in Employees Pays Off*, Wharton, University of Pennsylvania, March 2023.

74   'Why a Rhodes Scholar's Ambition Led Her to a Job at Starbucks', Noam Scheiber, *New York Times*, 19 June 2022.

75   'Inside the Effort to Unionize Every Starbucks in America', Sauruv Sarkar, *Progressive*, 22 August 2022.

76   'Municipalist Syndicalism: From the Workplace to the Community', Alexandar Kolokotronis, *ROAR*, Issue #9.

77   Wikipedia gives a good history of the occupation.

78   See more at Participedia.net: the Worker-Recovered Enterprise Movement (Argentina).

79   'Reddit 'antiwork' forum booms as millions of Americans quit jobs', Taylor Nicole Rogers, *Financial Times*, 9 January 2022.

80   *Psychopolitics: Neoliberalism and New Technologies of Power*, Byung-Chul Han, Verso, 2025.

81   *'How to Be Useless*, Helen De Cruz & Pauline Lee, Psyche, 12 January 2022.

82   Ibid.

83   Ibid.

84   Rachel Carson, *The Sense of Wonder*, Harper Collins, 1965.

85   'Top climate scientists are sceptical that nations will rein in global warming', *Nature*, 1 November 2021.

86   'Is green growth happening? An empirical analysis of achieved versus Paris-compliant CO_2–GDP decoupling in high-income countries', Jefim Vogel and Jason Hickel, *The Lancet Planetary Health*, Vol 7, 2023.

87   '1.5°C scenarios reported by the Intergovernmental Panel on Climate Change (IPCC) rely on combinations of controversial negative emissions and unprecedented technological change, while assuming continued growth in gross domestic product (GDP).' From '1.5 °C degrowth scenarios suggest the need for new mitigation pathways', Lorenz Keyßer and Manfred Lenzen, *Nature Communications*, 12, 2021.

88   'Decarbonising the energy system by 2050 could save trillions', Institute for New Economic Thinking, Oxford Martin School, 13 September 2022; 'Empirically grounded technology forecasts and the energy transition, Rupert Way et al, Joule, vol 6, Issue 9, 2022'.

89   See 'Technological improvement rate predictions for all technologies: Use of patent data and an extended domain description' by Singh et al, Research Policy, Vol. 9 2021.

90   See Timothée Parrique (timotheeparrique.com), 'Degrowth in the IPCC AR6 WGII', 5 March 2022.

91   Ibid. 'The voice of careful, rigorous science has spoken against the feasibility of green growth as a mitigation strategy ... But there is also another dangerous voice. It is the once of cherry-picked statements that give the illusion that developed nations have gotten green and that further economic growth is compatible with climate targets. This voice is made of vague claims and fuzzy definitions which can neither be proven true nor false. It is a pat on the back for regions, countries, and industries who use these arguments to turn a blind eye to the necessary degrowth of their economic activities'. See also Timothée Parrique, 'Sufficiency Means Degrowth', 24 April 2022 (available at timotheeparrique.com).

92 Polls in Europe show that the majority of people prioritise well-being and ecological objectives over growth (see: 'Europe's south and east worry more about emigration than immigration — poll', *The Guardian*, 1 April 2019). Polls in the United States and the United Kingdom show support for job guarantees and working-time reductions ('Majority of voters support a federal jobs guarantee', The Hill, 30 October 2019, and the YouGov poll).

93 Quoted from *The Anarchist Revelation* by Paul Cudenec, Paul Cudenec, Winter Oak Press, 2013.

94 Quoted 'Shrinking the Economy to Save the World', Kyle Paoletta, The Nation, 11 April 2022: 'But as Jackson demonstrates in *Prosperity Without Growth*, there's little reason to be satisfied with the diminishing returns that the Global North sees from its focus on growth when compared with developing nations. Using political scientist Ronald Inglehart's measure of 'subjective well-being', or SWB, as a proxy for life satisfaction, Jackson shows that as GDP per capita rises, SWB increases steeply for countries whose income is below about $15,000 per capita. The gains taper off as you move up the income spectrum, though, before flatlining at around $25,000—less than half of the United States' current GDP per capita'.

95 See *The Spirit Level: Why Equality Is Better for Everyone*, Kate Pickett and Richard Wilkinson, Penguin 2009.

96 Data.

97 'Providing decent living with minimum energy: A global scenario', *Global Environmental Change*, Vol 65, November 2020.

98 'Replicable for other countries, our framework is applied to the case of the United Kingdom where we find that reductions in energy demand of 52% by 2050 compared with 2020 levels are possible without compromising on citizens' quality of life'. From Barrett et al., 'Energy demand reduction options for meeting national zero-emission targets in the United Kingdom', *Nature Energy*, 7, 2022.

99   'Existing climate mitigation scenarios perpetuate colonial inequalities', Jason Hickel, *The Lancet Planetary Health*, Volume 6, Issue 7.

100 'Impacts of meeting minimum access on critical earth systems amidst the Great Inequality.' See Rammelt et al., *Nature Sustainability*, 6, 2023, on the need for redistribution to achieve SDGs for all.

101 'Amitav Ghosh: European colonialism helped create a planet in crisis', *The Guardian*, 14 January 2022.

102 *The Ecology of Freedom: The Emergence and Dissolution of Hierarchy*, Murray Bookchin, AK Press, 2005.

103 'Nature is a state of grace that can be experienced by anyone, anywhere', John Burnside, *New Statesman*, 5 January 2022.

104 World Land Trust, 'State of Nature 2023' report.

105 'The Theft of the Commons', Eula Bliss, *The New Yorker*, 8 June 2022.

106 From *The Promise of an Anarchist Sociological Imagination*, Erwin F. Rafael, The Anarchist Library, 2018.

107 'The Trouble With Race and Its Many Shades of Deceit', Subrena E. Smith, David Livingstone Smith, *New Lines Magazine*, 29 March 2023.

108 From *The Myth of Normal: Trauma, Illness & Healing in a Toxic Culture*, Gabor Maté, Penguin 2024.

109 *Anti-Semite and Jew (Réflexions sur la question juive)*, Jean-Paul Sartre, first published Les Temps Moderne, 1945

110 Quoted in the documentary film, *I am Not your Negro*, dir Raoul Peck, 2016.

111 *Memories, Dreams, Reflections: An Autobiography*, Carl Gustav Jung, Fontana, 1995.

112 'Nobel-Winning Physicist Wolfgang Pauli on Science, Spirit, and Our Search for Meaning', Maria Popova, *The Marginalian*.

113 This article is 'Anarchy = Love', *DOPE* a journal sold by the homeless who keep all proceeds.

114 From *Jung: A Very Short Introduction* Anthony Stevens, OUP, 2022.

115 Judith Butler: 'I was always drawn to radical thinkers' — *The Guardian*, 1 September 2021.

116 'Utopian thinking prompts us to get real about society's needs', William Paris, *Psyche Ideas*, 30 March 2022.

117 *Living in the Future: Utopianism and the Long Civil Rights Movement*, Victoria W. Wolcott, University of Chicago Press, 2022.

118 Quotes from *The Promise of an Anarchist Sociological Imagination* by Erwin Rafael, The Anarchist Library, 2018.

119 Open Society Barometer, 2023.

120 From *Demanding the Impossible: A History of Anarchism*, Peter Marshall, Harper Perennial, 2007.

About the Author

Carne Ross is a former British diplomat who is now a writer, diplomatic strategist, and advocate for anarchist principles. During an extensive diplomatic career, Ross served in Germany, Norway, Kosovo, Afghanistan, and the UK Mission to the UN in New York. He also served as speechwriter to two Foreign Secretaries, the second of whom fired him. His work covered many high-stakes global issues including counter-terrorism and Middle Eastern policy, and he was central to UK Iraq policy, for which he was responsible at the UN in the years before the Iraq invasion in 2003.

In 2004, Ross resigned from the Foreign Office after providing secret testimony to the first official inquiry into the Iraq War. His evidence raised critical questions regarding the government's presentation of the Iraqi threat and the exploration of alternatives to military action. Though he was threatened with prosecution when he resigned, the eventual publication of his testimony in 2007 was a key catalyst for the Chilcot Iraq Inquiry, to which he later provided further public evidence.

Following his resignation, Ross founded Independent Diplomat (ID), the world's first non-profit diplomatic advisory group. The organisation supports democratic countries and political movements—including in Ukraine, Syria, Western Sahara and Myanmar—in navigating international diplomacy. Notably, ID helped the Marshall Islands form the High Ambition Coalition, which was instrumental in securing the 1.5°C goal in the 2016 Paris Climate Agreement. ID also brought the first ever delegation of actual refugees into negotiations for UN refugee agreements.

Today, Ross continues his work as a strategist, advising countries and regions such as the autonomous administration in northeast Syria. A commentator for the Financial Times, the New York Times, Al Jazeera and the BBC, he writes extensively on political change and anarchism. He is currently developing a global network dedicated to "communalist" democracy—a practical application of his belief in self-governance and individual autonomy. His work seeks to offer an alternative to traditional state structures, proposing a philosophy of anarchism as a constructive way to address the world's multiplying crises.

For more information, please see Carne's website: carneross.com or Substack: @carneross

About the Publisher

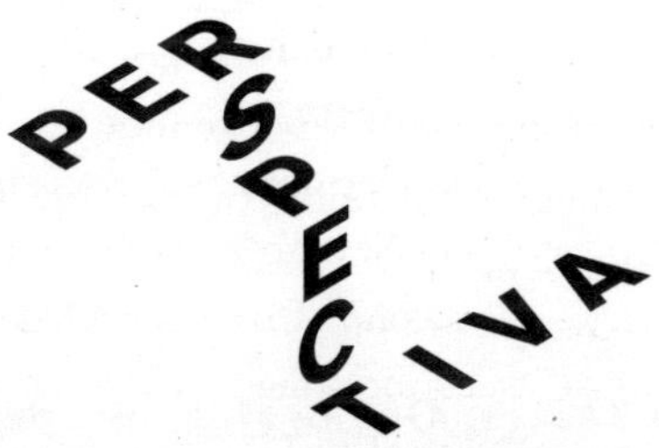

Perspectiva Press: Soul food for expert generalists

Perspectiva is a home for generative inquiry amid a great unravelling, a call to remember lost ways of looking, a harbour for those who sense that normality is destroying the world we love and are moved to act, a site of experiential reasoning where the heretical is welcome and valued as a gateway to cultural transformation. We are a research institute, a publishing house, a sandbox for innovation in social and spiritual practice. Perspectiva lays new foundations for political and cultural change, beginning with the blind spots in existing discourse. We look beyond systems change: because systems won't change until we acknowledge souls; beyond spiritual bypassing: because power dynamics can't be wished away; beyond fixation on narrative: because we ourselves must become the story; and beyond crisis rhetoric: because it's time for vision and method.

In our attempt to understand the relationship between systems, souls and society, we publish books to help readers develop skills of synthesis and epistemic agility, cultivate spiritual sensibility, and commit to shaping viable and desirable futures.

Selected titles by Perspectiva Press:

***Learning as If Life Depended on It:* Why we must see the world anew, and figure out what follows** — Olli-Pekka Heinonen (2025) How can we ensure that future generations enjoy the miracle of life? A work of planetary reckoning by the Director General of the International Baccalaureate.

***The Matter with Things:* Our brains, our delusions and the unmaking of the world** — Iain McGilchrist (2021) A vast and searching philosophical vision by a psychiatrist that returns the world to life, and invites us to a better way of living in it: one we must embrace if we are to survive.

***The Entangled Activist:* Learning to recognise the master's tools** — Anthea Lawson (2021) A seasoned campaigner on how your sense of agency changes when you realise 'getting the bastards' is not working.

***The Politics of Waking Up:* Power and possibility in the fractal age** — Indra Adnan (2021) A therapist and political innovator on putting the full spectrum of a consciously awakening humanity at the heart of society, economy and politics.

***Dispatches from a Time Between Worlds:* Crisis and emergence in metamodernity** — edited by Jonathan Rowson and Layman Pascal (2021) An anthology of metamodern scholars and writers on our world-historical context and pathways to cultural renaissance.

For all titles and more information, see systems-souls-society.com and perspecteeva.substack.com